PUBLIC

OPINION

and

CONGRESSIONAL

ELECTIONS

Recent books from the Bureau of Applied Social Research of Columbia University

COMMUNITY CONFLICT
  by James S. Coleman

POLITICAL SOCIALIZATION
  by Herbert H. Hyman

THE ACADEMIC MIND: Social Scientists in a Time of Crisis
  by Paul F. Lazarsfeld and Wagner Thielens, Jr.

UNION DEMOCRACY
  by Seymour Martin Lipset, Martin A. Trow, and James S. Coleman

DEVELOPMENTS IN MATHEMATICAL PSYCHOLOGY
  R. Duncan Luce, Editor

FORMAL THEORIES OF MASS BEHAVIOR
  by William N. McPhee

THE VOLUNTEERS: Means and Ends in a National Organization
  by David L. Sills

PUBLIC
OPINION
and
CONGRESSIONAL
ELECTIONS

Edited by

William N. McPhee

& William A. Glaser

The Free Press of Glencoe

To the regional research specialists who initiated this study:

Joseph Bachelder and Stuart Dodd,
Washington Public Opinion Laboratory

Ross Beiler, Department of Government,
University of Miami

John Emery and Edward Whittlesey,
Research Services, Inc., and the *Denver Post* Poll

Sidney Goldish, and the Minnesota Poll,
Minneapolis Star-Tribune

William Longman and Charles Parker,
Central Surveys, Inc., Iowa

ACKNOWLEDGMENTS

*T*his has been one of the vanishing race of studies started by individual initiative and carried on by personal persistence without visible means of support. The initiative in getting the field work done using local resources was that of the persons and organizations named in the dedication. The persistence in getting the analysis done on their own was that of the authors of the papers to follow.

Yet this exception proved that the contrary rule is necessary. For funds finally had to be diverted from foundation and government grants and from organizational resources to intervene, mercifully, in assisting the study across the finish line. Thanks for funds that could be used for this important unfinished business are due to the unrestricted nature of the grants made to the first editor by the Ford Foundation, and then the National Science Foundation (NSF G #13045); to the second editor by the Social Science Research Council; and to the Bureau of Applied Social Research by the Eda K. Loeb Foundation. In a field in which foundations have their own ideas about initiating new studies, we especially appreciate their leaving it to our judgment, which here was that free funds are better used for "finishes" than "starts."

The study was a cooperative undertaking of The American Association for Public Opinion Research, in which leading roles were played by Paul F. Lazarsfeld in instigating the idea and Bernard Berelson in organizing—with the people named in the dedication and the first editor—the actual venture. A grant to Berelson by the Rockefeller Foundation covered the costs of initial processing of the data contributed by the regional groups, and Lazarsfeld's students at Columbia did much of the early exploration of these data, especially Sylvia Gilliam, Charles Kadushin, and Jane Emery. Joseph Bachelder's students at State College of Washington also contributed valuable data-processing and analyses. Ralph Casey's students at the University of Minnesota contributed interviews with the candidates and campaign materials, also obtained in Colorado by Charleton Price of the *Denver Post* and in Iowa by Charles Parker's Central Surveys, Inc. The valuable work done by Ross Beiler and his students in Miami, including the raw data from that area, unfortunately could not be used in the present pooled analyses because of noncomparability, but were instructive qualitatively. It is not the fault of any of the persons above, rather, precisely the fact they could not find time to participate in the analysis, that the expertness of their regional knowledge is not always exploited in the analyses of the pooled materials here.

When those analyses were made, by different people with different purposes discussed in the Introduction, it took hard work by Sylvia Eberhart as editor and Myra Gordon as technical assistant, supported by publication funds of the Bureau of Applied Social Research, to make the collection coherent (in both senses).

Helmut Guttenberg's expert manipulation of the original data was matched by Clara Shapiro's of the subsequent deficits. We thank the Free Press's editor, F. Warren O'Reilly, and Lorraine Blake, chartist, for their labors in making a handsome book of it.

Thanks are due to *The Public Opinion Quarterly* for permission to reprint the substance of Freeman and Showel's "Differential Political Influence of Voluntary Associations" and Freeman's "A Note on the Prediction of Who Votes." Thanks go to *The American Political Science Review* for permission to use a revision of Glaser's "Intention and Turnout."

CONTENTS

INTRODUCTION

An interesting development in the years just after World War II was the emergence of regional survey research centers connected with universities, newspapers, and private enterprises. In 1950, a group of five pioneer centers, under the auspices of The American Association for Public Opinion Research, worked in collaboration with Berelson and Lazarsfeld's Elmira study of presidential voting to carry out smaller but comparable panel studies of congressional voting in each of five states.

A major purpose was to replicate current findings in different kinds of elections and in varying contexts. This effort was successful, and its results are summarized in a chapter of this book. But the regional survey organizations, which had freely contributed the considerable expense of field work, were unable to take on the additional burden of analyzing these valuable data as a voting study in its own right. Instead, the data were deposited at Columbia University for use in more general analyses of problems in public opinion and mass behavior, as opportunities and funds for the latter purpose arose in subsequent years. This book is a collection of those analyses.

The subject matter of the original materials gives the results a political content, which the chapter titles reflect. But most of the analysts represented here were not primarily interested in voting as such. Rather, they were attacking problems in attitude consistency, in the effect of varying community contexts, in the use of computer models, and so on, using the voting data only as examples. Curiously, however, this proved to be a good way to study voting as well; studies of attitude consistency, for example, suggested a way to formulate the "coattails" phenomenon in ticket voting. The third section of this introduction will discuss how these papers—many produced after analysis of this *as* a voting study was abandoned—perhaps have as much to say about voting as if they had resulted from a direct frontal attack on the subject.

The main purpose of this introduction, however, is to make explicit more general concerns of these analyses, beyond the concrete political results reported in the main text. To introduce them by an analogy that will surely be overworked by the time this volume appears, the complaints of the scholarly community about survey technology have been like asking, some years ago, when would rocket technicians stop "playing with nuts and bolts" and pay attention to, say, astronomy. The survey research technology may not reach any moons, of course, but the principle is the same: the "big" things scholars demand of this work are blocked by stubborn technical problems, nuts and bolts if one pleases, but whose significance in any event is not widely understood. For, if it were, we would not hear the constant complaints that work on such problems is a diversion from larger goals. The larger goals that everyone urges but seldom suggests how to reach are chiefly these three:

1. *Theory,* that is, more efficient forms of knowledge than the descriptive results which survey research is accumulating almost beyond assimilation today.
2. *Magnitude,* that is, capacity to deal with larger social structure and longer historical time than the microscopic results now typical.
3. *Substance,* that is, relevance to what matters more in subject disciplines and policy questions, than the simple behavioral correlations of which most current findings consist.

In the present case, we were specifically relieved of the third responsibility, which a sponsored voting study would have had, and simply recount in the third section of this introduction that attending to other interests does not neglect the substance of politics itself. It is in connection with the first two goals—theory and magnitude— that the baffling technical problems arise. And when analysts are given free reign to work on them, as they were here, implicit in what they do is an informed judgment of what the obstacles are. The purpose of the discussion below is to bring out these general aspects of the work, under the above headings of theory and magnitude, followed by an introduction to the third, the particular political content of the materials.

I. THEORY

To TAKE the goal of theory seriously when the dominant source of research information is the survey technology makes two questions much more explicit than they have been in discursive social and political theory based on earlier kinds of data. They are the questions: (a) whether what we want is idea elaboration or idea reduction, and (b) whether what we want is analytic theory or synthetic (that is, putting together) theory. Implicit in the background of some of these papers is interesting experience with each question.

A. Information Reduction

Sociological and political theory sometimes is individually parsimonious, but collectively it is a growing flood of insights, filling page after page in what are becoming large libraries. One might call this richness of insights *idea elaboration,* as contrasted to *idea reduction.* Tacitly, we have always assumed that the former was the chief problem of theory today, to get ideas to guide the developing research, because empirical testing would later handle the problem of reducing the number of such hypotheses, with a vengeance, to the one or two that are "true." Empirical studies like these voting series are making obvious, however, that it is not going to work out that way. An extraordinarily *large* number of assertions are going to be true, each in an unsatisfactorily *small* degree (that is, weak correlations).

An example is an inventory of some 200 propositions about voting, found in one or more studies (Berelson, *et al.,* 1954, Appendix A). All possible instances have been replicated in these data, in a paper called "Political Behavior in Midterm Elections," by William Glaser and Charles Kadushin. These are mostly low-level generalizations, of the kind that one would expect changes of time and place to winnow down to only a few reliable ones. Not so. Most come true again—but in the same weak correlations. And if we added all the ifs, ands, and buts that were suggested in the new testing, the empirical winnowing out added information, if anything.

Moreover, the reader who thinks that these too-particular propositions (as they deliberately were made to be) can be reduced to more parsimonious generalizations, should try it. One of the editors spent several months trying so to reduce them, and it came down to a series of very general propositions indeed. Such as: "people influence each other" (toward compatability). But this is the kind of common knowledge with which the studies began. The research function was to elaborate on them. Simple "generalization," then, seems to go back toward common observation, which itself is a form of generalization. But that means it tends to lose precisely what the research added.

An alternative, one not practiced much to date in the research side of the field that is concerned with empirical verification and scientific caution, is tried at several points here. It is not to seek safe generalizations, but to postulate more risky assumptions (even if out of the blue) that are *strong* enough to account for findings in a way that does not drop out but predicts the details that research found and common sense could not have.

The "strength" of an assumption is meant in a sense like that of mathematics, that is, its definiteness. As a simple example, a paper on "Fluctuations in Turnout" by Glaser, postulates the following about the relation of responses, like voting turnout, to changing motivation. Responses are not just "a function of" political motivation, but a definite *form* of function. Given this, which is verified as roughly correct, a number of previously separate findings follow as deductions from simple geometric reasoning, including as the main deduction, an explanation of why for nearly a century the party in power has tended to lose its majority again at midterm. A mathematical reader can see from the diagrams and statement of the assumptions here, and from consequences drawn from independent work reaching the same conclusion, that a model can easily be set down that connects an old mystery with a number of contemporary findings, as essentially one causal idea. (We do not carry out formalization here, however, but show the problem in "working" form.)

Another possibility in the problem of idea reduction is not to invent new theory of a substantive or content nature, but reduce that new content to existing formalisms, "empty" formalisms if one pleases, but for that reason *general*. For instance, a good deal of psychological theory is being elaborated around the problem that, in exposure to propaganda appeals between which people finally have to decide, there is a tendency toward increasing "consistency," "congruency," or "consonance" as it is variously called. By any name it is an increasing correlation among attitudes. For example, in a rising civil rights dispute, people who do not like several minority groups would tend to give responses increasingly more hostile to another minority. "Tend to" do so, however, expresses the state of affairs: the rule is weak and contrary instances are easily found. Moreover, if we followed the usual advice to specify the "conditions" under which the rule applies, the list would cover several pages. What one wants is a more powerful formulation in which the conditions take care of themselves in a natural way.

The paper, "Attitude Consistency" by Bo Anderson, Harry Milholland, and William N. McPhee is a progress report on a long and frustrating effort to find a manageable formulation in this domain. Since that formulation is deceptively simple, its history is worth recounting to show the technical difficulties, which those who only *urge* theory, underestimate. Earlier, Charles Kadushin had found that, in the politics of the early 1950's, the disturbances of foreign-policy attitudes (for example, due to Korea) did not correlate well with domestic political beliefs, so that change in attitudes during the campaigns of that period were a nightmare of inconsistencies. Next, an attempt was made to see whether psychological formulations in this domain (consonance, congruity, and so forth) would reduce the chaos to a few main ideas. But at least at the time of a review of the literature (1959), those ideas involved motivations implausible for such casual opinions and, in any event, could not reproduce the chief mystery, certain contradictory patterns in these data. Next a Markov-chain formulation was tried, which did have the necessary deductive power, but failed to fit the data. Yet it failed in an instructive way.

Precisely contrary assumptions, expressing simple reasons why attitude changes would *not* be Markovian, have been developed by Lee Wiggins (1955) and Lazarsfeld. Starting originally from considerations of the reliability of attitudes, Wiggins' final models are a motion or time version of Lazarsfeld's latent structure. A simplified version of such models finally seems to fit the consistency data. So, the problem promises to fit under existing formalisms. This reduces a chaos of findings to a few key changes in model parameters, as the remaining unknowns. At least one explanation of these changes, in turn, can be found implicit in the assumptions of the voting model in this volume, when generalized free of its content. So, while these formal ideas may organize the problem wrongly, the point is that they *compactly* organize, within existing formal knowledge, findings that one cannot prove right nor wrong and with which one can do nothing in their existing empirical multiplicity.

To sum up. For all that scholars ask for "insightful" theory, and that empiricists urge generalizing from research results in their hope for "true" theory, the technical puzzle as we find it in practice is to formulate *efficient* theory.

B. Synthetic Theory

In many situations, however, one seems doomed to numerous weak correlations, with even the best formulation, because that is the nature of the empirical case. An example is the influence of voters on one another in a short period, such as a single election campaign. Everyone knows that most vote changes in so short a period are due not primarily to social influences, but to current political stimuli and learning from the past. So, an influence theory cannot have major predictive results.

Suppose, however, that we *combine* such a social-influence process with another that portrays how political stimuli affect people, and a third that deals with the learning process. The combination of the three can be called a "synthetic" theory, in the technical sense of putting together, as opposed to the usual analytic hypotheses. Such a combination can be very powerful indeed, not just suggesting a tendency, "the more *X,* the more *Y,*" but, given certain parameters, generating the complete action, in this case the whole vote. A rudimentary theory that does just that is presented in a paper entitled "A Model for Analyzing Voting Systems" by Robert Smith and William N. McPhee. It does so by taking three very different analytic ideas about the three different topics above and combining them into one synthetic model. For, voting *is,* after all, an empirically synthetic act: one perceives, learns, discusses, and so on. In fact, when we stop to think of it, nearly all behavioral acts are synthetic phenomena in the sense that they combine what are theoretically very different topics, such as learning and social communication. So, in addition to good analytic ideas about each, there is an unsolved technical problem of combining them, a synthetic problem, implicit in any call for theory of "socially significant" (whole) behavior.

The paper mentioned above illustrates, however, that this kind of theory is fostered, not by calling for less use of "IBM machines," but, paradoxically, more. For, these are *logic* machines and, in fact, it takes a computer to make the synthetic combinations and then draw the consequences over time, the problem being beyond both intuition and algebraic manipulation. "Computer," however, is a misnomer here. Little calculating is done and one uses mostly non-numerical operations to "simulate," carry out the behavior literally. Although this model is simple enough to have proved easily translated into formal notation, which makes its assumptions clearer, we leave the paper in its original form to show how the model was in fact conceived and must in fact be operated, in "machine logic."

There is no need to stop the synthesis mentioned above at the boundary of a single individual. Indeed, in the model discussed just above, the theory of individuals is deliberately kept very simple because the model is intended to aggregate them to study how a community or electorate votes, over long time spans. So, the technology of synthetic theory has an intimate connection to the second of the three main objectives listed at the beginning of this introduction —namely, overcoming the "microscopic" character of interview observations. How can we draw from these details implications about large social structure and the historical time dimensions that matter in social theory and political policy?

II. MAGNITUDE

MERELY to focus criticism on the "triviality" of surveys in this respect, their irrelevance to aggregate magnitudes, is simply to reverse the direction from which one looks at the same ignorance— ignorance about the *connections* between individual acts and collective results—that has never been solved in broad scholarly work, either. Toynbee, for example, experiences the puzzle "from the other direction," that is, his knowledge of aggregate events but uncertainty about the individual acts that created them. In a recent discussion, he says:

> Let us recall the fundamental point that collective action is fiction, not fact. Why, then, do we talk in terms of collective action? . . .
> . . . The individual acts in question are innumerable, and the network of relations between them is immensely complex. Even where only few individuals are involved, it is quite impossible for an unaided human mind to perceive the relation between the "collective" result and the acts of large numbers of individuals that were the only genuine realities in the event.
> This ignorance of the relation between "collective" results and the underlying individual human acts is not an ignorance peculiar to us in our time. All human beings who have ever lived so far—

Leibnitz, Dante, Bede, Aristotle, and the rest—have been as ignorant as we are on this point . . ." (Toynbee, 1961).

So, if the air is cleared of complaints about *who* is ignorant here (everyone), we might examine as Toynbee does what can be done about it. He sees two technical problems involved: (a) observation of individual acts and (b) their synthesis into collective results. His utopia would be:

> Can technology come to our aid here? Can technology enable us to devise and construct computing machines that will record the myriad of individuals including the inner acts in the psyche of each individual as well as the interactions of each individual with every other? And could such a record be utilized by other computing machines for demonstrating in detail, point by point, exactly how these individual acts generated the "collective" results visible to an unaided mind? If computing machines can perform these two operations for us, our insight into human nature and life would be increased out of all recognition. . . .

Toynbee professes to be "out of his depth" on these two technical questions, and he is on one. For, his *observation* problem, knowing what individuals are doing "inside" the collective action, clearly belongs in the technology, not of computers, but of interviews, panels, diaries, records, content analysis, and the like. For example, the utopian solution implied by Toynbee's wanting to know about "every individual" is actually being solved by sampling. But if the individual observation problems are being solved, in principle, then why are their results proving so irrelevant to precisely the larger concern that motivated them, collective action? It is the unsolved second puzzle, the *synthesis* problem of showing how "individual acts generate collective results," that has been unresolvable even in principle. For we now appreciate, as it is surprising to hear a humanist like Toynbee agree, that it requires what is only now becoming available: a technology capable of reasoning about the millions of interactions involved.

He meant machines seriously and we do too, but here the reader must descend from the sublime to what can be done now. As a primitive illustration of computer synthesis of collective implications, a paper on "Political Immunization" by Jack Ferguson and William N. McPhee, takes the voting model based on the inventory of survey findings mentioned above and subjects the model to "historical disturbances." The substantive outcome is a kind of immunization tendency discussed in the next section. Here we continue with the technical problems this new opportunity for synthetic aggregation is itself raising.

One chief difficulty is implicit in the fact that the results are now obtained with hypothetical electorates, only indirectly checked by testing implications in real data. This removal from the real world is true of all theory. But it neglects to exploit what was implicit in the Toynbee discussion above: the *combination* of technologies, one for observing individuals (here, interview) and the other for synthesizing the collective consequences (here, computer model). This combination is actually being tried in current work. For example, the respondents in a Roper survey of the Wisconsin presidential primary election in 1960 were used in place of a hypothetical electorate in a short-term version of the model (McPhee, 1961). But current experience here simply reveals that we are missing a different kind of empirical information.

What the computer does is synthesize in only one direction, "up." From individual interactions it aggregates the collective consequences, which are indeed logical consequences. But there the dynamics stop. To go on, to complete the theory, we need processes that go "down" again, make these aggregate consequences come back and affect individuals again, thus continuing the action. Today, some *deus extra machina* must now intervene, technically to decide for the model what new stimuli the aggregate outcome would have set in motion for individuals in the next cycle. One has, then, only a "half system" and cannot complete the loop back to individual action again. The reason is simple. Aggregating the social consequences of individual acts *is* primarily a logical question, something computers can do. But how these consequences come back to affect individual behavior involves new behavioral, that is, empirical questions. Research papers by Philip Ennis and by Howard Freeman and Morris Showel illustrate this reverse kind of problem: how do aggregates influence individuals?

Ennis' paper, "The Contextual Dimension in Voting," was analyzed almost a decade ago, and was one of the first examples of what has later become something of a fashion. It is "contextual" analysis, studying the effects on otherwise nearly identical individuals, interviewed when nonindividual or aggregate conditions are varied from place to place. For example, Ennis finds that political majorities (in a district) tend to give certain issues dominant circulation. These tend to become the "frame of reference" for individual decisions, bringing into play attitudes favoring the perpetuation of the district majority. Thus, simultaneously in two adjacent districts in Minnesota, the incumbent congressmen were able to create by their campaigns elections that the constituents in one district perceived to be about foreign (Far Eastern) policy and to those in the other about domestic (labor) policy. This is because the interests and reputations of the incumbent candidates were supported by dominant majorities in each district, which in effect "resonated" what the incumbents said or stood for. We have long known that all politicians try to do this— hold elections according to their own frame of reference—but Ennis suggests that they succeed when there is (indeed it may be the psychological unfairness of) dominant majority rule.

Size of the aggregate is another condition Ennis finds makes for systematic differences in individual behavior. There is a great convenience in these kinds of variables. For, the aggregate stimuli affecting an individual are logically *other* individuals, their number, their divisions, and so on. So, a model thereof would "loop back" on itself: its own aggregate consequences imply the stimuli again for individuals. The knotty problem, however, is this: how to complete the loop when stimuli from aggregates have independent origins in institutional and organizational leadership?

For instance, a paper on "The Political Influence of Voluntary Associations" (contributed to this collection by Howard Freeman and Morris Showel, then of the University of Washington) can be interpreted as follows for present purposes. They suggest a correlation whereby the more the members of a controversial organization such as the CIO or the Catholic Church say they would be *for* what it endorses, the more nonmembers say they would be *against* what the same organizations endorse. This is not so for innocuous organizations, for example, the Chamber of Commerce, but they are innocuous to voters precisely because they do not intervene much at the voting level of politics. So, this hypothesis suggests that where there *is* noxious potential for effective intervention in voting, that very fact provokes its own counterforce by other voters. If so—if we can verify the behavioral assumptions in historical interpretations to this same effect—then in an interesting way one may be able to circumvent details of organizational and institutional maneuvering, to write a larger theory of self-balancing capacities in the aggregate as a whole. For, in the long run, whatever such organizations do that is effective will be reflected in support, that is, *votes* of certain groups for them. And then in a theory or model, these votes can be made the contrary stimuli for other groups in opposition to the first groups.

Work on such a "self-balancing" version of the voting model is beginning. But the problem of completing (rather than circumventing like this) the institutional level of these synthetic models is unsolved, generally.

To sum up. If we stop complaining about "IBM machines" and findings that are "microscopic," and appreciate that the latter microscopism is just what makes the problem difficult for everyone, scholars included, then emerging technologies like the former machines could make reasoning about significant aggregates easier for everyone, survey analysts included. For the combination of sample interview as data source and computer model as combinational theory is, in principle, equal to the twin tasks of observation and synthesis that aggregate magnitudes consist of as technical problems. In practice, however, the reader will find we have not got far; not because the models are primitive, since they can be made as complex as we wish, but because they run into unfinished empirical business like that touched on by Ennis and by Freeman and Showel.

III. SUBSTANCE

THE READER will recall the three main disappointments noted by critics who say that political surveys lack significance: lack of theory, lack of magnitude, and the lack of substantive relevance to the reader's discipline or policy problem, which we now discuss. The first two were the chief early disappointments, particularly to psychologists and sociologists. Then those disciplines entered political survey research, and the effort to direct that research toward their own problems has in recent years brought from political scientists and from policy makers an even louder outcry on the third ground, namely, disregard of the political subject matter itself.

Some of the papers in this book do bear upon important political problems. But we are not attempting to provide facts about the political events of a particular time, nor attempting to provide a comprehensive analysis of electoral behavior, a voting study. Rather, the analyses here are addressed to highly selected questions, chiefly centering around the following two technical problems: (a) how to extend these data in *time,* at best, into "process" formulations and at least, by empirical time extension, for example to the four years between elections; (b) how to translate their topical political content in *form,* that is, give clearer and more general, if possible logical, meanings to political concepts like "independent voter" and "coattails effect." The latter is so closely connected to the above technical problems in theory—replacing particular political content with more general formulations—that we discuss it first.

Reformulations

Certain papers have almost no other purpose than to clarify the meanings of some old political terms in *general* form. It is a problem in translating lore into logic.

Alan Meyer's "The Independent Voter," for example, specifies a meaning for a widely idealized but never well-defined type of person in other fields as well as voting. His article develops numerous indicators that fit the classic concept of independent voter. The number of independents would vary considerably with different possible definitions. But most definitions and discussions of the topic imply a type of voter who, as Meyer illustrates, is inherently scarce because the type is a *deviant* combination of substantial interest but low bias or partisanship. The opposite combinations of interest and bias, lack of bias and lack of interest or participation, are the dominant cases. And the data suggest the former deviant combination is unstable: it won't last. So, it is psychologically unsound to expect of the majority really durable habits of independent voting, on which some early political philosophers have felt democracy must rest.

In a paper called "A Reformulation of the 'Coattails' Problem," John Meyer has re-examined another historical topic that has always seemed simple common sense until one tries to subject it to disciplined research. It is the relationships between separate choices of alternatives on the same slate or ticket, or as the general form of the problem, "parallel decisions." We have always assumed that certain candidates or offices can be viewed as "leading" the ticket and exercising "coattail" effects on others. But as several modern analysts including the editors have discovered, it is a frustrating problem to try to demonstrate any such effect, because we are unclear as to precisely what it is supposed to be.

The approach finally adopted was to specify two different statistical models for what the effect might be and then determine empirically which of them led to meaningful (patterned, dependable) results. Most time was wasted on the one that most literally catches up the "coattails" idea. Namely, that it is a *pair interaction* formulation, whereby A's effect on B and B's effect on A can be measured. Its failure, incidentally, shows the value of replication: it would work in data from one state, but reverse itself in data from the next. What finally brought order to the problem was a different formulation, one that represents the idea not that candidates affect one another, but that all are "in the same boat" so to speak. This approach is the same formulation as the attitude-consistency work mentioned earlier, that is, it explains the consistency of choices on a political ticket by the same formalisms that make any series of parallel opinions tend to consistency. It is true the effect of individual candidates, for example presidential candidates, on that consistency of choices is yet to be demonstrated. But the problem now seems "formulatable,'" and thus measurable.

Finally, perhaps more than any other, the old political concept that is found misleading here is that of "the" nonvoter. We will discuss below certain long-term dynamics implicit in sizable fluctuations in and out of the electorate, but short-term changes are found here as well. Voting turnout—or more generally, the implementation of attitudes—is a source of dynamics equally as important as the direction of choices, once made. Indeed, pollsters know turnout is the more difficult problem to predict, and Howard Freeman and Arnold Simmel and Murray Gendell devote two technical notes to showing what a difference it makes to reformulate such prediction questions probabilistically. For example, take pollsters' method of predicting who will vote, in dichotomies contrasting "the" voter with "the" nonvoter. The above authors replace this concept with the idea of a sequence of probabilities, a function, along a semicontinuous scale of disposition to vote. Then they show that, if one does not handle the problem this way but only in dichotomies, the error is asymetrical, for example, the polls biased to the Republicans. The effect on the polls is not large, however, and in any event it seems a "small" problem. Not so. It is primarily due to Simmel's reformulation that measurement problems implicit in theories here, for example, in the voting model, are being handled in current work (McPhee, 1961).

Time and Process

Turning now to the second kind of political content, we note that critics rightfully complain that surveys restrict us to single points of time instead of describing the dynamics of the moving electorate through various types of elections over long periods. It is only too true that single elections cannot be described meaningfully in isolation from previous and subsequent elections. But it is only too true, also, that it is expensive to do otherwise! In good part, the time must be supplied by *analytic* extension rather than empirical measurement.

The fact that the Regional Panels surveys were conducted during a midterm election in a period of political transition frequently reminded analysts of this problem of time extension. For example, "Fluctuations in Turnout" by Glaser is addressed to the widely discussed political puzzle about whether the drop in turnout from the presidential to the midterm elections has any meaningful pattern, and whether this drop in turnout bears on the fact that the party in power usually declines at midterm. From certain basic findings that some members of the electorate are more sensitive to changes in stimuli than others, one can derive the implication that fluctuations in campaign stimuli affect subgroups in the electorate differently. As the electorate cyclically expands and contracts between presidential and midterm elections, for example, the most variable subgroups are, concretely, women, the young, the lower class, and the politically less involved. The hard-core partisans are stable in both their turnout and their candidate choices in successive elections. Now, popular presidents usually gain their landslide victories by attracting more marginal voters of indifferent interest than their opponents. Since these marginally indifferent voters are more likely than the partisans to fluctuate in turnout between presidential and midterm elections, the president's (that is, the popular) party gains and loses proportionately more of its support from this source than does the opposition. Or put another way: the party in power gets in power in the first place by obtaining more of the marginal increment in the presidential year, and that is lost in the midterm sequel. These conclusions were reached independently from other data by Campbell (1956).

There is something curious in this. Political theory customarily locates "dynamics" in the most active people. But we are finding in electoral cases that the mobility or fluidity comes from the least active, from their undependability. For instance, a companion paper to that mentioned above, "Intention and Turnout," shows that the potential electorate even changes size and composition during the short campaign. This is chiefly due to failure of good intentions. Again women, the young, the lower class, and the less interested abandon intentions to vote, and this generally strikes the parties unequally, for example, the Democrats and/or the previously popular party are more vulnerable.

As another example of this fresh appreciation of the dynamics inherent in apathy, so to speak, consider the "Political Immunization" problem of Ferguson and McPhee. Immunization means that experience with political disturbances generates resistance to further disturbances, both directly in the model and indirectly in a test on American data back to 1936. But in both, the immunization effect turns out to be only academic in degree, not enough for practical safety. Under what conditions, then, would it be enough for safety? In the process of analyzing that problem, Ferguson found an answer to a question that we, at least, have never been able to answer unambiguously: Why is apathy dangerous? His answer is: It is impossible to foster an immunity of electorates to being suddenly overwhelmed by new political winds that blow tomorrow so long as there is sizable indifference or nonparticipation today.

The reason is that resistance to new disturbances is due to the effects of previously strong stimuli in generating contrary *commitments,* for example, to parties whose goals are opposite to the way the new winds will be blowing. "The enemies of my enemy will be my protection." But any large pool of indifferent people in the population will not have this positive check on them, and under strong new stimuli, strong enough to threaten the system, they could come into the electorate and overwhelm the previous balance among committed people. That they do so even now is the implication of Glaser's (and Campbell's) results, and some data on the Nazi case in 1928-1932 suggest that, with truly violent stimuli, a re-entry into the quarrel by previous nonparticipants might be a major factor in overwhelming the previous balance. So an old question "why is apathy bad?" gets a theoretic answer, if we study how two political armies checkmate each other. Then one notices that the checkmate is illusory when there is a third, uncommitted army among the spectators.

Finally, we come to the specifically political assignment of the original materials on which these papers were based, to investigate the midterm period between the presidential elections studied to date. Surprisingly, there is little difference in the findings. This is suggested by the replication of the inventory of findings of presidential studies mentioned earlier, "Political Behavior in Midterm Elections," by Glaser and Kadushin. Precise quantitative comparisons were impossible, but the qualitative directions of correlations and trends were surprisingly similar. Except that the characteristic findings all seemed, so to speak, "less so."

In comparison to the presidential electorate, the midterm electorate is obviously less interested in politics, discusses politics less intensely, and is apparently subject to fewer pressures to make orderly, consistent, and stable decisions. For, compared to the presidential electorate, the midterm electorate seems to make somewhat more random and contradictory opinion changes, and polarizes less into mutually exclusive partisan camps. Midterm campaigns apparently have less power than presidential campaigns to crystallize new trends in their own right. Rather they seem, here at least, to be mixed records of unfinished disputes from the previous presidential election and of new underlying trends that will only be crystallized in the next presidential election. A brief note included for topical background, "Hindsight and Significance," shows that the 1950 period was actually an important turning point historically: that, for example, the shift from the old, New-Deal issues to "Communists, Korea, and Corruption" began then. But this "critical turning point" was not evident in the casual voting at the time. So, like the voters who settled the question along party lines at that time, we have preferred the general rather than the topical approach in the analyses to follow.

I

ANALYTIC

REDUCTION

1

FLUCTUATIONS IN TURNOUT

By William A. Glaser

*T*wo of the persistent mysteries about midterm elections have been (a) the causes of declines in turnout and (b) the effects of these declines upon voting results. This paper will suggest some hypotheses about cyclical fluctuations in turnout between presidential and midterm elections, and it will suggest other more basic hypotheses that may account for these fluctuations. The hypotheses will be illustrated with data previously gathered by the Regional Panels Project and by other surveys. Part I of the paper will suggest some relationships between people's reasons for voting and turnout. From these simple premises, Part II will derive implications about how the American electorate expands and contracts between presidential and midterm years. Part III will suggest consequences for the outcomes of elections.

I. REASONS FOR VOTING AND TURNOUT

Turnout and Its Determinants among Individuals

Voting in America is the kind of act that is easy for many individuals and difficult for others. Voting is easy for those who have

Adapted from a paper first written in 1956. Some of the findings about the expansion and contraction of the entire electorate were discovered independently and reported in Campbell (Fall, 1960).

considerable competence in many areas of social participation, who know the location and procedures of polling booths, who possess the necessary time and transportation, and who have the requisite information and freedom from barriers. But there are others who possess little political competence and knowledge, who encounter overriding work or family obligations, and who lack the skills, knowledge, and opportunities that make voting a simple matter.

Since the difficulty or ease of the voting act varies considerably among individuals, they react differently to the same political motivations or stimuli. If each individual has a particular probability of voting at each level of motivations or social stimuli, then we may imagine each has a distinctive probability function showing how he would respond to the complete range of forces. Figure 1-1 presents the curves for a few typical probability functions. Among individuals for whom voting is very easy (as curve A illustrates), the first few increments of motivation produce a rapid increase in the probability of action, and additional increments tend to be redundant according to the principle of diminishing returns. When voting is very difficult (as in the case of individuals represented by curve D), the first increments of motivation produce only slight increases in voting probability, and many additional increments are needed before the likelihood of voting rises substantially. For those persons who find voting moderately easy (represented by curve B), voting probability steadily increases as reasons for voting rise, but the increments in voting steadily diminish with each successive increment in motivation. (For simplicity throughout this paper, I shall assume that the basic *forms* of the motivation-turnout relationships for individuals and electorates remain the same in all elections, and that variations occur only in motivations and social stimuli.)

Empirical confirmation of such probability functions must await future research about the political behavior of single individuals under varying conditions. Such generalizations about individuals seem theoretically plausible. In addition, these relationships seem valid because they resemble well-established findings from experimental research about task performances and learning, as reported by Hovland (1949, pp. 153-158), Krueger (1946, pp. 247-249), Lord (1953, pp. 520, 528-529), and other psychologists. This research has yielded families of curves showing performance and learning according to the difficulty of the tasks and the skills of the individual subjects. In the performance of easy tasks by all persons or average tasks by able persons, the first few increments of stimulation or ability

1-1—Reasons for Voting and Individuals' Turnout Probabilities

Probability of Voting

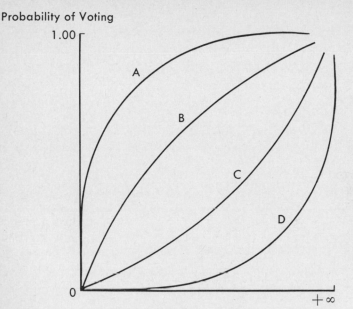

Number and Strength of Reasons for Voting

are associated with a rapid increase in the rate of success, and then the success rate levels off. But when an action or questionnaire item is difficult, the first few increases in stimulation or ability produce only small gains in performance.

A General Rule about Turnout and Its Determinants within the Electorate

The following statistical proposition about the electorate can be derived from the foregoing assumptions about individuals:

> **If the electorate at any one time is ranged in groups according to strength of disposition to vote, from low to high, the turnout along this range will first rise slowly, than rapidly, and then with successively smaller increments.**

This generalization can be derived mathematically as follows. At the time of any election, people's political dispositions—both their internal motivations to vote and the social influences exerting pressure on them to vote—range from very weak to very strong. At each level of disposition, the individuals vary among themselves according to whether they find voting easy or difficult. The proportion of people who vote at each dispositional level is calculated by adding the voting probabilities of all individuals at that level and dividing this total by the number of individuals at that level. The curve in the left half of Figure 1-2 connects the turnout frequencies of the successive levels and is the graph for the basic generalization. Since voting is easy for most people, the major part of this curve in Figure 1-2 resembles curves *A* or *B* in Figure 1-1. But since the American electorate contains some people who are weakly motivated and who find voting difficult, a slight dip occurs at the left extremity. The proposition and the left half of Figure 1-2 mean that highly but unequally motivated groups in the electorate contain nearly the same proportions of voters; among groups with medium or low motivation, differences in motivational strengths are associated with large differences in rates of behavior; but aggregates of very weakly

1-2—Reasons for Voting and Turnout Frequencies in the Entire Electorate

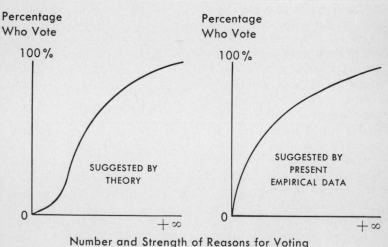

Number and Strength of Reasons for Voting

motivated people tend to have nearly the same low voting proportions despite measurable differences in motivation.

The available data from the Regional Panels Project and from other studies confirm part of this theoretical generalization. For illustration, Table 1-1 describes the relation between interest and turnout in the Colorado sample. The greater the level of interest in the campaign (expressed in the pre-election interview), the higher the rate of voting on Election Day. In addition, differences among low levels of interest produce larger increments in voting than differences among high levels. For example, the increase from "no" to "not much" interest produces a large jump in turnout from 22 per cent to 61 per cent, but the increase from "quite a lot" to a "great deal" of interest results in a turnout increase of only 8 percentage points.

Table 1-1—*Interest and Turnout (Colorado)*

Levels of Interest	Per Cent Who Voted	Difference in Turnout between Levels: Percentage Points	Number of Cases
Great Deal	89%		(83)
Quite a Lot	81	8 pts.	(101)
Not Much	61	20	(121)
None	22	39	(27)

Table 1-1 and the other available data do not show the initial slow acceleration in turnout among the extremely apathetic, and they fail to confirm the dip at the left end of the left-hand curve in Figure 1-2. Perhaps this failure results from inadequate measurement of very weak motives and social stimuli, or possibly the initial slow acceleration does not actually take place. Instead, Table 1-1 and the available data support a simpler rule— *as reasons for voting increase, turnout rises with successively smaller increments.* This generalization is represented by the curve in the right half of Figure 1-2. For simplicity and because of the empirical findings, I shall base the rest of this paper on this simpler rule, but eventually the more elaborate proposition might prove to be empirically true as well as theoretically plausible. (Readers also should note that the arguments in the rest of this paper are based on the statements about social aggregates graphed in Figures 1-2 and 1-3 rather than on the statements about individuals' voting probabilities graphed in Figure 1-1.)

The pattern of smaller increments in turnout usually can be found when other motivations and social stimuli increase. Table 1-2 lists the turnout increments for all the other attitudes and exposures to social stimuli included in the Regional Panels data.[1] When the separate samples are combined in Table 1-2, the decline in turnout is seen to accelerate as interest, candidate involvement, mass-media exposure, and conversational exposure decline; and the same result holds true in two state samples for issue involvement.

The general pattern in Tables 1-1 and 1-2 can be summarized by means of a simple index that classifies respondents by whether they had many or few reasons to vote.[2] Table 1-3 shows that differences between high levels of the index produce smaller turnout changes than do differences at low levels. Or in other words, as reasons for voting increase, each additional reason tends to produce a smaller increment in turnout.

Tables 1-1, 1-2, and 1-3, of course, simply suggest a hypothesis and are not enough to prove a sweeping law about the determination of turnout. One reason is the occurrence of exceptions; an even more

---

1. The questions eliciting interest and amount of exposure to political conversations were included in the pre-election interview and are reproduced in Appendix B, *infra*. Construction of the indexes of candidate involvement, issue involvement, and mass-media exposure is described in Appendix C. Candidate involvement and issue involvement are calculated from pre-election interview reponses, and media exposure from the postelection interview. The question about conversations was taken from the postelection interview in Minnesota and from the pre-election interviews elsewhere.

2. The index is based on the heterogeneous list of reasons in Table 1-2 and simply rates each respondent by the number of reasons for which he has high values. The index has no theoretical meaning aside from furnishing a crude way of classifying people into those with strong, and those with weak, political dispositions. The weights of the various motivations and social stimuli are:

Reason for Voting	Scored 1	Scored O
Interest	Great Deal, Quite a Lot	Not Much, None
Issue Involvement	High, Medium High, Medium	Low, Medium Low
Candidate Involvement (Colorado, Minnesota, Iowa)	High, Medium High	Low, Medium Low, Medium
Difference if Respondent's Candidate Lost (Washington)	Lot, Some	Not Much, None, Not Yet Decided on a Candidate
Mass-Media Exposure	High, Medium High	Low, Medium Low
Conversational Exposure	Actively Discussed	Did Not Discuss, Did Not Hear

For each respondent in Colorado, Minnesota, and Iowa, the total score may range from 0 (if he has low levels of every motivation and stimulus) to 5 (if he has high values throughout). Because no questions about mass-media exposure were asked in Washington, only a five-point scale exists for that sample.

basic reason is that we do not know whether all our levels of motivation and social influence are equal distances apart. For example, in the case of "interest," clearly, turnout rates have been computed over

Table 1-2—Differences in Turnout between Successive Levels of Motivation and Social Stimuli*

		PERCENTAGE-POINT DIFFERENCE BETWEEN LEVELS			
Reasons for Voting	All States Combined		Separate States		
		Colo.	Wash.	Minn.	Iowa
Interest					
Great Deal					
Quite a Lot	9 pts.	8 pts.	7 pts.	17 pts.	10 pts.
Not Much	17	20	22	10	19
None	37	39	29	43	29
Candidate Involvement†					
High and Medium High					
Medium	8	0	12	11	15
Low and Medium Low	13	24	23	17	4
Issue Involvement					
High and Medium High					
Medium	12	12	5	20	16
Low and Medium Low	7	17	9	2	8
Mass Media Exposure					
High					
Medium High	8	16	‡	—1	10
Medium Low	9	8		17	—2
Low	19	23		19	20
Conversational Exposure					
Heard and Actively Discussed					
Heard and Paid No Attention	7	13	10	—16	17
Did Not Hear	13	7	8	38	7

* To economize on space, Table 1-2 omits the turnout rates and the numbers of respondents, which appeared in Columns 1 and 3 of Table 1-1. Table 1-2 lists the percentage-point differences in turnout between each level of each attitude or social stimulus—that is, the kinds of numbers that appeared in the second column of Table 1-1. Each positive number in Table 1-2 shows the decline in turnout rate between the higher level and the level at which the number is entered; a negative number shows that turnout increased when the disposition declined.

† An index of candidate involvement was computed for Colorado, Minnesota, and Iowa. The first column in the table combines the results for these three states alone. In addition, the table contains the data from Washington, where respondents were asked how disappointed they would be if their favorite candidate for Senator should lose. This item may test the same attitudes as the index. In the Washington data, respondents who reported they would experience "a lot" or "some" disappointment had subsequent turnout rates which were 12 per cent higher than those who predicted "not much" or "no" disappointment; and the latter voted at rates which were 23 per cent higher than those who had not yet decided on a candidate choice at the time of the pre-election interview.

‡ Data on media exposure were not obtained in Washington.

an "ordinal scale" of interest (in which strength levels are simply ranked) but not upon a "ratio scale" (in which strength levels are numerically equal distances apart, beginning from an absolute zero). However, our hypothesis is supported repeatedly with many different scales of motivations and social influences, some of which resemble ratio scales with equally weighted additive components.

Table 1-3—Reasons for Voting and Turnout*

	COLORADO, MINNESOTA, AND IOWA COMBINED			WASHINGTON		
Scale Value	Per Cent Who Voted	Number of Cases	Differences in Turnout between Levels	Per Cent Who Voted	Number of Cases	Differences in Turnout between Levels
5	88%	(104)				
4	87	(186)	1 pt.	89%	(55)	
3	79	(195)	8	87	(87)	2 pts.
2	66	(196)	13	74	(115)	13
1	57	(176)	9	54	(78)	20
0	39	(119)	18	37	(40)	17

* In the second and fourth columns, the numbers in parentheses are the total cases. For example, in the three states, 104 persons had scale value 5, and 88 per cent of them voted.

The table presents the aggregate differences for the six-point scale for three states. The following are the differences in turnout rate from one level to another for each state separately:

Scale Value	Colorado	Minnesota	Iowa
5			
4	1 pt.	4 pts.	4 pts.
3	5	11	9
2	20	14	5
1	8	13	10
0	27	6	26

Important support for the generalization that successive reasons for voting add successively smaller turnout increments can be found in other published data about predispositions and turnouts. Most of this material fits the rule more consistently than do the Regional Panels data.

Interest. Nearly every time that interest in politics has been correlated with turnout in a particular election each increment of interest is associated with a steadily smaller increase in turnout. The result is generally true even though studies use different scales of interest. See Lazarsfeld (1948, p. 46, Chart 14), Berelson (1954, p. 31, Chart 11), Campbell (1954, p. 35, Table 3.6), Kornhauser (1956, p. 140, my recomputation of Table 4.19). My Regional Panels finding is based on four independent samples during a midterm election. The confirmations listed above come from four different samples in three separate presidential elections. The Campbell table comes from a representative national sample. The only exceptions I have found are Benney (1956, p. 177, my recomputation of Table 49) and Miller (1952, p. 396, Table 6). The Benney relationship (based on a British sample) is linear; a graph of the Miller data would be S-shaped.

Mass-media exposure. In other studies using other indexes of media exposure (some of which are true ratio scales), the identical relationship appears. Whether the variable is number of different mass media used, frequency of hearing candidates over radio or television, percentage of news and radio stories subsequently recognized by the respondent, or some other measure of media exposure, generally, as the use of and recollection from the mass media during the campaign increase, turnout rises with successively smaller increments. See Campbell (1954, p. 32, Table 3.3), Kornhauser (1956, p. 78, my recomputation of Table 3.2), and unpublished data gathered during the presidential campaign of 1948 in Elmira, New York. Also, with a slight statistical irregularity, Kornhauser (1956, p. 82, my recomputation of Table 3.5).

Candidate involvement. In the 1952 national sample, the Survey Research Center's "extent of candidate orientation" follows the rule consistently. As the index increases from low to high, the successive turnout increments are 16 percentage points, 7, 5, and 1. See Campbell (1954, p. 139, Table 9.1).

Issue involvement. In the 1952 presidential data reported by Campbell (1954, p. 133, Table 8.10), the Survey Research Center's "extent of issue orientation" follows the rule with one irregularity. As the index increases, the successive turnout increments are 24, 5, 11, and 7.

Concern about the outcome of the election. In the 1952 national sample, as concern increases, turnout increases at a decelerating pace. See Campbell (1956, p. 37, my recomputation of Table 3.8).

Political involvement. In a sample of Detroit citizens, increases in an index measuring "sense of political efficacy" are associated with successively smaller increments in turnout in each of the following: the 1948 presidential election, the 1952 presidential election, and the 1953 Detroit mayoralty election.[3] In a 1952 representative sample

3. Unpublished data supplied by Professor LeRoy Ferguson of Michigan State University from Survey Research Center Project Number 816. For permission to use these data, I am indebted to Dr. Harry Sharp, Director of the

analyzed by Eulau (1956, p. 139, Table 13), an index measuring "sense of political relatedness" shows the same kind of relation to turnout rates.

The "diminishing returns" relationship between dispositions and turnout is not as "obvious" as it seems on first reading. Past research has never, specified the form of the relationship, but many authors may have assumed linearity—that is, as dispositions grow stronger, turnout steadily increases. Voting turnout in other contexts may be more difficult for most participants and therefore may not follow the law of diminishing returns; for example, the disposition-turnout curve for most union and corporation elections may be concave upward. Dispositions and frequencies for other kinds of social action may be correlated according to many different patterns.

To sum up the basic hypothesis of this section, *as reasons for voting increase, each additional reason elicits a successively smaller amount of voting in the electorate.* Later, from this simple relationship and from the curves in Figure 1-2, I shall derive a series of implications about fluctuations in turnout by the entire electorate.

Some Intensifying Effects Associated with Social Roles

There is one additional reason for voting that affects how other motivations and social stimuli determine turnout. Besides the opinions, social influences, and other reasons that arise out of the particular election of the moment and that fluctuate from one election to the next, people are subject to certain long-term and stable social norms regulating their turnout regardless of their other motivational states. Men, older persons, and the upper class are *expected* to vote, in response to causes described by Lane (1959, pp. 209-234 *passim*). These expectations will restrict decline in turnout in these groups when their other reasons for voting diminish. Consequently, the effects of variation in other motivations and social stimuli are more intense for persons who lack such social-role prescriptions, namely women, the young, and the lower class. The variations in turnout as reasons change, which were described in previous sections, are intensified or moderated according to the absence or presence of social norms. In summary:

Detroit Area Study at the Survey Research Center, University of Michigan. Construction of the efficacy scale is described in Campbell (1954, pp. 187-189).

**As motivations and stimuli increase, turnout differences
between groups with strong and groups with weak role
prescriptions grow smaller.**

The general pattern can be seen in Table 1-4, which relates
turnout, sex, and interest for all the Regional Panels respondents
combined. Men and women who are highly interested in the campaign
have much closer voting frequencies than men and women with
lower levels of interest. Between high and low levels of interest, the
voting rates of men vary over a narrower range of percentages than
do the voting rates of women—that is, men's turnout varies between
88 and 60 per cent, while women's ranges between 84 and 48
per cent.

Table 1-4—Sex, Interest, and Turnout (All States Combined)

	MEN		WOMEN		
Levels of Interest	Per Cent Who Voted	Number of Cases	Per Cent Who Voted	Number of Cases	Differences between Men and Women in Percentage Points
Great Deal	88%	(192)	84%	(179)	4 pts.
Quite a Lot	80	(222)	75	(241)	5
Not Much, None	60	(230)	48	(280)	12

The effects of role prescription associated with sex and age
can be seen generally in Table 1-5. In the Regional Panels data,
social classes fail to show an increasing inequality in turnout as other
reasons decline, but we should expect such a pattern to exist, and
perhaps it will appear in other research using different class variables.
In summary, if a social group is subject to role prescriptions inducing
it to vote, its turnout will vary less than the turnout of other groups,
when variations occur in the motivations and social stimuli that are
aroused by the election campaign. The people whose voting is more
sensitive to statistical variations in these other stimuli are groupings
like women or the young, who vote as often as men and the old
when they have many reasons to vote, but who are not subject to
strong social norms guaranteeing a minimum level of participation
when they are unmotivated. Figure 1-3 shows the relation among
other reasons and turnout for persons who are and are not subject
to such norms. Like the other rule stated in the previous section,
this simple and almost "obvious" finding will soon lead to some
new results.

Table 1-5—Differences in Turnout between Social Categories at Various Levels of Motivations and Social Stimuli (All States Combined)

Reasons for Voting	PERCENTAGE-POINT DIFFERENCES	
	Between Men and Women	Between Persons Older and Younger than Forty
Interest		
Great Deal	4 pts.	7 pts.
Quite a Lot	5	12
Not Much, None	12	24
Issue Involvement		
High and Medium High	—2	14
Medium	15	26
Low and Medium Low	14	13
Candidate Involvement		
High and Medium High	3	11
Medium	9	23
Low and Medium Low	15	21
Mass-Media Exposure		
High	2	5
Medium High	7	14
Medium Low	4	17
Low	14	22
Conversational Exposure		
Heard and Actively Discussed	5	14
Heard but Paid No Attention	7	15
Did Not Hear	16	24
Combined Index of Reasons—		
Scale Values		
5 and 4	0	10
3 and 2	6	16
1 and 0	12	19
Turnout Behavior of the Rest of the Household (Minnesota)		
All Other Members Voted	2	0
Household Split	10	19
No Other Members Voted	44	30

* These data are computed from a large number of tables like Table 1-4, but only the differences between sex and age categories (that is, the numbers in the fifth column of Table 1-4) are reproduced in Table 1-5. The numbers might be interpreted as the increments in turnout that role prescriptions give to men and to persons over forty, when other more ephemeral reasons for voting are held constant. The one negative number indicates the exceptional case where, among persons with high and medium high issue involvement, women voted slightly more frequently than men.

Because some of the necessary variables were not obtained in Washington, candidate involvement, mass-media exposure, and the combined index are based on three samples. Interest, issue involvement, and conversational exposure are computed by combining all four samples. The construction of the combined index of reasons is described in Footnote 2, *supra*.

II. INFERENCES ABOUT FLUCTUATIONS IN TURNOUT

CERTAIN IMPLICATIONS about variability and change in turnout can be derived from the rules presented in Part I. Part II will show that when individuals are classified into social categories, some of these groups have larger responses to stimuli than others. Consequently, when the strength of campaign stimuli fluctuates from one election to the next, the turnout of the more sensitive groups will fluctuate more than the turnout of the less sensitive ones. Part III will show how these fluctuations in turnout may affect the results of successive elections.

1-3—Reasons for Voting, Role Prescriptions, and Turnout

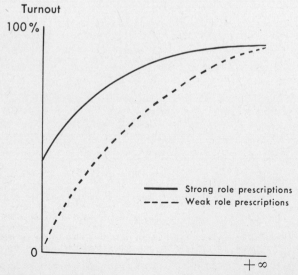

Number and Strength of Motivations and Social Stimuli

Group Responses to Influence

The simplest and most basic implication from Part I is the fact that categories of individuals react differently to stimuli, according to their prior states:[4]

If people are classified by the strength of their motivations, social stimuli, and role prescriptions, the weaker these variables the larger the group shifts in turnout in response to change.

The foregoing proposition about group shifts follows from the first rule stated in Part I, as can be seen by simple geometric reasoning. Figure 1-4 performs certain operations with the curve that earlier appeared in Figure 1-2. The curve is the graph of the function by which predispositions correlate with turnout in the electorate as a whole, and its shape signifies that successive increases in reasons for voting produce steadily diminishing increments in turnout.

Let us compare two categories of people during an election campaign consisting of people with strong and weak dispositions to vote and located at points A and B on the horizontal axis. In this initial state more members of group A vote than members of group $B,$ as can be seen from the fact that point C represents a larger proportion than point D. If we stimulate members of both categories an equal amount, increasing their motivational states to A' and B', the turnout of each increases (from C to C' and from D to D'), but these gains are not equal. The more apathetic group B has gained *more* than the interested group A—that is, the increment from D to D' is larger than the increment from C to C'. In other words, the weaker the predispositions among the members of any social category, the larger their response to changes in stimuli.

Survey data readily confirm that influencing a weakly motivated group during a campaign will yield greater results than equivalent stimulation of a more politically conscious group. A familiar example is the impact of canvassing upon turnout at various levels of interest.

---

4. To simplify the presentation, I shall often omit an important qualification implied by the propositions in Part I. If it is true that turnout rates are nearly the same at very low motivational levels, then the addition or reduction of stimuli should produce very little change. Consequently, my inferences about declines in reasons for voting always should be understood to apply to medium and low levels of motivation, but not to the lowest range.

Previous research by Berelson (1954, pp. 175-176) and Gosnell (1927, pp. 78-79) has established that when people are highly interested in politics party contact does not increase their already high proportion of voters, but canvassing will produce a large increment among those with little interest. The same result appears in the Regional Panels data. Table 1-6 combines respondents from the three states where they reported contact by canvassers. Contact does not add any turnout gains for those who expressed great interest in the campaign at the pre-election interview, but it does add increments for those who had less interest. In other words, the lower the interest, the larger the proportion of people affected by canvassers.

The same difference in response can be found when any other reason for voting is added to or subtracted from the reasons that

1-4—Reasons for Voting and Turnout

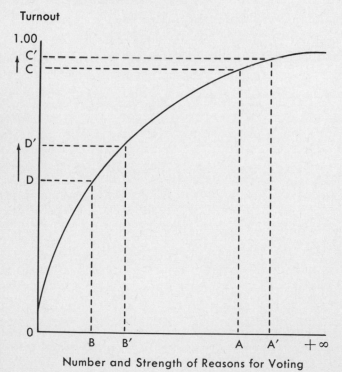

Number and Strength of Reasons for Voting

members of a category already possess. When a group consists of weakly motivated individuals (according to any attitudes or social influences), adding or subtracting any other reason will produce a greater change in their likelihood of voting than within another group whose motivational state is stronger. Regional Panels data show these results, but I shall omit these tables for the sake of brevity.

This finding about individuals' differential sensitivity to influence has important theoretical implications for understanding changes in the character of the electorate, as I will show in the rest of this paper. The finding also has immediate practical applications. For example, if apathetic people are more responsive to stimuli than the politically conscious, canvassers should concentrate on the former. A given investment of canvassing and propaganda will produce a larger return if it is directed toward individuals and groups with low motivational levels than if it is directed toward those with high levels.

Table 1-6—Party Contact, Interest, and Turnout (Colorado, Minnesota, Iowa)

Levels of Interest at Pre-Election Interview	CANVASSED		NOT CANVASSED		Difference between Groups in Percentage Points
	Per Cent Who Voted	Number of Cases	Per Cent Who Voted	Number of Cases	
Great Deal	85%	(74)	89%	(175)	—4 pts.
Quite a Lot	87	(70)	75	(245)	12
Not Much, None	69	(80)	53	(327)	16

Parenthetically, we may note that these findings imply another practical lesson about the costs of canvassing. As canvassing increases, turnout increases at a decelerating rate. Thus, if party and civic organizations should try to arouse maximum public turnout by personal contact and propaganda alone, the volume and costs of such effort would soon rise very steeply. For each additional equal increment of turnout, the cost of canvassing increases at an accelerating pace. This is simply the law of increasing marginal cost in economics, described in Boulding (1948, pp. 506-508) and elsewhere.

These inferences and Figure 1-4 refer to changes in the turnout frequencies of collectivities, and they do not yield descriptions or predictions about individuals. In order to predict the effects of canvassing or other stimuli upon individuals, one must identify the probability patterns for each person, as they were summarized in the first section of this paper and in Figure 1-1. Because the survey category of less-interested people contains many who could easily vote if aroused, canvassing can produce more new voters in that category than among those with high interest, since most of the latter are already very likely to vote. Not every uninterested individual is sensitive to turnout stimuli; some are chronically apathetic. And on the other hand, some highly interested persons might still need additional stimuli to overcome barriers. Canvassing the less interested is most profitable on balance because more of them can be changed.

Group Fluctuations in Turnout in Successive Elections

This unequal group response to changes in stimuli leads to an important implication about fluctuations over time:

The weaker a social group's average level of motivations, social stimuli, and role prescriptions, the more variable will be that group's turnout from one election to another.

In this section, I will first show how this rule can be derived from the basic postulates that were set forth in Part I. Then, I will show that weakly motivated social groups are in fact more variable in their turnout as between presidential and midterm elections.

The effects of an unequal distribution of motivations and social stimuli among social groups. Geometric reasoning again can easily show how this new implication follows from the rules presented earlier in this paper. In the analysis of Figure 1-4 in a previous paragraph, the points *A* and *B* were interpreted as the average dispositions of strongly and weakly motivated groups, and the points *C* and *D* were interpreted as their proportions of voters in an election. Suppose the initial points describe a dull election. If a more exciting election occurs at a later time, the furor causes both groups to increase in involvement and in interest, from *A* to *A'* and from *B* to *B'*. For each equal increment in motivation, the turnout of the weakly motivated group increases *more* than the turnout of the stronger group; on the vertical axis, the distance *D'* minus *D* is larger than the distance *C'* minus *C*. For each equal drop in motivation between an exciting and a subsequent dull election, the voting rate for the low turnout group drops *more* than does the rate for the high turnout group. Consequently, the graph implies that *the weaker a social group's reasons for voting, the more variable is its turnout from one election to another.*[5]

A final problem in the analysis of Figure 1-4 is to give it an empirical interpretation and to predict what kinds of social groups are most likely to fluctuate in turnout. Previous research has repeatedly established, and the Regional Panels data again confirm, that women, the young, and the lower class have weaker reasons for voting than men, older persons, and the upper class.[6] Our survey data could document this well-known fact with hundreds of tables too numerous for reproduction in this chapter, but Figure 1-5 presents

5. Figure 1-4 and the foregoing paragraph make the simple assumption that changes in stimuli are equal for all groups in the electorate. An important but still untouched research problem is to discover whether campaign stimuli and motivations increase more for one group than for another between minor and major elections. If the increases and decreases in stimuli are larger for the weakly involved groups, their turnout fluctuations are very much larger than those of the more strongly motivated groups. This assumption may be more realistic empirically than the assumption of equal changes in motives and stimuli. If the oscillations in predispositions are larger for the strongly involved group, the strong and weak would have similar turnout fluctuations.

6. In every Regional Panels sample, men exceed women in interest, issue involvement, candidate involvement, and exposure to politics in mass media. In two samples, men exceeded women in exposure to politics in conversation, but in the other two samples women reported such involvement more frequently. In nearly every sample, for each of these motivations and stimuli as age increases, possession of high values of these reasons increases too. In the case of conversation exposure, an exception may exist for age groups as it did for the sexes—in two samples the young are at least equally likely to participate in political conversations as are older persons, although in the other two samples the latter exceed them. In every sample, for each of the foregoing motives and stimuli, as social-class standing increases, possession of high values of those attitudes and social influences also increases. For each reason or predisposition, the difference from one social class to another is usually large. The only consistent exception to the rule about the comparative frequency of motives and stimuli is party contact—since most electioneering is now done by women party workers at the voters' homes, women respondents report more contacts than do men. On the combined scale of reasons described earlier in Footnote 2, in all four samples the index values correlate with sex, age, social class, socioeconomic status, breadwinner's occupation, and education. The Index of Social Class used in this paper is described in Appendix C. The Regional Panels data are confined to the familiar survey categories of motivations (such as interest and mass media use) and of demographic categories (such as age, sex, and class). Greater differences in reasons for voting and in political behavior might result if our data differentiated between groups of people who were actually organized as units, who occupied different positions in a social structure, and who possessed contrasting series of motives and stimuli.

one concrete example. The chart gives the slightly curvilinear relation between motivations and turnout for all the Colorado, Minnesota, and Iowa respondents on the six-point scale of reasons for voting, according to the data in Table 1-3. Figure 1-5 then shows the average position of upper-, middle-, and lower-class persons along the curve, according to the arithmetic means for each group.

As a result of all the aforementioned differences in reasons for

1-5—Social Class, Predispositions, and Turnout

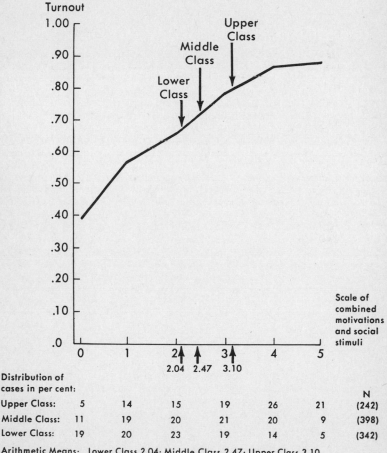

Distribution of cases in per cent:							N
Upper Class:	5	14	15	19	26	21	(242)
Middle Class:	11	19	20	21	20	9	(398)
Lower Class:	19	20	23	19	14	5	(342)

Arithmetic Means: Lower Class 2.04; Middle Class 2.47; Upper Class 3.10

voting, we would expect that, when the glamour of campaigns and public concern vary, women, the young, and the lower class will fluctuate more in turnout than will men, the middle-aged, and the upper class.

The effects of unequal role prescriptions. In Part I, I said that the presence or absence of role prescriptions regulates the intensity of a person's reaction to any changes in his other reasons for voting. From this fact one can also derive some implications about the tendency of one social group to fluctuate in turnout more than another group. The group with weaker role prescriptions will fluctuate more than the other group in response to changes in other motivations and social stimuli, *even if the two groups are similar in these other reasons.* The two groups react with *different* intensity to the *same* attitudes and stimuli.

This implication can be seen in Figure 1-6, which reproduces the same pair of curves that were presented in Figure 1-3. In Figure 1-6, the solid line represents the more politically involved group (such as men, persons over forty, and the upper class), while the broken curve represents the less involved group (such as women, persons younger than forty, and the lower class). If everyone should register a single motivation or combination of motivations whose value falls at point A on the horizontal axis, members of the first group would vote at turnout rate $B,$ and members of the second would vote at turnout rate $C.$ Since B is larger than $C,$ the graph shows the result suggested earlier by Tables 1-4 and 1-5—the first group has a higher turnout than the second, because at the same level of motivation or social stimulation members of the former are more likely to be moved to act.

When motives and stimuli increase from A to $A',$ from dull to exciting elections, the turnout of each group also increases. Just as in the case of the less arousing election, the turnout by the first group is still higher than the turnout by the second group—that is, just as B was larger than $C,$ so B' is larger than C'—but the *same* increase in motives and stimuli has increased the turnout of the second group *more* than it has increased the turnout of the first group. On the vertical axis, the distance C' minus C is larger than the distance B' minus $B.$ Similarly, when the reverse process occurs between an exciting and a dull election, the participation rate for the low-turnout group drops more than the rate for the high-turnout group. Therefore, different social groups have different "response mechanisms" determining how intensely they will react to the variations in motivations and social stimuli that commonly occur from one election to the next in America.

Group differences in inconsistent voting. If the foregoing argument holds, we should expect to find in the politically least-motivated groups the highest proportions of occasional voters—people who vote only when particularly stimulated; and we do find such corroboration in survey data, both from the Regional Panels Project and from other sources.

In our pre-election questionnaire, every respondent was asked whether he had voted in the presidential year of 1948, and in the postelection interview he was asked whether he had voted in the midterm year of 1950. Such data are not ideal for inferring regularities about turnout. The 1948 election had the third lowest

1-6—Predispositions and Turnout for Groups Responsive to Different Role Prescriptions

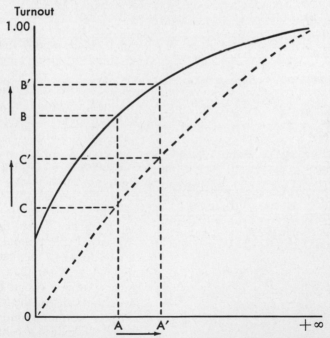

Number and Strength of Motivations and Social Stimuli

turnout of any presidential balloting in American history; questionnaire responses about past turnout may contain substantial error. However, I shall not depend on the Regional Panels data alone for testing the theory. From the possible response patterns in our data, the following typology can be constructed:

Type	1948	1950
Consistent Voter	Voted	Voted
Inconsistent Voter	Voted	Did Not Vote
Consistent Nonvoter	Did Not Vote	Did Not Vote

The typology and all the tables in this section omit the respondents who voted in 1950 but not in 1948. They comprise only 8 per cent of the Regional Panels samples. Their inclusion would strengthen my findings—since they are usually female, young, and lower class—but I am excluding them because many may not be properly classifiable as "inconsistent." (They may have been too young to vote in 1948 or they may have lacked residential eligibility.)

An important step in the empirical test is to see whether irregular voting is more frequent as reasons for voting weaken in midterm election years. Table 1-7 shows the relation between interest in the 1950 campaign and the three voting patterns. As the middle row of the table reveals, the weaker the interest in the midterm election, the higher the frequency of irregular turnout. The same result can be found in any other tables that correlate reasons for voting and turnout patterns over time. In all such data, when persons are classified by the number of reasons for voting in the midterm election year, as such reasons decline there are higher proportions showing a voting history of participation in the more arousing presidential balloting and abstention in midterm elections.

Table 1-7—Interest in the 1950 Campaign and Turnout in 1948 and 1950 Elections (Four States Combined)

| | AMOUNT OF INTEREST | | | |
	Great Deal	Quite a Lot	Not Much	None
Consistent Voter	85%	76%	56%	18%
Inconsistent Voter	8	11	20	31
Consistent Nonvoter	7	13	24	51
	100%	100%	100%	100%
	(n = 345)	(n = 419)	(n = 381)	(n = 78)

As our next step, we must show that the social groups with the highest proportions of weakly motivated people have the highest frequencies of inconsistent voting. Table 1-8 lists the proportions of inconsistent voters in each group—that is, it lists the kinds of percentages that appeared in the middle row of Table 1-7.[7] In confirmation of the reasoning in this paper, the social groupings with the weakest political motivations, social stimuli, and role prescriptions (such as women, the young, and the lower class) have the highest rates of inconsistent voting.

In three of the four samples in Table 1-8, women are slightly more likely to be irregular voters than are men. Although in these particular samples the differences appear small, that they are real seems to be supported by other data regarding fluctuations in turnout. Between 1952 and 1954, women's turnout rates declined slightly more than men's, according to a comparison of the two representative national samples interviewed by the Survey Research Center and reported in Campbell (1956, p. 21). The Survey Research Center's Detroit Area Study of 1954 asked respondents whether they had voted in the presidential election of 1948, the presidential election of 1952, and the mayoralty election of 1953; women were more likely than men to have voted irregularly. (Unpublished data supplied by Professor LeRoy Ferguson from Survey Research Center Project Number 816.) In a recent French public opinion poll reported by Duverger (1955, p. 169), women are slightly more likely than men to vote irregularly. In Norway throughout the twentieth century, women have shown greater fluctuations in turnout rate than men between parliamentary and municipal elections and also from one parliamentary election to the next (Duverger, 1955, pp. 26-28). Finally, the greater variability of women may be confirmed by American election statistics. Before the introduction of women's suffrage, fluctuations for the entire American electorate were less than

7. The differences between the percentages in Table 1-8 and 100 per cent are the frequencies for consistent voting and consistent nonvoting. Men, persons older than forty, and the upper class are more likely to be consistent voters and less likely to be consistent nonvoters. For brevity and in order to concentrate on the causes and consequences of inconsistent voting, I shall omit these data. These findings are not surprising and could have been guessed in view of the well-known facts that men, the middle-aged, and the upper class are always more likely to vote in any *one* election, in comparison with women, the young, and the lower class.

Table 1-8—Demographic Characteristics and Inconsistent Voting

PER CENT WHO VOTED IN 1948 BUT NOT IN 1950

	All States Combined		Colorado (SEPARATE STATES)		Washington		Minnesota		Iowa	
	Per Cent	Number	Per Cent	Number	Per Cent	Number	Per Cent	Number	Per Cent	Number
Sex										
Men	13%	(580)	17%	(161)	10%	(148)	15%	(179)	11%	(92)
Women	15	(651)	17	(149)	12	(189)	17	(181)	17	(132)
Age										
40 and Over	10	(707)	10	(185)	6	(188)	14	(193)	11	(141)
30 to 39	19	(317)	26	(87)	12	(84)	18	(95)	18	(51)
21 to 29	23	(207)	29	(38)	23	(65)	18	(72)	25	(32)
Social Class										
Upper	12	(313)	12	(77)	10	(89)	18	(74)	10	(73)
Middle	15	(515)	18	(124)	13	(149)	17	(151)	12	(91)
Lower	16	(407)	20	(107)	10	(104)	13	(136)	23	(60)
Socioeconomic Status*										
A and B	10	(106)	11	(36)	5	(55)	13	(39)	6	(31)
C-plus			13	(94)	16	(141)			11	(83)
C-minus			20	(136)	6	(55)			18	(85)
C-plus and C-minus combined	16	(590)					17	(192)		
D	18	(192)	21	(44)	10	(71)	16	(126)	27	(22)
Occupation of Family Breadwinner										
White Collar	12	(180)	11	(52)	10	(40)	16	(74)	0	(14)
Business and Farm	15	(412)	16	(99)	8	(120)	21	(86)	16	(107)
Labor	15	(554)	19	(159)	14	(154)	13	(191)	14	(50)

* In Washington interviewers asked respondents for their income instead of rating them on SES. The four categories used in the table are "over $5,000," "$3,000-5,000," "$2,000-3,000," and "under $2,000." In Minnesota, no division was made between "C-plus" and "C-minus" respondents on SES. The first column combines respondents from Colorado, Minnesota, and Iowa on three levels of SES.

they have been since. Table 1-9 takes a few states from the North and Middle West.[8]

Table 1-9—Fluctuations in Turnout between Presidential and Midterm Elections before and after the Beginning of Women's Suffrage*

| | AVERAGE DIFFERENCE IN TURNOUT, IN PERCENTAGE POINTS | |
	From 1888 through 1918	From 1920 through 1958
Massachusetts	9 pts.	15 pts.
New York	10	17
Pennsylvania	10	14
Ohio	14	18
Minnesota	8	12
Iowa	13	25
North Dakota	10	14

* The entries were computed by comparing the number of eligible voters and actual voters for each election, calculating the turnout rates and then taking the mean of all the differences between each election and the next one. The number of eligible voters for each state for each year was estimated from the decennial census statistics. The total number of voters for each state at each election was obtained from many sources. Robinson (1934), Burnham (1955), Gallup (1952), Professor V. O. Key's unpublished Election Statistics File at Harvard University, and the *World Almanac*.

The age differences in irregular voting also can be confirmed by other data. A comparison of the Survey Research Center's national samples of 1948, 1952, and 1954 shows that the aggregate turnout rates of people under thirty-five fluctuated more from one election to another than the frequencies of all higher age brackets (Campbell, 1956, p. 22). In the unpublished data from the Detroit Area Study mentioned earlier, respondents under thirty-five were more likely than older respondents to have voted irregularly during the series of elections in 1948, 1952, and 1953.

Finally, certain social-class variables showed a limited correlation with inconsistent voting in Table 1-8, and some corroborating data exist. In the unpublished Detroit Area Study data cited in previous paragraphs, the lowest-income levels and blue-collar occupations have higher frequencies of inconsistent turnout than do higher-income levels and higher-status occupations.

---

8. The increase in fluctuations for the entire country before and after women's suffrage can be seen in the statistics published by Ewing (1947, pp. 33, 36). Turnout fluctuations before women's suffrage might have been even smaller if there had been popular election of United States Senators, a twentieth-century innovation that has presumably given midterm elections more popular appeal.

In summary, *women, the young, workers, the lower class, and less motivated people in general are most unstable in their political involvement between presidential and midterm elections.* Other evidence shows that these same groups are most unstable *during* the campaign, too. When they intend to vote at the beginning of the campaign, women, the young, the poor, workers, the lower class, and people with weak political involvement are less likely to carry through their intentions than men, the middle-aged, higher-status persons, and more politically motivated people. (See Glaser, "Intention and Turnout," this book, pp. 225-239.) Women, the young, the poor, workers, and the lower class are the groups most likely to vacillate in deciding upon a candidate preference during the campaign, according to Mosteller (1949, pp. 280-284).

III. CHANGES IN THE CHARACTER OF THE ELECTORATE AND THE OUTCOME OF ELECTIONS

THE FINAL PROBLEM is to identify some consequences of our findings for the explanation of the behavior of the American electorate. Since our theory has explained some of the reasons for the turnout fluctuations between presidential and midterm elections, it might shed some light on the connections between these fluctuations and the often contradictory outcomes of presidential and midterm balloting.

As I have tried to show throughout this chapter, changes in the general level of motivations and stimuli affect the constituent groups in the electorate in an unequal fashion. If one election is duller than its predecessor, all groups decline in turnout to some extent; if an election is more arousing, all groups increase in turnout to some extent. But some demographic groups and less-motivated persons in general show a greater propensity to fluctuate than the others. Compared to the presidential electorate, the midterm electorate is slightly more male, older, wealthier, and more elite in its occupational status. Compared to the midterm electorate, the local electorate is probably also slightly more male, older, and more elite. The more glamorous a campaign and the more important an election, the more female, the younger, the less wealthy, and the more "blue collar" will be its electorate. Since American presidential, midterm, and local elections follow each other at fixed intervals, the American electorate periodically expands and contracts in size, and at the same time it cyclically changes in composition. There exists a functional interdependence between size and composition.

Inconsistent Voting by Party Identifiers and the Effects on Election Outcomes

What relationships exist among the size, composition, and outcome of elections? Do these fluctuations in size and in composition of the electorate determine year-to-year changes in the outcome of elections, in the sense that supporters of one party or candidate vote in one election but not in the next?

At first consideration, this seems very plausible, and a simple hypothesis often is advanced. It is well-known that lower-class persons have tended to be Democratic in recent decades, they are one element in inconsistent voting, and during the Roosevelt-Truman period Democratic strength usually declined at midterm. In all four Regional Panels samples, those who identify themselves as Democrats have higher rates of inconsistent voting than those who identify themselves as Republicans. In addition, the Democrats include a larger proportion of consistent nonvoters and a smaller proportion of consistent voters. Table 1-10 lists the rates of inconsistent voting alone.

Table 1-10—Party Identification in 1950 and Inconsistent Voting: Respondents Who Voted in 1948 but Not in 1950

	All States Combined		Colorado		Washington		Minnesota		Iowa	
	Per Cent	Number	Per Cent	Number	Per Cent	Number	Per Cent	Number	Per Cent	Number
Democrats	17%	(528)	20%	(148)	13%	(156)	18%	(165)	17%	(59)
Republicans	11	(381)	20	(83)	8	(80)	15	(110)	12	(108)
No Party	14	(323)	18	(77)	11	(105)	13	(84)	16	(57)

The same contrast between Republicans and Democrats has been found by Campbell (1954, p. 101) and Hastings (1954, p. 307, my recomputation of Table 4B), the former source using a representative national sample. Both these studies report that "independents" have higher rates of inconsistent voting than Democrats, a result that contradicts the Regional Panels data but that is probably correct. The essential thing about irregular voting is its performance by people with weak political involvement, regardless of whether they call themselves Democrats, Republicans, or independents.

If turnout fluctuations determine electoral results by a simple translation of party identifications into ballots, then as turnout declines in a single district or in the entire country, the Republican share of the vote should increase; and as turnout grows, the Democratic share should rise. Past studies of election statistics by Mosteller (1949, pp. 186-190), Key (1952, pp. 521-522), Lazarsfeld (1945, p. 264), and Press (1956, pp. 692-694, 697) have shown that such a simple correlation does not exist. One reason why the sheer size of turnout fails to determine the election result according to party lines is the obvious fact that among the consistent voters some change their minds from time to time, and many electoral switches arise from this.

Another reason that increased turnout will not automatically produce a predictable electoral outcome simply according to party lines is the weak kind of partisan loyalty to be expected from the irregular voters. These are people who ordinarily have a limited interest in politics, they tend to live in an apolitical personal environment, and their preferences in parties and in candidates are not as fixed as the preferences of the more politicized consistent voters. As is shown by the data partially reported in my Table 1-10, in Campbell (1954, p. 101), and in Hastings (1954, p. 307), inconsistent voters do not identify with political parties or they express weak identifications. When an exciting campaign or a national crisis draws these people into an election, it is attracting a politically fickle element. If the turnout of such persons is particularly sensitive to changes in stimuli, probably their candidate preferences also are more changeable than those of the more politicized persons. Previous research by Mosteller (1949, pp. 280-284), Lazarsfeld (1948, Chaps. 6 and 7 *passim*), and Benney (1956, Chap. 12 *passim*) reveals that the kind of politically marginal person who is an inconsistent voter also vacillates more than others when deciding among candidates.

Popular Presidential Candidates and Inconsistent Voting

The voting psychology of the inconsistent voters suggests one way in which the size of turnout affects the outcome. If it is true that inconsistent voters are less controlled by party allegiances and by sophisticated political discriminations than are consistent voters, perhaps they are particularly susceptible to glamorous presidential candidates, salient issues, and political bandwagons. Possibly the following hypothesis[9] is true about presidential campaigns:

An arousing presidential candidacy attracts more new support among the weakly motivated citizens than among the politically alert.

If this assumption proves true in future research, it will have certain practical implications, such as the advantage of nominating candidates and emphasizing issues that can appeal to the normally less interested. In addition, this assumption has certain important theoretical implications for our argument.

If strong candidates are more *popular* with the less interested, then usually they get more *votes* from these citizens than do their opponents. Since so many Americans have a limited number of political motivations, social stimuli, and other reasons for voting, the less-involved persons will always make up an important fraction of a victor's support. Under some conditions a successful presidential candidate may break even or perhaps even lose among the politically more alert voters, while winning his majority from the ballots of the less interested. Some miscellaneous evidence suggests that these politically marginal people have become an important element in recent presidential elections, particularly when crises occur or when glamorous candidates like Roosevelt and Eisenhower run.[10]

9. Because past surveys have not been designed for an adequate understanding of the political behavior of various types of weakly motivated people in different kinds of campaigns, we presently lack sufficient data to test the assumption. Roosevelt always was far more popular than his Republican opponents among the politically apathetic citizens, but this may have resulted from the coincidence that both apathetics and traditional Democratic support come from the lower class in large numbers. The data about Eisenhower's appeal to the apathetics are inconclusive. In 1952, according to Campbell (1954, p. 34, my recomputation of Table 3.5), Eisenhower and Stevenson shared almost equally in popularity and votes among those who said they were "not much interested in following the political campaign." More consistent with my hypothesis is Kornhauser's finding (1956, p. 37) that the unpoliticized segment of Detroit auto workers who did not vote was more pro-Eisenhower in 1952 than the auto workers who voted.

10. Harris (1954, pp. 35-37, 107-117, 146) reports that in 1952, when the Republicans nominated an attractive candidate during a period of crisis, women (who have higher rates of inconsistent voting) participated in large

If such people do mark the rest of their ballots, probably they would tend to approve all the anonymous candidates sharing the ticket with their hero.

Two years later, the midterm campaign would seem duller to the inconsistent voters, no single prominent candidate could simplify and personalize the ticket, and they would not vote. Thus, the more popular a president, and the more successfully he attracted inconsistent voters, the more vulnerable his party when the midterm dip occurs. Our reasoning thus leads to a prediction of differential loss by the two parties:

> **The more stimulating a president's appeals, the larger the losses his party will suffer between the presidential and the next midterm election; and the larger the gains for his party between the midterm and the next presidential election, if he or someone like him runs again. The president's party nearly always loses more votes between presidential and midterm elections than does the opposition party.**

To summarize the argument, the mere size of total turnout does not correlate with the magnitude of Democratic Party victories, but it may correlate with the magnitude of victories for the political parties which nominate glamorous presidents and emphasize important issues. An arousing presidential candidacy owes much of its electoral victory to inconsistent voters, and their failure to vote in the subsequent midterm election automatically subtracts much from the party's strength. The presence or absence of presidential coattails (see John W. Meyer, this book, pp. 52-64) has been suggested as a reason for year-to-year changes in outcome by Bean (1948, p. 36) and Key (1952, p. 521), and our theory predicts a kind of coattail effect for a certain part of the electorate. The argument certainly casts doubt

---

numbers and contributed to the Eisenhower victory both by their votes and by personal influence. Since the beginning of women's suffrage, according to Moos (1952, pp. 16-22), the larger the total turnout in a presidential election, the larger the proportionate discrepancy between the total vote cast for president and the total vote cast for the rest of the ticket, a fact indicating that politically unsophisticated persons have been drawn by the fame of the presidential candidates. After the publication of Moos's book, the same fact again occurred in 1952 and 1956. In Germany inconsistent voters may have supplied much of the electoral support for the arousing Nazi candidates (Bendix, 1952, pp. 369-373).

on the hypothesis, reported by Key (1952, pp. 214 and 520) and others, that the president's losses at midterm are usually due to disillusionment and militant protests by his followers. As I have tried to show, many of his losses are the unintended results of his supporters' complacence and apathy.

Because the stimuli arousing inconsistent voters vary among different presidential elections, the outcomes will differ. Since the consistent voter is more likely to have stronger political feelings and identifications than the inconsistent voter, possibly the smaller the turnout the more likely the election will be decided by a straight party vote. In periods of nation-wide apathy, weak presidents, and minor issues, year-to-year fluctuations in turnout and in electoral outcomes should be smaller than fluctuations during times characterized by crisis and by idolization of presidents.

Fluctuations in Candidate Choice

As Press (1956) correctly observes, turnout alone cannot explain electoral changes between Presidential and midterm elections. This chapter does not present all the reasons for such shifts but only suggests how turnout contributes to change. However, some of our findings about turnout have implications for the question of identifying the sources of change in candidate choice by persons who vote in both presidential and midterm elections.

As Table 1-7 and many other survey data show, not all politically uninterested people are inconsistent voters or consistent nonvoters. Many of them drift into both the presidential and midterm electorates, as if they voted contrary to their normal dispositions. On the basis of my argument in this chapter and on the basis of previous research I have cited, one would expect the less interested to be more susceptible to persuasion by friends, family, candidate appeals, and other sources than the kinds of people who constitute the bulk of the consistent voters. Lazarsfeld (1948, Chap. 16) and Berelson (1954, pp. 138-139) report that the less motivated are very sensitive to personal influence and are the group most responsive to the main currents of political change.

Midterm voting must be particularly puzzling to the uninterested, since the amount of publicity and private discussion is less than during presidential campaigns, and no salient candidates lead and personalize the ticket. In midterm voting, the uninterested might have to depend on personal advice more often than during presidential elections, and also random choices are more likely to occur. If many of them voted for the president's party (as I have argued in the last section), then some of them are likely to change to the opposition at midterm without fully realizing that they are weakening their hero. The less motivated thus may be the principal source of vote changes between major and minor elections.

If the kinds of people who are inconsistent voters do vote, they are more likely to change parties between presidential and midterm elections than the kinds of people who are consistent voters.

This implication is supported by Regional Panels data that compare the candidate preferences of the consistent and inconsistent voters in both 1948 and 1950. (The irregulars did not vote in 1950, but their candidate preferences were reported in the Regional Panels postelection survey.) The inconsistent voters were more changeable in their candidate preferences than the regular voters. While the regulars shifted 10 percentage points in their choices for national office (from 57 per cent for Truman to 47 per cent for Democratic congressmen), the irregulars showed an even larger swing of 15 percentage points (from 67 per cent to 52 per cent). In Colorado, Minnesota, and Iowa, the irregulars swung toward the Republicans even more heavily than the regular voters in the balloting for state offices. Consequently, if the Regional Panels irregulars had voted in 1950, they would have accentuated the losses suffered by the president's party.

CONCLUSION

IN SUMMARY, two simple premises have been developed about the determination of turnout in the electorate, and they have led to some generalizations about turnout fluctuations over time. First, increases in reasons for voting (except possibly in the lowest range) produce successively smaller increments in turnout. Secondly, different social groups will react differently to variations in other immediate motivations and social stimuli, according to whether they have a sense of duty to vote irrespective of their more voluntary and ephemeral reasons. Consequently, except in the lowest range containing the most apathetic people, the weaker a social group's motivations, social stimuli, and role prescriptions, the greater its sensitivity to changes in reasons for voting and the more variable its turnout between one election and the next. The cyclical increase and decrease in interest between presidential and midterm elections therefore bring about higher rates of inconsistent voting by women, the young, the lower class, and people with medium and low motivations. Because their partisan commitments and political sophistication are weaker than those of the consistent voters, the irregular voters' participation may contribute much to the electoral victories of an arousing president and their abstention may contribute to the decline of his party in the midterm balloting.

2

A REFORMULATION OF THE
"COATTAILS" PROBLEM

By John W. Meyer

*I*n most election studies, analyses involving candidate preference are based on data concerning the voters' choice for a single
office. This paper will make use of data on the relations between
voters' choices of different candidates for several offices, in order to
examine topics noted in the voting literature (under names such as
"ticket" voting) in regard to casting whole ballots. One such topic
is the increase in consistency of the voter's choices over the period
of a campaign—that is, the tendency to move toward the straight
ticket. The other is the notion of the "coattail effect"—the ability
of one candidate at the head of a ticket to win votes for fellow
candidates during the course of a campaign.

INCREASE IN CONSISTENCY

IN EACH of the three Regional Panels states where appropriate data
were obtained, the tendency for the voter to choose all his candidates
from one party showed an increase from the October to the November
interviews. In Colorado, 47 per cent made all one-party choices in
October, 61 per cent in November. In Minnesota the figure rose

52

from 51 per cent to 53, in Iowa from 62 per cent to 72. These figures represent the voters who chose at least three candidates out of a possible five from a single party and none from the opposition party. By applying other standards, the figures can, of course, be varied. If only those respondents who indicated choices for *all* offices are included in the tabulation (that is, if everybody who gave a don't-know answer regarding any office is eliminated), the percentages of straight-ticket choices become considerably higher at both times. The increase between October and November persists, however, which is the main point for our present purposes.

Still another measure may be taken by testing the voter's party consistency with regard to each *pair* of offices. This is done in Table 2-1. Here every office is paired with every other office, and the "per cent consistent" shows the proportion of the respondents who chose candidates from the same party for both offices, the tabulations being made separately for October and November. Respondents who gave don't-know answers at either time for either office in a pair are eliminated from both October and November calculations for that pair.

The fact that every figure in the "per cent consistent" columns is well over fifty demonstrates that, both at the beginning and at the end of the campaign, the majority of voters made one-party choices for *all* offices for which they made a choice at all. Since in twenty-six of the thirty comparisons in the table the percentages are higher in November than in October, the table is also another demonstration that consistency grows during the campaign. It is this phenomenon that we are interested in—as the first step in attacking the coattails problem.

A FORMULATION OF THE

COATTAILS PROBLEM

IT IS OFTEN HELD that the lesser candidates on a party's ticket "ride into office on the coattails" of a personally popular candidate at the head of the ticket. There are more complications to this hypothesis than may be evident immediately, and specifications for it could be proliferated. But clearly an underlying assumption is that, during the course of a campaign, the voter's choice of candidate for a major

Table 2-1—Change in Voter Consistency on Pairs of Offices Compared

	COLORADO				MINNESOTA				IOWA			
	Per Cent Consistent			Number of Cases	Per Cent Consistent			Number of Cases	Per Cent Consistent			Number of Cases
	Oct.	Nov.	Diff.		Oct.	Nov.	Diff.		Oct.	Nov.	Diff.	
Senator-Governor	77%	85%	8%	(246)					89%	93%	4%	(123)
Senator-Congressman	80	83	3	(223)					90	94	4	(143)
Senator-Lt. Governor									96	95	—1	(85)
Senator-Sec. of State	74	82	8	(200)								
Senator-Atty. Gen.	75	80	5	(201)					91	92	1	(124)
Gov.-Congressman	80	84	4	(217)	75%	74%	—1%	(277)	89	88	—1	(129)
Gov.-Lt. Gov.					79	80	1	(271)	94	97	3	(89)
Gov.-Sec. of State	76	79	3	(199)	73	75	2	(316)				
Gov.-Atty. Gen.	76	79	3	(229)	77	82	5	(270)	97	93	—4	(118)
Cong.-Lt. Gov.					78	80	2	(240)	92	99	7	(90)
Cong.-Sec. of State	75	87	12	(188)	61	73	12	(271)				
Cong.-Atty. Gen.	76	81	5	(205)	71	78	7	(248)	88	94	6	(134)
Lt. Gov.-Sec. of St.					75	82	7	(270)				
Lt. Gov.-Atty. Gen.					82	84	2	(255)	96	99	3	(90)
Sec. of State-Atty. Gen.	73	81	8	(191)	78	84	6	(279)				

Totals: Number of Positive Differences = 26

Number of Negative Differences = 4

Total Comparisons = 30

office will tend to decide his final choices for the minor offices. It is this assumption that we shall test here.

Such a phenomenon could account for the growth in party consistency we find in our data. If it exists, we should expect to find that the respondents who make shifts from inconsistent to consistent positions do so by bringing their choices for minor offices into conformity with their choices for major offices, rather than the other way around. The method of ascertaining whether or not they do so depends upon the successive pairings introduced in Table 2-1. It consists of a series of "sixteenfold tables" classifying voters by their choices for two offices at two time points.[1] Table 2-2 will illustrate.

Table 2-2—Mutual Effects of Voters' Preferences for the Offices of Governor and of Secretary of State (Minnesota)

OCTOBER		Governor Sec. of State	Dem. Dem.	NOVEMBER Dem. Rep.	Rep. Dem.	Rep. Rep.
Gov.	Sec. of State					
Dem.	Dem.		37	3^a	4^b	3
Dem.	Rep.		18^c	35	0	7^d
Rep.	Dem.		3^e	0	15	8^f
Rep.	Rep.		10	13^g	8^h	152

In looking at such a table, we are primarily interested in what happens to voters who in October had inconsistent preferences for the two offices. Looking at the second row, which represents those who in October preferred a Democrat for governor and a Republican for secretary of state, we find that in November eighteen changed their preference for the latter office, and only seven for the former. Similarly, of those who first preferred the Republican for governor and the Democrat for secretary of state (third row), eight changed their minds regarding the latter and only three regarding the former. Thus, in this example most voters who moved from inconsistent to consistent positions did so by altering their choices for secretary of state (a minor office) in favor of the party of their choice for governor (a major office).

This finding could be due, however, to a *generally* higher rate of change of opinions on the election for secretary of state due to some other factor. To eliminate this possibility, we look at changes in the other two rows of the table, representing voters who were con-

1. The sixteenfold analysis here was initiated and in large part carried out by William McPhee. The method and index used are due to Paul F. Lazarsfeld.

sistent in their October choices. We ignore those who changed their choices for both offices, as nothing can be deduced there regarding distinctions between the offices. In the other cells, among those who in October preferred the Democratic candidates for both offices, four changed their minds regarding the candidate for governor, while three changed regarding the secretary of state; among those who preferred the two Republicans in October, thirteen changed as regards the governor, only eight as regards the secretary of state.

Our first result, then, was not due to any greater volatility of preferences for secretary of state as such. Taken together, the two sets of data lead to the conclusion that voters' preferences for governor tended to influence their preferences for secretary of state.

In reaching such a conclusion from a sixteenfold table, we use only the information contained in the eight cells indicated in Table 2-2 by the letter superscripts. *Indexes of mutual effects* are available which combine this information into one statistic. The index we shall use is derived as follows, the small letters referring to the cells lettered in Table 2-2, and N being the total number of cases in the table:

$$\text{Index of mutual effect} = \left(\frac{cf - de}{c + d + e + f} - \frac{ah - bg}{a + h + b + g} \right) \frac{8}{N}$$

For Table 2-2, the index proves to be $+ 0.112$. The positive sign indicates that the office of governor tended to influence that of secretary of state. Had the reverse occurred, the sign would be negative. The larger the number, the greater the dominance of one office over the other.

If such indexes are assembled for each pair of offices in a given election, a number of results are possible:

1. One or two major offices may appear to dominate all the others. This finding would provide evidence of the existence (and importance) of influence by these offices on the voters' other choices, and would lend support to the coattails idea.

2. Minor offices may appear to dominate major ones. Unless we had some reason to believe that the minor offices in question were important to the voters, we would take this result to be evidence of the inadequacy of the coattails model as an explanation of the growth in consistency.

3. No results, or random results, may appear. This would suggest the inadequacy of the model.

4. Influence may be seen to run in a clear hierarchy, with more important offices dominating lesser ones and with the most important offices exercising the greatest influence. This would suggest the pervasive importance of office influence—not just of one office with popular candidates, but in general.

We performed the statistical computations in question with our data on voter preferences in the Colorado, Minnesota, and Iowa samples. The results are shown in Table 2-3. The figures in the table are indexes of mutual effect and show the extent to which the office listed at the *side* of the table tends to dominate the office listed at the *top* of the column. Thus, the figure —.071 in the top row, being negative, means that in Colorado voters' choices for senator were influenced *by* their choices of congressman more than the reverse.

Table 2-3—The Mutual Effects among Offices*

Influencing Office — INFLUENCED OFFICE

COLORADO	Senator	Congressman	Governor	Sec. of State	Atty. Gen.
Senator		.071	—.047	—.041	.047
Congressman	.071		.002	.037	—.071
Governor	.047	—.002		—.030	.051
Sec. of State	.041	—.037	.030		.034
Atty. Gen.	—.047	.071	—.051	—.034	

MINNESOTA	Congressman	Governor	Lt. Gov	Sec. of State	Atty. Gen.
Congressman		.043	.085	.095	.110
Governor	—.043		.059	.112	.150
Lt. Gov.	—.085	—.059		.118	.136
Sec. of State	—.095	—.112	—.118		.015
Atty. Gen.	—.110	—.150	—.136	—.015	

IOWA	Senator	Congressman	Governor	Lt. Gov	Atty. Gen.
Senator		.070	.022	.071	.056
Congressman	—.070		—.089	—.030	.051
Governor	—.022	.089		.000	.016
Lt. Gov.	—.071	.030	.000		.059
Atty. Gen.	—.056	—.051	—.016	—.059	

* The figures are indexes derived by means of the formula explained in the text. They are based on very few cases, and while precise measures of their statistical variability are not available, it is clear that the results are to be taken very tentatively.

Scanning each state's figures as a whole, we find that the Colorado results show no clear pattern—certainly no tendency for major offices to dominate minor ones. The index values tend to be low. We may conclude that office influence was not an important factor.

The Minnesota results, on the other hand, show a clear example of a hierarchy—major offices tend to dominate minor ones. And with the offices ranked in the order shown, each office tends to dominate the ones below it in the list. Even here, however, there are problematic results. Choices for lieutenant governor appear to play an important role in influencing choices for the other minor offices, a result it is difficult to take seriously.

The Iowa results could be made to show a consistent pattern. Except that the index values are lower, the pattern would be similar to the Minnesota one if the office of congressman were moved farther down on the list—less important than lieutenant governor. But this, too, is difficult to accept as a substantive result, especially in view of the importance of this particular congressional race (Seventh District) to the Iowa voters in 1950 in that district.

Thus, while some suggestions of a pattern of office effect are found in two of the samples, sharply anomalous results are found in all three, and the figures do not conform to what we would expect on the basis of our formulation of the coattails effect. We conclude that the model, essentially a measure of "pair" effects, is not adequate to account for the observed behavior of the voters in a dependable way.

THE PARTY-DISPOSITION EXPLANATION

THE COATTAILS THEORY tells us that the voters' choice for office *y* results from their choice for office *x*. The image this calls up is that of interaction within a *pair*—that is, the choice for office *x* acts upon the choice for office *y*. Hence, we adopted the sixteenfold table as the statistical model.

The search for a different formulation of what happens to voters' choices during a campaign suggests an entirely different imagery. It is dominated not by the figures of *pairs* of candidates but by the phenomenon of *general* partisanship as brought out in a campaign. Visualize a "party-bias continuum" from Democratic to Republican, with some voters scattered all along the scale, but many voters clustered near each of the two poles—the dependable party voters.

The campaign can then be postulated to *polarize* the scattered voters—that is, draw them outward toward one or the other of the parties—and also to *intensify* the party feelings of voters already near the poles, namely, increase the likelihood of their manifesting their party biases in votes for any and all candidates of that party. Both these effects imply that observed votes are due to a latent variable, namely, party disposition. At any time, the voter's candidate preferences are closely related to his position along the party continuum. The two propositions noted above specify ways in which this relation is *increased* through a campaign: (1) The dispersion of the voting population toward the opposite poles in party disposition (polarization) leaves fewer voters near the ambiguous middle point, where inconsistency and "neutrality" in candidate preference—random and don't-know answers—are most likely to be found. (2) The rallying effect of the campaign crystallizes the expression of party dispositions (intensification). At any given level of underlying party disposition, more people vote in accord with it.

Just as the "coattails" imagery corresponded to the sixteenfold logic, the above ideas have a formal analogue in latent structure analysis, the theory and computational methods of which have been described by Lazarsfeld (1950, 1954a, 1959). A set of observed indicators, and their statistical interrelations, are used in mathematically deriving measures of the underlying variable. Individual cases are distributed along this "latent" variable in such a way that the statistical relation of each indicator to the variable accounts for the observed interrelations among the indicators (responses). This is done without reference to external criteria: the analysis starts with the observed indicators and derives from them both a classification and the relation between this classification and each indicator.

We have as the observed indicators here, voters' responses about their candidate preferences on five offices. As latent structure analysis is usually employed, interest is focused on measuring the latent variable and ranking people along it; usually the indicators are relevant only as devices for measurement. But our primary interest is in explaining the indicators themselves, by their relations to the latent variable and changes in that relation through time.

It must be stressed that the use of latent structure analysis here cannot *prove* the accuracy of the conceptual model. It only provides a statistical analogy for our ideas, and it is a question that can only be answered pragmatically whether that will account for phenomena of voter consistency in a more satisfactory (less contradictory) way than the former coattails model did.

We employ the model to study the two propositions about party disposition that have been stated earlier: (1) how the distribution of voters on the underlying party disposition variable changes (for example, polarization), and (2) how the relation between the choices for each office and the underlying variable changes (for example, intensification).

1. *Polarization.* To facilitate computational solution, we use a model in which individuals are usually assumed to lie, not on a continuous distribution, but in an ordered set of discrete classes, here Democrats, Republicans, and those uncommitted or with weak party dispositions. We wish to show that the size of the uncommitted class decreases through time. For stable results, the available three-class models required larger samples and less highly correlated indicators than are provided by the Regional Panels data. Consequently, we derived our three classes as follows: Each candidate choice was dichotomized, with don't-know and Democratic responses combined as together "not Republicans." A simple dichotomous latent structure was fitted; this gave the proportion of individuals in the latent Republican class. Then each indicator was dichotomized the other way, with don't-know and Republican responses combined. Another dichotomous latent structure was fitted; this gave the proportion in the latent Democratic class. The proportion in the class with no identifiable party disposition was derived by subtraction, since the three classes must together include the whole population.

Thus, voters' preferences on five different offices are used to develop a classification on the underlying party-disposition variable. This was done for October and November separately, since we are interested in changes in the distribution through time. The results are given in Table 2-4. Each row shows the derived distribution of voters for one state at one time—the results, that is, of one latent structure analysis. Thus, in Colorado 26 per cent of the voters are

Table 2-4—Distributions on Latent Party Disposition*

	Republican	None	Democratic	Number
COLORADO				
October	26%	35%	39%	(336)
November	44	8	48	(336)
MINNESOTA				
October	52	21	27	(397)
November	54	11	35	(397)
IOWA				
October	43	45	12	(251)
November	59	14	27	(251)

* It must be remembered that the October and November results are completely independent of each other. Thus, it is formally possible that many Democrats became Republicans, in terms of latent party disposition, or vice versa. This is known to be empirically infrequent, however.

classified as Republicans in October, while 39 per cent are classified as Democrats.

The major point of Table 2-4 lies in the comparison of the two times within each state. In each case, from October to November, there is a sharp decline in the size of the class estimated to manifest no party disposition. In Colorado, for example, this class decreases from 35 per cent of the sample to 8 per cent. In the other states there are similar sharp declines. This means simply that in November there are fewer don't-know answers and less *mixing* of parties in the candidate choices of individual voters. Large numbers of people are moving from uncommitted positions to committed ones as the campaign progresses. This illustrates the "polarization" proposition. It would produce, in manifest data, greater consistency of choices, as if they were interacting. But it is because more people are joining the ranks of party voters and fewer are making independent choices.

2. *Intensification.* We can now turn to the second proposition—that inconsistency decreases because voters who are disposed toward one party or the other become more likely to *manifest* this disposition on each and every office as the campaign progresses.

The statistical solutions give the probabilities in question—the probability that a voter with a Republican disposition will prefer the Republican candidate for a given office in October and the comparable probability for November. The same information is given for those with Democratic dispositions.

Table 2-5 contains the relevant findings. The probability of voting in accord with party disposition is shown for each office in each state at each time. For example, in Colorado in October, latent Democrats had a probability of voting for the Democratic senatorial candidate of .87. Latent Republicans had a probability of voting for the Republican senatorial nominee of .95. (The probabilities of Democrats voting don't-know or Republican and vice versa are not given by our particular way of using latent structure analysis. This is also true of all response probabilities for the uncommitted class.)

We are interested in comparing, for each office and each party-disposition group, the October and November probabilities of voting in accord with party disposition. The difference between these—which is the relevant statistic in the comparison—is entered below each pair of figures.

Table 2-5 contains thirty such comparisons. In twenty-four of them, the results are in the predicted direction. That is, in twenty-four

Table 2-5—Change in Likelihood of Manifesting Party Disposition from October to November: Proportion Who Choose in Accord with Own Party Disposition for Offices

COLORADO	Senator	Congressman	Governor	Sec. of State	Atty. Gen.
Democratic					
Oct. (131)*	.87	.82	.93	.76	.83
Nov. (161)	.90	.91	.89	.91	.84
Increase	.03	.09	—.04	.15	.01
Republican					
Oct. (87)	.95	.95	.90	.75	.80
Nov. (148)	.93	.90	.91	.78	.85
Increase	—.02	—.05	.01	.03	.05
MINNESOTA	Congressman	Governor	Lt. Gov.	Sec. of State	Atty. Gen.
Democratic					
Oct. (107)	.98	.82	.80	.55	.73
Nov. (139)	.93	.79	.87	.70	.83
Increase	—.05	—.03	.07	.15	.10
Republican					
Oct. (206)	.61	.86	.85	.91	.88
Nov. (214)	.75	.87	.89	.96	.92
Increase	.14	.01	.04	.05	.04
IOWA	Senator	Congressman	Governor	Lt. Gov.	Atty. Gen.
Democratic					
Oct. (30)	.92	.84	.88	.84	.88
Nov. (68)	.98	.89	.89	.91	.90
Increase	.06	.05	.01	.07	.02
Republican					
Oct. (108)	.91	.98	.91	.63	.93
Nov. (148)	.93	.95	.95	.95	.97
Increase	.02	—.03	.04	.32	.04

* This figure is the number of cases.

cases the probability of voting in accord with party disposition increased from October to November. This result occurs in spite of the *dilution* of the November samples through the addition of a number of previously "unidentified" voters.[2] And it provides an illustration of the second proposition about voter consistency, that is, that those voters who are disposed toward a party become more

2. Because of the polarization effect, the November samples are larger than the October samples, and hence are "diluted." It would be possible to classify each voter by his October and November positions on the latent trichotomy and thus to show these results for each group separately. In this way it would also be possible to separate the cases of "conversion"—that is, October Republicans who became November Democrats, and vice versa.

likely to express this disposition in their choices of candidates for specific offices. This also would produce greater consistency between choices, again as if they were interacting. But it is because, as probabilities of voting for the party candidates increase all down the line, the non-party choices involved in the previous inconsistency decrease.

COMMENTS

WE HAVE FOUND empirically that voter consistency increases through the campaign. This increase is apparently not due to pair interactions, for the influence of choices for one office over choices for others does not have a dependable pattern. Since such influence is an essential ingredient of what is commonly called the coattail effect, it can be said that such effects were not found in any uniform way.[3] Rather, increases in voter consistency between offices can better be formulated by a different imagery. The choices are not individually related, but become so from the increasing importance to all of them of *party* disposition as a determinant of votes. This tendency can be formulated and measured with latent structure analysis, which provides a statistical analogy to the substantive ideas involved.

This accounts for the increasing consistency of choices for different reasons, but does not rule out the coattail effect. There appears to be no reason why such an effect could not play a role, along with the basic party disposition, in the interrelations of votes for several offices. Obviously it sometimes does play a role, as in our Minnesota data. It is interesting to speculate about the conditions, therefore, under which the effect will and will not occur.

The central aspect of the coattail effect is the influence of one office on voting for another. This office influence is likely to be greatest when voters see the candidates for the influencing office as

---

3. The findings on the importance of party disposition also suggest an explanation for some of the negative and anomalous results found earlier on office influence. Party disposition could act as a spurious factor on sixteenfold tables testing for the influence of one office on another. If candidates for major offices had images in the minds of voters distinct from party, a major result of a campaign might be to pull these images partially back into line with party disposition preferences. In such cases it could appear that the voters are changing their opinions on the major office to conform with opinions on minor offices (which were in correspondence with their party dispositions).

Alternately, it is also possible that where it appears voters are bringing their opinions on minor offices into conformity with those on major offices, there are also spurious factors of the same basic type (i.e., party disposition).

party representatives, for we have shown that the crystallization of party voting is the main dynamic or change-producing force in the situation. But when such a candidate is seen in party terms by voters, he is already likely to be evaluated by voters in party terms. A candidate for minor offices is likely to be evaluated in party terms, too. Indeed there is no other way to choose him. But that would mean, with both getting party votes, there would be little difference between the offices in voter preference. With neither having votes the other does not have, how could either help the other?

This can be put in another way. If the candidate for a major office remains strongly identified with his party, he gets primarily a party vote, and will not have many additional supporters whom he can bring to the ticket and whom it would not get otherwise. If, on the other hand, he is a popular individual who gets many supporters on other grounds than party, or is seen in nonpartisan terms, he may have much potential coattails influence but he will lack the party image necessary to effect the transfer, or deliver the votes to the *party*. An example is Eisenhower, who apparently could not deliver his personal votes to the party.

A suggestion of this picture is shown by the present findings. We found, in Table 2-5, that "intensification" of partisan voters occurred in twenty-four of the thirty comparisons. *All* six deviant cases were *major* offices—senator, governor, or congressman—although such offices made up only slightly over half the offices involved. This finding suggests that candidates for such offices may become well enough known by the voters to be seen in personal rather than partisan terms. Such candidates may be gaining support that they could bring to others on their tickets but simultaneously losing the basis —the identification with a single party—on which the transfer could be effected.

These ideas suggest that certain limitations are necessarily placed on the possibilities for coattail effects. Of course, a candidate might conceivably develop enough popular force to change the voters' image of his party, and thus escape these limitations. That this can occur during the short period of a campaign seems unlikely, however; that is, it is probably a historical rather than a campaigning phenomenon.

In any event, an obvious next step is to begin studying the effect of these individuals—Roosevelts who succeed and Eisenhowers who apparently do not—in transferring their popularity not to other individual candidates but to the only force we find clearly *can* carry in individual candidates, the crystallizing party vote.

3

THE INDEPENDENT VOTER

By Alan S. Meyer

*T*hroughout the evolution of our election system, some concept of flexible, independent voting has been included in democratic theories and has guided political tacticians. Independence of choice is an assumption underlying much of our creed. Elections would serve little purpose if no voters made independent and novel decisions and if everyone were rigidly tied to one political party throughout his life.

Some philosophers have held that rational, independent choice in opinions and in votes is the central condition for the success of democracy. For example, according to Viscount Bryce (1929, Vol. I, 47-48) the Ideal Democracy will depend on the following kinds of behavior by its citizens:

> The average citizen will give close and constant attention to public affairs, recognizing that this is his interest as well as his duty. He will try to comprehend the main issues of policy, bringing to them an independent and impartial mind, which thinks first not of his own but of the general interest. If, owing to inevitable differences of opinion as to what are the measures needed for the general welfare, parties become inevitable, he will join one, and attend its meetings, but will repress the impulses of party spirit. Never failing to come

---

Written in 1952 and revised for this volume by the editors, with the original analyst's permission.

to the polls, he will vote for his party candidate only if satisfied by his capacity and honesty.

The same ideas can be found in many other classics in democratic theory, such as Mill (1910).

However, recent research summarized by Hyman (1959, pp. 74-81) and Campbell (1954, pp. 98-106) shows that a large proportion of the electorate "inherits" or adopts political-party allegiance and thereafter stays with it fairly rigidly and persistently. The original assumption that *most* men would behave flexibly and adaptably has now been narrowed to the hope that at least *some* men will do so, and that these "independent voters" will exert decisive influence over election results. But in all these recent discussions, the meaning of "independent voter"—who and what he is supposed to be—remains vague.

This paper will consider two problems raised by these discussions: (1) what definitions are implicit in uses of the term "independent voter," and (2) if the independent voters are located by use of these implicit definitions, how numerous they are and what they are like. This paper will attempt to add some new ideas about the nature and sources of independent voting to the recent literature, which has concentrated on the kinds of electoral choice made by persons who do not identify with any party. So far, the principal articles have been written by Eldersveld (1952) and Agger (1959).

WHAT WE MEAN BY "INDEPENDENT"

Irregularity in Voting

The implicit assumption in democratic ideology that at least some voters can and will be independent in their choice-making suggests one criterion by which such people can be defined and located. Since political action is organized by parties, the independent voter must be one who is not regularly committed to a single party. He is *flexible* in some way with regard to political parties.

Flexibility or irregularity in this sense can be defined in many ways. One criterion might be *lack of persistence over time*. For example, if a voter chooses different parties in successive elections, he can be considered flexible in his vote. As an illustration of this and other definitions, data will be presented from the Regional Panels studies to give some idea of the number of voters who behave in the manners described.[1] In these studies of Western and Midwestern states, 20 to 25 per cent of the potential voters whom we interviewed chose different parties for national office in 1948 and 1950.

A second criterion of flexibility might be *withholding commitment to a party*. In October of 1950, a midterm election, about 25 to 30 per cent of the potential voters in these samples identified themselves with neither major party when the interviewer asked, "All in all, do you consider yourself mainly a Democrat, mainly a Republican, or neither one?" This figure is somewhat larger than that reported nationally for presidential years. It is interesting to note, however, that in the few weeks between October and November 1950, the percentages of those who did not identify with a party in our sample in the state of Washington decreased from 32 to 18. The percentage of potential voters who withhold identification with a party is probably influenced by the closeness to the election of the date of questioning, and thus, probably by the political heat and polarization generated at the time.

A third definition of flexibility might be *split-ticket voting*, in which a voter discriminates among candidates on the same ticket in any one election by choosing men from different parties. In the five leading contests in each state, from 20 to 45 per cent of the respondents split their choices on the second wave of interviews in November.

Finally, flexibility might be defined as *lack of agreement with one's "party line" on issues*. The largest amount of flexibility found in our samples was of this kind. About 45 to 65 per cent of potential voters did not agree with their party on at least one of five issues selected as samples of the questions at issue between the parties at the time. (We estimated these proportions by comparing respondents'

---

1. Throughout this paper, the percentages are general estimates of magnitude rather than exact proportions in the populations from which our data came. In the first place, the percentages are based on operational definitions selected from many possible ones that might fit the concepts of regularity and interest. Furthermore, these percentages are influenced by situational factors inherent in the particular time and place the study was made. The number of voters who identify with a party and who express interest in politics will depend to some extent on whether the question is asked during an election campaign, whether the election is in a presidential year, and whether the campaign is heated. Finally, the Regional Panels samples do not perfectly represent the populations from which they were drawn. Consequently, the figures are only illustrative.

party identifications with their scores on the Index of Issue Opinion, described in Appendix C.)

In summarizing the foregoing series of figures, it can be said that, although voters tend to be persistent in their party choices, anywhere from 20 to 65 per cent of the members of these samples are in some degree flexible, depending on how one defines flexibility and in what areas of decision the flexibility is measured.

All these measures of flexibility are found to be related to each other. Voters who are flexible in one way tend to be flexible in the other ways, although the correspondence is far from perfect. It is likely, however, that there is a meaningful dimension of party flexibility, or lack of party regularity, underlying all these measures, that could be represented by scales and indexes not entirely arbitrary in their definition and not dependent alone on how the voter likes to see himself. Until now, voting analysts have usually accepted the respondent's self-description of whether he is independent.

Comparisons of our measures of flexibility may yield certain interesting theoretical byproducts about the conditions governing voting flexibility. The fact that more flexibility was found with regard to issue opinions than with regard to ticket choices and more on ticket choices than on party identification suggests that flexibility is perhaps most likely to occur in making decisions that are less important to one's basic party commitment. Regional Panels samples provide further data in substantiation of this hypothesis. Party regulars are more likely to vote for the opposition in minor contests such as for state secretary of state or attorney general than in major contests such as for senator and congressman. Further corroborative evidence from national surveys shows that both Democrats and Republicans are more likely to cross party lines while voting for local offices (other than mayor) than while voting for state or national offices (Roper, 1952; Campbell, 1957, p. 306). Thus, it is likely that the less important a decision is to the voter, the more often he will deviate from his main commitments when making it.

A Second Dimension—Involvement in Politics

A second dimension underlies much contemporary thinking about independent voters. From earliest days to now, Americans have assumed that politics is the province of men who believe, think, and act *strongly*. This theme appears throughout the writings of the

American Founding Fathers, such as *The Federalist,* Nos. 6-10; and Adams (1850-1856, Vols. IV-VI). The American governmental system, with its checks and balances, is based on the assumption that politics is the concern of men who care too much, not too little, about the outcome of policy decisions. Political history is written about great debates and decisive elections, and current political reporting deals almost exclusively with those who care about politics. For example, consider the strong phrases used by a veteran reporter to describe independent voters in 1952:

> The true "independents"—and there are millions .of them— . . . are now *disgusted* and *indignant*. . . . What these true "independents" want to do is to register their protest . . . (Lawrence, 1952).

Consequently, an implicit distinction is made in most discussions of political phenomena, the uninterested portion of the public being ignored. The "independent voter" must therefore be distinguished from the person whose nonpartisanship or variability is associated with indifference; and research techniques for locating independent voters in a sample electorate must include some sort of measure of "involvement" in politics. Such a measure might be based on the extent of political knowledge a respondent displays, the amount of political activity he reports (talking politics, following the news, and so forth), the interest or concern he expresses in regard to political issues or election results, and so on.

The following measurements are among those that can be made using the Regional Panels data.[2] If we consider as generally involved those who voted in 1948 and who in October 1950 had at least a moderate interest in the election as well as an intention to vote (that is, if we make *interest in participation* our criterion), then we find about 40 to 50 per cent of our samples involved at the time of the 1950 campaigns.

Secondly, when we take people who made choices in all of the five leading contests and felt strongly about their candidates in at least two of them (that is, if our criterion is *breadth and strength of feeling about candidates*), we find that 45 to 75 per cent of the potential electorate in each of our various samples were involved.

---

2. The measurements are made from the Indexes of Participation Involvement, Candidate Involvement, and Issue Involvement described in Appendix C. Because "participation bias" and "panel mortality" in surveys result in oversampling the politically interested people and undersampling the apathetic persons, the percentages in the following paragraphs overstate the amount of political involvement that actually exists in the population.

Finally, if we take those who had opinions on all of five leading issues and felt strongly about at least two of them (if the criterion is *involvement in issues*), it is found that about 35 to 55 per cent of these samples were so involved.

To summarize these findings, somewhere around 35 to 70 per cent of that portion of the population that is easily accessible to surveys became involved in one or another of the above aspects of politics during the 1950 campaign. Each of these measures is related to the others empirically, and this fact suggests that, here again, an underlying dimension of political behavior exists—in this case, that of involvement—for which rather precise scales and indexes could be developed.

Flexibility versus Involvement

We have defined the independent voter as one who combines nonpartisanship with political involvement. How compatible would we expect two such characteristics—one implying political detachment, the other its opposite—to be? What is the relation of one to the other?

While our data do not afford precise scales for either of these dimensions of political behavior, we can arrive at a crude approximation by applying additively the criteria we have described. This is done in Figure 3-1, which is based on a classification of all Minnesota and Iowa respondents according to the number of criteria of partisanship and the number of involvement criteria they meet. The three indexes of party flexibility in Figure 3-1 are (1) "party habit," a combination of "lack of persistence over time" and "withholding commitment," which is selected as the measure for the later analysis of the independent voter in this paper; (2) split-ticket voting; and (3) lack of agreement with one's own "party line" on issues. The three measures of involvement are (1) participation involvement; (2) candidate involvement; and (3) issue involvement. All these measures except "party habit" are indexes described in Appendix C.

In view of the known propensity for the direction and intensity of attitudes to be correlated, it is not surprising to find that Figure 3-1 shows a U-curve. It indicates that the more inflexible (partisan) the respondent, the more likely he is to be involved; the more involved he is, the more likely he is to be a rather inflexible devotee of one party. Thus, most people who are variable or uncommitted as regards party are seen to be not so much independent as *indifferent*.

The independent voter, then, is a deviant in the electorate, for he violates the rule that partisanship goes with involvement, nonpartisanship with apathy. This is the sense in which the independent voter was described as a "deviant case" in Berelson (1954, p. 27). His implication that the independent condition may also be temporary or unstable is explored later.

APPLICATION OF THE DEFINITION

Locating the Independent Voter

For our working definition in this paper, we shall use only two of the possible criteria of party flexibility described earlier, and only one of the involvement criteria. The measure of flexibility will be a combination of *lack of persistence* and *withholding commitment;* that is, if a respondent said in the October, 1950, survey that he did not identify himself with any party, or if he identified himself at

3-1—Partisanship and Involvement in Politics

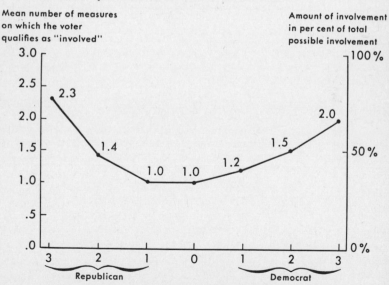

Number of measures on which the voter qualifies
as an "inflexible" partisan.

that time with a party different from the one he had supported in 1948, he is taken as meeting the flexibility criterion in our working definition of an independent voter. The measure of involvement will be based on his *interest in participation*. If he scored "high" or "medium high" on the Index of Participation Involvement described in Appendix C, he will meet the involvement criterion in the definition.

Cross-tabulating now produces four voter types, as in Table 3-1. In each of the four Regional Panels samples, between 10 and 20 per cent of the respondents are irregular in party commitment but highly involved in politics (according to the foregoing definition). These are the *independent* voters. The other 80 to 90 per cent in each sample are not independent and fall into one of the other types. Those who are involved in politics and are also party regulars are labeled "partisan" voters. Those who are neither involved in politics nor committed to a party we refer to as "apathetic" voters. The party regulars who are not involved are a familiar type we call "habitual" voters.

Table 3-1—Four Familiar Voter Types Defined by Party Regularity and Political Involvement

	Regular	Irregular
Involved	"Partisan Voters" (25-30%)	"Independent Voters" (10-20%)
Indifferent	"Habitual Voters" (25-40%)	"Apathetic Voters" (20-30%)

Validation—Some Characteristics of the Independent's Political Behavior

These operational definitions of voter types correlate plausibly with various other kinds of political behavior described in the survey data. Such checks validate our definitions and permit us to specify further the complex of behavior that distinguishes our independent voters from the other types (Table 3-2).

Table 3-2 shows the following similarities and contrasts among the four types of voters. Independent voters resemble the partisans and differ from the other types in ways indicating high political involvement, such as voting turnout, exposure to the mass media, discussing politics in conversations, knowledge about the candidates, and "caring" about whether their favorite candidates win. Independents differ from partisans and resemble the apathetics in some ways that reflect freedom from (or lack of) partisan convictions, such as the infrequency of their attempts to convert others to their own political opinions. Finally, independents give more evidence of

Table 3-2—Behavior of Four Voter Types*

	Independents	Partisans	Habituals	Apathetics
Voted in 1950	91%	91%	61%	46%
"High" or "Medium High" in Exposure to Mass Media	49	53	32	29
Actively Discuss Politics in Conversations	54	49	31	28
Know names of Both Senate Candidates	51	54	31	23
Would Care "a Lot" or "Some" if Favored Senate Candidate Were Defeated	51	66	24	21
Try to Convert Others In Conversations	6	20	5	5
Believe the Two Political Parties Have Equally Good Programs	43	20	21	31
Seriously Considered Voting for Other Senate Candidate	35	24	22	25
Voted a Partly or Completely Split Ticket	50	28	33	39

† All the voter types are defined on the basis of responses given in the October interviews. The variables listed in the lefthand column are taken from responses given in various states either in October or November. Participation in conversations is based on October interview responses in all four states combined; turnout in 1950 is based on November interviews in all four states combined. Mass-media exposure and ticket voting are secured from November answers In Colorado, Minnesota, and Iowa combined. The following are taken from October responses in Washington: knowledge of Senate candidates; amount of difference to the respondent if his Senate candidate lost; whether the respondent tries to convert other people; and whether the two parties have equally good programs. Consideration of voting for the other Senate candidate is taken from November responses in Washington. The following is the total number of cases in each sample for the two sets of interviews. The differences between the total numbers in October and November are due to the fact that some respondents were not reinterviewed.

	Independents	Partisans	Habituals	Apathetics
Colorado, October	63	130	181	99
Colorado, November	44	91	131	70
Washington, October	82	138	118	103
Washington, November	72	120	99	87
Minnesota, October	77	158	81	176
Minnesota, November	58	123	72	144
Iowa, October	53	130	136	157
Iowa, November	32	79	69	71

making *considered* choices than do any of the other types. They are most likely of all voters to see merit in the programs of both parties, they are most likely to consider rival candidates, before making their choice, and they are most likely to split their tickets.

Mixed Stimulation in the Independent Voter's Environment

Let us look into the immediate social environment of the voters and see what factors are related to independence. An illustration is the question of the voter's friends. In Washington, respondents were asked whether their friends were definitely going to vote and for which party. The answers may be grouped to describe social circles with four different kinds of political behavior: a circle of friends in which the party affiliations are mixed but in which voting is expected; one in which everybody is of the same party and in which, also, voting is expected; a one-party situation where voting is not taken for granted; and a mixed or undefined party situation in which voting is not taken for granted.

As may be seen in Table 3-3, independents characteristically describe their friends as being in the first kind of circle, where political affiliations are mixed but voting is the rule. Partisans are most commonly in one-party circles where voting is the rule. Seldom do either independents or partisans say they don't know whether their friends will vote, whereas such a statement is common among the

Table 3-3—Political Characteristics of Friends of the Four Types of Voters (Washington, October)

	Independents	Partisans	Habituals	Apathetics
Friends Will Vote, All for One Party	34%	50%	36%	25%
Friends Will Vote, for Both Parties or for Parties Not Known	53	40	22	31
Don't Know Whether Friends Will Vote, Friends All for One Party	2	6	30	20
Don't Know Whether Friends Will Vote, Friends of Mixed or Unknown Parties	11	4	12	24
	100%	100%	100%	100%
	(n = 82)	(n = 138)	(n = 118)	(n = 108)

habituals and the apathetics. The latter two groups differ in that the habituals more often describe their friends as favoring the same political party as themselves.

In short, each type of voter is found most often in the personal environment most consistent with his own political behavior. Table 3-3 does not, of course, indicate whether the nature of one's friends determines what type of voter one will bceome, or whether a voter projects his own political image on to his friends. Both processes surely operate. The relationship does suggest, however, that exposure to conflicting pressures in one's social milieu, pressures for political interest but not in one party alone, is associated with maximum independent voting.

Another social situation indicating cross pressures at work is that is which a voter for one reason or another breaks away from his parents' party. In the two samples for which data on parents' party are available, it may be seen that most voters vote the party of their parents (Table 3-4). In both samples, the proportions of independent voters are higher among those respondents whose current voting choices disagree with those of their parents; when respondents are voting in the same way as their parents, smaller proportions of independent voters result. One may conjecture that where new influences have produced a break with family political loyalties, old ties may inhibit the process of change, with a resulting irregular party commitment rather than an all-out loyalty to a new party. One of the possible sources of change is suggested by some previous research by Havemann (1952, pp. 117-120), who finds that desertion of the parents' party for an independent position may result from upward social mobility by the respondent.

Detailed analysis of our own data suggests further that whether deviation from the parents' party results in independent voting depends on the community context. If the context supports the

Table 3-4—Deviation from Parents' Party and Independent Voting: Comparison of Independent Voters' Voting Choices and Parents' Voting Habits

	VOTED FOR OPPOSITE PARTIES		VOTED FOR SAME PARTY	
	Per Cent Independent	Number	Per Cent Independent	Number
Washington	28%	(89)	9%	(247)
Iowa	15	(97)	10	(270)

deviation, independent voting will be encouraged. Washington voters who deviate from their parents in either a Democratic or Republican direction have high rates of independent voting. Urban areas of Washington support a Democratic deviation, while rural areas support Republican deviations. But in the overwhelmingly Republican Seventh Congressional District of Iowa, only the deviators from Democratic parents show the high political involvement that produces independent voting. In Iowa, those who deviate from Republican parents in a Democratic direction run counter to both parents and community; they have a low frequency of independent voting, and they have a very high frequency of apathetic behavior.

Transient Instability of Independent Voting

The data in the previous section also suggest that independents may be in transition from backgrounds in one party (such as the party of their parents) to eventual commitment to the opposite party. This would make the independent position *transient*. Some evidence exists for such transience even in short spans. Our Washington respondents were asked their party identification in both the October and November interviews. Table 3-5 shows that over half the respondents who identified themselves with no party in October adopted a party identification in November; but among those who selected a party in October, very few changed to independence in November.

Table 3-5—Stability and Change in Party Identification
(Washington)

RESPONSE IN NOVEMBER INTERVIEWS	RESPONSE IN OCTOBER INTERVIEWS	
	Identified Self with a Party	Identified Self with No Party
Identified Self with a Party	89%	56%
Identified Self with No Party	11	44
	100%	100%
	(n = 258)	(n = 120)

The independent voter's temporary position follows from his deviant combination of involvement and nonpartisanship. Such strong correlations as those in Table 3-1 and Figure 3-1 between involvement and partisanship are not accidental but are likely to result from a circular process of considerable force. Partisanship leads to interest and interest leads to partisanship. Consequently, if the independent voter remains involved in politics, he should tend to lose his flexibility and nonpartisanship, especially at election time. Or if he remains flexible and nonpartisan, on the other hand, he should tend to lose his involvement and become indifferent, especially in the quiet periods between elections.

Our data do not afford a direct test of this hypothesis, but it may be noted that if a voter who identified himself with no party in October said, nevertheless, that he was interested in the campaign, he was more likely than not (58 per cent to 42 per cent, n equals 79) to have adopted a party identification by November. If he had little or no interest in the campaign, he was less likely (47 per cent to 53 per cent, n equals 38) to do so.

In summary, it is possible to define and measure what seems to have been implied in the long-used but hazy notion of the classic "independent voter." Other familiar types of voters can also be specified and fitted into a typology in which the independent seems the numerically smallest category.

In the process of exploring this problem, several ideas are suggested about independent voting. First, it is a deviant and probably, transitional position. Secondly, it may arise out of configurations of social environments and political traditions that guide the voter into political activity but that provide contradictory pulls with regard to the direction of that activity. Thirdly, for both of the foregoing reasons, it is an unstable position.

4

ATTITUDE CONSISTENCY

William N. McPhee, Bo Anderson,
and Harry Milholland

*T*his is a progress report on work toward an explanation
of the following kind of phenomenon: if people are interviewed
before and after a mass-communications campaign calling attention
to certain ideas, afterward their opinions on those ideas tend to
become more consistent. Field studies[1] define "consistent" opinions
as those in agreement with the usual correlation, for example, liking
Kennedy and liking the Democrats are positively correlated. So, it
is "inconsistent" not to like one without liking the other. This
inconsistency tends to be reduced by the campaign.

In the last decade or so, similar phenomena found in laboratory

Section I of the text summarizes portions of an original empirical analysis
by Anderson, with the assistance of Jane Emery, in a program of methodological documentation supported by a Ford Foundation grant to P. F. Lazarsfeld.
The data used are from all four states combined. The work in Section II was
supported by a Ford Foundation grant to McPhee for research on mass behavior, and benefited especially from the ideas of Lee M. Wiggins. The work of
Section III drew on funds from National Science Foundation grant, G #13045,
to McPhee for computer simulation of social processes; and it benefited from
related work by Milholland under NSF G #11085, to Lazarsfeld for latent
structure analysis.

1. See, for example, "Introduction" in P. Lazarsfeld, B. Berelson, and
H. Gaudet, *The People's Choice* (1944).

experiments have become the basis of perhaps the most active new theoretical work in social psychology.[2] In this theory there are many definitions of consistency, under names such as "congruence," "balance," and "consonance." Festinger defines consonant opinions as cases in which one opinion "follows" as a plausible inference from the other. For example, in the 1960 campaign, if one liked Nixon it would "follow" that one believed that we should defend Quemoy and Matsu. But one might not believe this; in that event, to oversimplify, these theories predict that the voter is likely to change his opinion on Quemoy and Matsu, or in rarer cases his opinion of Nixon, so that one belief will be in harmony with the other.

We have not been able to connect the present work with those theories, except that the variables in each are similar, because the psychological work does not deal in any formal way with the three principal features of the problem in field data. These are:

1. *Turnover* (change of opinion) in such field data of real life is, in the first place, large and chaotic; a quarter to a third of the opinions may change when only one-half change would lead to a diagnosis of completely random responses. In the second place, when the statistics of all this "flux of opinion" are related to psychological variables, the patterns one finds are so anomolous as to strain credulity that they are psychologically motivated. In a word, one needs a model to diagnose what underlies all this turnover before he can even know what it *is* that requires substantive explanation.

2. *Independence* (in the sense explained below) of two opinions from one another at the same time and, to a surprising degree, of the same opinion at two different times, is implicit in the kind of models that, alone of those we have tried, actually will fit and make sense of all this turnover. But that fact tends to rule out the "interactions" between opinions that the above theories properly postulate are crucial in the psychology of other attitudes that do matter to the individual. So, what one needs is a theory that can explain how *casual* responses that apparently do not interact with one another or with new responses at a later date, nevertheless become increasingly correlated.

3. *Attention* to the subject matter (independent of motivations like strength of conviction or "pain" of contradiction or "discord"

---

2. The work of Heider, Festinger, Osgood, Abelson, Newcomb, and others in this area is summarized, and detailed references given, in the special issue on "Attitude Change" of *The Public Opinion Quarterly,* Summer, 1960.

with the opinions of others around one) is what emerges as the apparent cause of trends toward consistency in the statistics of turnover, once we do have a model to diagnose the latter. So, what one needs for these opinions, so casual as to defy explanation as "motivated" change, is a theory of why simply calling attention to them alone increases their consistency (correlation) (Glock, 1952).

We do not intend this paper as argument contrary to the psychological-interaction theories, however, but as an effort to solve the three mysteries discussed above at their own level, in the statistics of casual public opinion and popular culture, leaving open the question of their connection to the detailed mechanisms being studied in corresponding work in individual psychology.

The paper is in three parts corresponding to the three problems, namely:

1. The first part of the paper illustrates the anomalies in *observed* turnover data that make it so difficult to interpret anything substantively at this (observed) level.

2. The second part then presents a *diagnostic* model of such turnover, which points to "attention" as the source of changes in the model's parameters affecting opinion consistency.

3. The third part, the main theory of the paper, then presents an *explanatory* model in the sense that it shows how attention would cause changes in parameters like those in number 2 that account, in turn, for the data in number 1.

This is called a "progress report," however, because, as an appended Technical Note makes clear, there are difficulties still to be solved in these models; the paper itself, while it uses some elementary algebra, is an account of the substantive ideas for nontechnical readers.

I. ANOMALIES IN TURNOVER DATA

WHAT WE MEAN by "casual" opinion is illustrated in the following list of items. The first three are to be used for the analysis immediately to follow and the others later (items were selected in each case for a priori reasons of content and party that turned out to be irrelevant in the face of formal similarity of all turnover in these domains). People were read the statements on the left in random order and to each statement they were asked to give an "agree" or "disagree" reaction, for instance as they might have been reacting to such ideas, say, at a dinner party around 1950:

	THE ANSWER CONSIDERED "CONSISTENT" IF VOTER IS	
	Democratic	Republican
Used in the Initial Analysis		
The Republicans would cut down waste and bureaucracy in government.	Disagree	Agree
We need strict price controls and excess profits taxes immediately (that is, for Korea).	Agree	Disagree
We should go even farther with government welfare benefits such as housing, medical care, and farm price supports.	Agree	Disagree
Used Later		
The Taft-Hartley law is unfair to the working man.	Agree	Disagree
Democrats have been too easy on Communists in America.	Disagree	Agree

Initial work on this problem (by Charles Kadushin) was a study, in large combinations, of the interaction of these opinions and changes therein with each other. For reasons reported in detail in a closely related paper in this volume—the "coattails" analysis of the consistency of choices on a political ticket—such a conception of specific preferences interacting with *each other* finally had to be abandoned in favor of the formulation that any two of these opinion responses were related to each other only indirectly through their relation to a *third* factor common to both, party disposition.[3] Why will become more clear in the later sections of this essay, but for now we proceed directly to a consideration of the analysis of the interaction between opinion on an issue and *party vote* as the initial problem to solve. This analysis used an index illustrated in Figure 4-1 where party vote is used as "item *i*." "Item *j*" is an issue. "Plus" opinion is the answer consistent with plus on vote, for example, both Democratic.

For simplicity, we classify the party-vote item such that for practical purposes it can be assumed to be *constant* in both interview waves, namely, "vote" is the party for which a majority of choices on the ticket were made (which majority rarely changes, although

3. We are indebted to Kadushin for making this fact evident.

4-1—Gains and Losses in Consistency

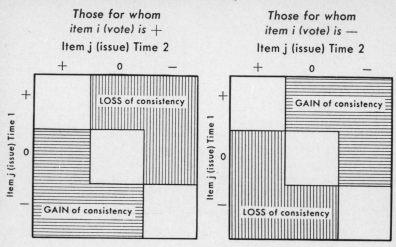

Those for whom
item i (vote) is +
Item j (issue) Time 2

Those for whom
item i (vote) is —
Item j (issue) Time 2

single choices do).[4] Given a classification by this stable attitude, what the detailed tables in Figure 4-1 show is the turnover of the other item, one of the opinions on *issues* above, in a direction toward less consistency or toward more consistency with the vote item.[5]

The following definitions of change in consistency become obvious from Figure 4-1, and these will be the *dependent* variables of the analysis:

INITIAL CONSISTENCY = Proportion of people whose opinion on the issue at Time 1 is consistent with their vote

GAIN = Proportion who change opinion on the issue toward greater consistency

LOSS = Proportion who change opinion on the issue toward less consistency

TURNOVER = Gain + loss

NET = Gain — loss (with plus sign being more consistent)

---

4. We use the Index of Straight-Ticket Voting in the Appendix.

5. Logically, vote at Time 1 should be used, but because of the excessive don't-knows then in some states, we were forced to use Time 2 as the index of general party bias.

The *independent* variables that will be used, because they are the ones out of a number tried that dependably affect the changes in consistency above,[6] are of two kinds: "motivation" and "attention."

"Motivational" Variables:

Partisanship, or the "internal motivation" to adopt or hold beliefs consistent with the party line, this being indicated by the proportion of five candidates chosen from one's own party ticket (all from the same party is considered plus partisanship, one or more from the opposite party being non- or minus-partisanship).

Environment, or the "external motivation" to adopt or hold beliefs consistent with the party line, this being (crudely) indicated by the proportion of people in the respondent's county voting for his party (a majority for that party in recent history is a plus environment, a minority, minus).[7]

"Attention" Variables:

Interest, or the "internally originated" attention to the topics of opinion involved, this being indicated by how much interest the person reported in the 1950 election ("a great deal" or "quite a lot" is plus interest, "not much" or "none" or DK [don't know], minus).

Salience, or the "externally originated" attention to the topics of opinion involved, this being indicated by answers to the following question: "According to your impressions of the election campaign, which of these issues or questions were talked about most often right here in (*place*)?" An issue named is considered salient, not named not salient.

If one or another of the above indicators is crude, as they are, it apparently does not matter in the statistical average; for each "motivation" indicator above has virtually identical effects on consistency of opinions, and each "attention" indicator also has virtually the

---

6. Other independent variables tried were measures of campaign exposure, discussion with others, and feeling that issues were important (rather than, say, candidate). These did not seem to have effects independent of the motivational and attention variables used here.

7. It should be appreciated that a Republican county, for example, means more than simply surrounding the Republican individual with compatible associates. It usually means also a Republican newspaper, better Republican publicity and canvassing, usually better-quality or better-known Republican candidates, and so on. These corollaries probably account for the fact that our crude index of the environment stimuli has good results. The index used is described in Philip Ennis' paper in this volume.

same effect as the other. But the two former and two latter kinds of effect are distinct and, we might add, distinct puzzles. A brief discussion of each kind of perplexing result follows.

Motivational Effects

We will later give a formal meaning to the "effect" of a substantive condition like partisanship as a partial difference idea substantive condition like partisanship as a partial difference idea like the partial derivative in the continuous case; for example, $\Delta T/\Delta P$ will be the change in turnover due to a change in partisanship. So, it is important to emphasize now what the empirical counterparts of these partial differences look like in raw data. The first step is illustrated in Table 4-1, using the example of the effects of favorable environment.

Table 4-1—Effect of Environment When Partisanship and Salience Controlled (Both +)

		PROPORTION OF SAMPLE THAT SHOWS CHANGES TOWARD		
	Gain in Consistency	Loss in Consistency	Turnover	Net
Averages for Issues Where Initial Consistency Was High in				
Favorable Environment	.09	.11	.20	—.02
Unfavorable Environment	.25	.12	.37	+.13
Δ = Difference Due to Environment	—.16	—.01	—.17	—.15a*
Averages for Issues Where Initial Consistency Was Low in				
Favorable Environment	.23	.13	.36	+.10
Unfavorable Environment	.17	.17	.34	.00
Δ = Difference Due to Environment	+.06	—.04	+.02	+.10a

*a = algebraic difference, throughout subsequent tables as well.

Note the Net trend to consistency on the right of Table 4-1. As the negative figures of difference in the upper and positive in the lower half of the table indicate, when considering any motivation variable, it is essential to control the degree of *initial* consistency of opinion. Initially "high" consistency on an issue occurs when over 60 per cent of those who choose a party also support their party's position on the issue at Time 1, in this particular party-issue combination (for instance, Democrats and the Democratic side of, say, the "welfare-benefits" issue). This is like the degree of *support* for the party line on the issue. We do not distinguish which party is involved, however, because close analysis shows that apparent party differences are usually due to this degree of initial consistency of the given party's voters on the given issue. The same independence of content applies to the topic of the issue, although minor differences were found with other foreign issues that were not due to purely formal considerations such as this degree of initial skew. Since no such foreign issues are included, we *average* all issue-party combinations having similar initial consistency, high or low (low is really moderate), to obtain sufficient sample sizes for refined control of other variables. In every analysis, matched comparisons considering party and issue separately have confirmed results in detail.

Table 4-1 is a selection, however, that shows only the case when two other variables were also favorable, the other motivational variable, "partisanship" and the specific attention variable, "salience." To consider *all* combinations of these control variables and the test variables simultaneously, it is too cumbersome to present all the details as in Table 4-1. We instead compress as in Table 4-2. It gives only the figure that matters, the partial *differences* in turnover, ΔT, and so forth, comparing data for the favorable environment with the unfavorable case. The sign of the difference (favorable — unfavorable) is positive when the effect of favorable environment is to increase the magnitude of some turnover category, negative, when it reduces the magnitude of this kind of turnover, as in Table 4-1. For example, the differences previously derived in the top half of Table 4-1 now make up the first row in the summarizing Table 4-2. The controls being partialed out are shown on the left.

In the upper half of Table 4-2, the predominance of negative numbers means that here the effect of favorable environment is to make all categories of turnover *less* than in the comparable sample for an unfavorable environment. The third column, for gross turnover, is boxed to highlight this. But note the fourth column in the upper table, giving the net effect of all changes on the consistency of issue opinion with vote choice. Favorable environment—like living in Iowa for a Republican—apparently has no dependable effect on reducing inconsistency of opinion. Rather, such an environment reduces *change* of opinion.

One no sooner makes such a statement, however, when the

opposite trend becomes evident in the lower half of the table. It shows the average turnover for items on which the voters in the particular party did *not* initially support its position on this issue item so well (typically about 50 per cent, with the rest divided between opposition and undecided). In that event, the favorable environment does not reduce turnover. And more important, as the right-hand column for net is boxed to emphasize, a favorable environment is a plus factor making for net change toward *greater* consistency during the campaign. Matched comparisons in detail confirm these results.

Environment was considered above as a kind of "bias" pressure, the local scene being one-sided (not only in numbers, but usually in newspaper bias, party organization, quality of candidates, and so on). The other bias considered is a one-sidedness within the respondent himself, "partisanship." Table 4-3 presents the same summary of differences as Table 4-2, but 4-3 shows "the effect of

Table 4-2—Effect of Favorable Environment (Respondent's Party in Majority Locally)

CONTROLS		$\Delta =$ DIFFERENCES (Favorable environment)—(Unfavorable)			
Partisanship	Saliency	in Gains	in Losses	in Turnover	in Net
When Initial Consistency of Item with Party Was High					
+	+	—.16	—.01	—.17	—.15a*
+	—	—.01	—.08	—.09	+.07
—	+	—.20	.00	—.20	—.20
—	—	.00	—.06	—.06	+.06
$\Delta =$ Average Differences Due to Favorable Environment		—.09	—.04	—.13	+.05a
When Initial Consistency of Item with Party Was Low					
+	+	+.06	—.04	+.02	+.10a
+	—	+.01	+.01	+.02	.00
—	+	—.02	—.08	—.10	+.06
—	—	+.07	+.05	+.12	+.02
$\Delta =$ Average Differences Due to Favorable Environment		+.03	—.02	+.01	—.05a

* a = algebraic differences in net. They show the effect *toward* consistency (+). See Table 4-1.

partisanship." That is, the table entry is: difference = (movements to or from consistency among·partisans) — (among not-partisans). Again, this effect has a plus sign if partisanship increases the given category of turnover, a minus sign if it reduces it, with the algebraic sign of the net the final effect toward consistency.

The reader should note the predominance of minus signs summarizing gross turnover in the upper half of the table, which we again emphasize by boxing the third column. Here, when the item is one already well supported, that is, if a condition of high initial consistency exists, the effect of partisanship is to *reduce turnover*. But again, it is a different story in the lower half of the table, which summarizes cases where the party position on an issue is not initially so well supported. Here, the effect of partisanship is, if anything to *increase* turnover; but especially, again, to increase *net* trend to consistency. Detailed matched comparisons confirm these results.

So, these are the same effects as in the case of favorable cn-

Table 4-3—The Effect of Partisanship (Partisanship = All Choices Same Party)

Controls			Δ = DIFFERENCES (Partisans)—(Not-partisans)		
Saliency	Environ-ment	in Gains	in Losses	in Turnover	in Net
When Initial Consistency of Item with Party Was High					
+	+	—.05	—.15	—.20	+.10a
+	—	—.09	—.14	—.23	+.05
—	+	—.06	—.00	—.06	—.06
—	—	—.05	+.02	—.03	—.07a
Δ = Average Differences Due to + Partisanship		—.06	—.07	—.13	+.01a
When Initial Consistency of Item with Party Was Low					
+	+	+.08	+.01	+.09	+.07a
+	—	.00	—.03	—.03	+.03
—	+	+.07	—.04	+.03	+.11
—	—	+.13	.00	+.13	+.13
Δ = Average Differences Due to Partisanship		+.07	—.02	+.05	+.09a

* a = algebraic differences in net show the effect toward consistency (+).

vironment. It is plausible to say that partisanship has a "preservative" effect against any change of opinion when consistency with the party line is already high, but a "generative" effect stirring up new increments in consistency when it was not previously high. But this apparent teleology, different results where different effects of the variable would be "needed," begins to strain credulity when we now consider the effects of attention where, we shall see, one would have to invent a wholly different rationale (in which initial consistency plays no role, for example).

Attention Effects

The reader will recall that what we called partisanship was an internal bias; environment, a bias in external influences. The "attention" variables correspond: interest being the internally motivated attention to a topic, and salience, its prominence in the external environment. The latter will be measured for each tissue, but the former interest is unfortunately only measured in general for the whole election. Results are much the same in either event.

Table 4-4 gives "the effect of interest." That is, the table entry is the difference: (movements to and from consistency among the more interested) — (among the less interested). Again, a plus sign means that interest increases the turnover magnitude in question. For example, the predominance of minus signs in Table 4-4 is evidence of an effect of interest noticed in other studies as well (Berelson, *et al.,* 1954), in sharply *reducing* turnover.

However, note a change from earlier tables. In the case of the previous "motivation" variables it was the *initial condition* of high or low consistency that controlled the direction of effect of the substantive variables. Now, in the case of the "attention variables," that does not matter. Rather, it is the subsequent *interaction* between the two attention variables, salience and interest, themselves. Each makes all the difference in the other's effects. Table 4-4 accordingly shows the effect of interest when the issue involved was salient in the upper half of the table, in the lower half when the item was not salient.

The interaction of interest and salience is not the expected one, however. For example, it would be nice if salience of the particular topic were found to be a necessary condition for general interest to have a specific effect on that topic, but the actual result is the opposite. Interest promotes more net trends to consistency on an issue when that topic is *not* salient locally (compare the right-hand columns highlighted in boxes). When the topic involved is salient, detailed data not given here show that the interested people usually do make minor changes toward consistency, it is true, but *less* than the uninterested do in the same salience situation. This result is due to the fact that the gain column on the left is markedly reduced by interest in the upper or salient case; that is, there the uninterested are the ones who show active gains. What the combination of interest and salience apparently does, then, is *not* to promote consistency of opinion but resistance to *change* of opinions (when, as the lower part of the table shows, such changes would otherwise have been toward consistency). Matched comparisons confirm all this.

Finally, Table 4-5 shows "the effect of salience." This means that now the table entry is the difference: (movements to and from consistency when the issue is salient) — (when not salient). The effect of salience is the mirror image of the effect of interest. When the one is *not* operative, the operation of the other promotes net

Table 4-4—The Effect of Interest on Changes to and from Consistency

Controls		Δ = DIFFERENCES (Interested)—(Not interested)			
Parti-sanship	Initial Consistency	in Gains	in Losses	in Turnover	in Net
		When the Issue Is Salient Locally			
+	Hi	—.06	—.03	—.09	.03a
+	Lo	—.13	—.05	—.18	—.08
—	Hi	—.10	—.10	—.20	.00
—	Lo	—.25	+.02	—.23	—.27
Δ = Average Effect of Interest		—.13	—.04	—.17	—.09a
		When the Issue Is Not Salient Locally			
+	Hi	+.10	—.07	+.03	+.17a
+	Lo	—.02	—.10	—.12	+.08
—	Hi	+.05	—.10	—.05	+.15
—	Lo	+.01	—.03	—.02	+.04
Δ = Average Effect of Interest		+.04	—.07	—.04	+.11a

trends toward consistency. This is chiefly because when one is inoperative, turnover is then active and this permits gains (lower left column) in consistency of opinion with vote. But when *both* interest and salience are operative, the result is less turnover, and especially less "gain" type of movement toward consistency, which means less net trend to consistency than otherwise.

Again, one could invent plausible interpretations. But these become increasingly unparsimonious in the light of the earlier results. There, initial consistency played the critical role; now it is irrelevant. Here, the attention variables interact, which the motivation variables did not do before, but this interaction is peculiarly inverse. And we find that in every detailed matched comparison, the above anomolies persist.

This briefly illustrates extensive experience with these data and those for the other issues as well: they apparently cannot be interpreted parsimoniously at this observed level, and one is forced to postulate models of underlying processes to diagnose what could and would generate these peculiar patterns in observed turnover.

Table 4-5—The Effect of the Topic's Salience (Salience = Recall It Discussed Prominently

Parti-sanship (Controls)	Initial Consistency (Controls)	in Gains	in Losses	in Turnover	in Net
		Δ = DIFFERENCES (When Topic Salient)—(Not Salient)			
When Interest in the Election Is High					
+	Hi	—.07	—.02	—.09	—.05a
+	Lo	—.04	.00	—.04	—.04
—	Hi	—.03	+.13	+.10	—.16
—	Lo	+.01	—.01	.00	+.02
Δ = Average Effect of Salience		—.03	+.03	—.01	—.06a
When Interest in the Election Is Low					
+	Hi	+.09	—.06	+.03	+.15a
+	Lo	+.07	—.05	+.02	+.12
—	Hi	+.12	+.13	+.25	—.01
—	Lo	+.27	—.06	+.21	+.33
Δ = Average Effect of Salience		+.14	—.01	+.13	+.15a

II. A DIAGNOSTIC MODEL

MARKOV CHAINS, for example, are formally similar to some of the theories of psychological "states" in this domain, for instance, unstable states, but will not fit these data.[8] The only kind of formal model we can find that makes sense of these patterns and others in the turnover data is a type often used as a measurement model. But when taken as a substantive theory, this type of model expresses exactly the ideas with which we began the analysis. Namely, it is a picture of *casual* opinion responses that endlessly change, but for reasons virtually the exact opposite of change motivated by "tensions," "contradictions," and the like. For present purposes, let us interpret the general idea in the following way:

The person has an observable opinion *only* when he is prompted to react, for example, by a dinner party, interview, or whatever. Thereafter, "out of sight, out of mind," that is, he soon forgets these casual responses (in theory, even if this is not wholly true). In the idealized case, in any event, when some months later he is again prompted to respond on this topic, it is a *new* response independent of the first except in a sense discussed below. If another opinion on a related topic was also elicited at the first time, it is not only independent of the first opinion, again in the sense indicated below, but independent "of itself" when a new version of it is given at some second time a month or two later. No "dynamic interactions" could have gone on between the two topical opinions meanwhile, for neither really existed in the interim as a continuous entity. No more than, if we observe a man tipping his hat to a lady on two occasions a month apart, we assume he held his hat that way all month as one continuous response.

Yet, if the two hat tippings were independent responses, why did they take the same form? We may answer, for example, that the man is "polite." That is, we mention some much more general state

---

8. The failure to fit the present data of only two interview waves is cumbersome to show, but a decisive test with similar data from three or more interview waves is this. A Markov-chain implies steadily increasing turnover with increasing time periods; but in opinion data the turnover is not markedly greater comparing, say, Time 1 and Time 2 and Time 1 and Time 4. See Wiggins (1955). Higher order Markov chains would fit, but resemble the simple model below.

that does endure and that each of the otherwise independent responses expresses. But if, on a third occasion, the man is in a rush and happens not to tip his hat, we do *not* say he has "changed in his degree of politeness." For everyone appreciates that states such as politeness or, for that matter, liberalism are only probabilistic tendencies.

Models of turnover of opinion responses under conditions like these have arisen from two different considerations. In one case, starting from the problem of the behavior over time of partly unreliable data (for example, our casual responses), Lee Wiggins later developed a family of substantive models of processes in which response is not "unreliable," but in the nature of the situation probabilistic. These fit the turnover of opinion data (Wiggins, 1955, and Lazarsfeld, *et al.,* 1962). The assumptions involved are formally identical to Lazarsfeld's earlier measurement models, latent structure, where in the same sense explained below two or more opinions given at a *single* time can be visualized as independent. These models have also been extended over time (Stouffer, *et al.,* 1951) and used for empirical indexes of turnover whose rationale is the same as the model below (Kendall, 1953). The present data are not in a form and do not have sufficient interview waves for Wiggins' more detailed models; but we derive a solution for the simpler Kendall version to diagnose a portion of the present type of data. This diagnosis will then suggest an explanatory theory using latent structure measurement ideas in the concluding section.

A situation like that in the earlier raw data can be portrayed by letting A stand for the proportion of *adherents* to their party's line on the particular issue, among that party's voters. That is, A is the proportion of people who in many tests would be found "basically" favorable to their party's position on this kind of issue. The rest of the party's voters are $1 - A$, those who on this issue are basically contrary or indifferent, if by repeated test we found out what they "really" thought.

However, these are only *tendencies.* Each category of people expresses its underlying general sentiment in a specific situation only with probability. Let p_1 be the probability that the adherents happen to express their tendency, the party line, on this issue at Time 1. And as a simplification to solve the model for only two interview waves, assume that the nonadherents on this issue also express their tendency (the contrary one or indifference), with the same probability, p_1. Put another way, they both make the same "error" or have the same "unreliability" in expressing their underlying dispositions, namely $1-p_1$.

For example, what was referred to earlier in the data analysis as the "Initial Consistency" of opinions with the party position, call it *I,* would be simply:

$$(1) \qquad I = p_1 A + (1 - p_1)(1 - A)$$

As a simplification that also happens to make a critical substantive point explicit, let the A and $1 - A$ numbers of people remain constant over time, that is, there is *no change,* really, of the underlying division of opinion. But assume the probability of manifesting these dispositions at the second time, call it p_2, can, and usually will, be different from p_1. (Again, we have to simplify by assuming that p_2 is the same for adherents expressing their view as for nonadherents expressing their contrary view.)

Next, as the fundamental idea p_2 operates *independently* of p_1; technically, this means the probability of giving the same answer both times is $p_1 p_2$ or $(1 - p_1)(1 - p_2)$. But, heuristically, it means that the first answer is virtually forgotten or otherwise irrelevant in the second situation a month or two later. The two answers will be highly correlated at the *observed* level, nevertheless, because the A type of people will tend to give the same pro answers, the $1 - A$ people the same con answers, both times. Nevertheless, because of the distinctness of two responses over time, turnover will be substantial. Namely, if we call it T, turnover will be:

$$(2) \quad T = A\left[p_2(1 - p_1) + (1 - p_2)p_1\right]$$
$$+ (1 - A)\left[(1 - p_2)p_1 + p_2(1 - p_1)\right]$$
$$= p_1 - 2p_1 p_2 + p_2$$

By analogous operations one can define expressions for the approximate equivalent in this model of the other observed quantities in the earlier analysis (although the foregoing analysis would have to be entirely redone, with a different handling of some of the don't-know changes, exactly to conform to the dichotomous model that can be solved here). What looks in observed data like gain and loss in "consistency" with *party's* position, will be:

$$(3) \quad \text{Gain (to party line)} = G = A(1 - p_1)p_2$$
$$+ (1 - A)p_1(1 - p_2)$$
$$= A(p_2 - p_1) + p_1(1 - p_2)$$

(4) Loss (from party line) $= L = Ap_1(1 - p_2)$
$$+ (1 - A)(1 - p_1)p_2$$
$$= A(p_1 - p_2) + p_2(1 - p_1)$$

(5) Net (in favor of party) $= N = G - L = (p_2 - p_1)(2A - 1)$

A technical appendix shows how the model can then be solved for the unobserved A, p_1, and p_2 in terms of these observed G, L, N, T, and I quantities. The exact solutions will be used only for guidance, however, not only because of the discrepencies already noted and the difficulties noted below, but because a less simple version is developed as the main theory in Part III. We are only interested now in getting an idea of how the solutions for A, p_1, and p_2 *differ* when substantive variables like partisanship or salience differ in the original data.

Underlying Effects of the "Motivation" Variables

Table 4-6 shows the difference that favorable environment makes on the parameters. (Here, based on data when initial consistency was high, that is, the solutions interpret data from the top half of Table 4-2, where favorable environment reduced turnover.) Concern

Table 4-6—Effect of Favorable Environment on Parameters (for Original Data When Initial Consistency High)

Parti-sanship	Sali-ency		A	p_1	p_2	(p_2-p_1)
+	+	Favorable Environment	.96	.86	.92	+.06
		Unfavorable Environment	.73	.65	.93	+.28
Differences Due to Environment			+.23	+.21	—.01	—.22a
+	—	Favorable Environment	.85	.77	.87	+.10
		Unfavorable Environment	.77	.74	.73	—.01
Differences Due to Environment			+.08	+.03	+.14	+.11a
—	—	Favorable Environment	.82	.69	.87	+.18
		Unfavorable Environment	.69	.63	.81	+.18
Differences Due to Environment			+.13	+.06	+.06	.00

A = Proportion of underlying "adherents" of their party position on the issue item.
p_1, p_2 = Probabilities of adherents expressing party position, nonadherents the contrary (or no opinion) at Times 1 and 2.
* No solution for — + case (unusual turnover involving don't-knows in the three-classification data, makes a two-class solution impossible).

here is not with the absolute magnitudes but the difference between solutions for samples in a favoráble environment versus those in an unfavorable one, other things controlled in the original data. Results are clearest if one first examines the differences for A down the leftmost column and then for p_1 down the next column. The first is the number of party-line "adherents" to start with, the other, the probability or "reliability" of such adherents in giving the party-line response at Time 1. Both are initial conditions, and what a favorable environment seems to affect is these *initial* conditions.

The campaign changes themselves are represented by changes p_1 to p_2, shown in the far right column. In these short-run changes, favorable environment is always associated with increases in p, but the increase is often greater where previous environment was *un*-favorable, that is, where environment is irrelevant.

The majority environment, then, seems to have its essential effect on long-term learning of the consistent or "correct" party line in the *first place;* but is not essential to, nor alone effective on, short-run *changes* to consistency.

Table 4-7—Effect of Partisanship on the Parameters (for Original Data When Initial Consistency High)

Sali-ency	Envi-ronment		A†	p_1	p_2	p_2-p_1
+	+	Partisan	.90	.86	.92	+.06
		Not Partisan	.88	.82	.66	—.16
Difference Due to Partisanship			+.08	+.04	+.26	+.22a .
—	+	Partisan	.85	.77	.87	+.10
		Not Partisan	.82	.69	.87	+.18
Difference Due to Partisanship			+.03	+.08	.00	—.08a
—	—	Partisan	.77	.74	.73	—.01
		Not Partisan	.69	.63	.81	+.18
Difference Due to Partisanship			+.08	+.11	—.08	—.19a

The header "CONTROLS*" spans Saliency and Environment; "SOLUTIONS FOR" spans A†, p_1, p_2, p_2-p_1.

* No solution for + — case. See Note to Table 4-6.
† For definitions, see Note to Table 4-6.

In Table 4-7 we see that this is true of partisanship, the other motivation variable, as well. Again, the differences, between solutions for samples of partisans versus those not-partisan, are dependable in the two left columns, not dependable in the two right, which means that partisanship is associated, like environment, with *initial* conditions fostering consistent opinions. It is true that there are further gains in forces toward consistency (p_2 greater than p_1 has this effect) in two out of three instances, as there were in all three instances for favorable environment. But these are usually less than the corresponding gains in consistency in giving the party line among those *not* previously so favored by environment or disposition. In the campaign, the previously disadvantaged tend to "catch up," and what partisanship and environment do, instead, is to make people advantaged (consistent) from the start.

But why would all this have the paradoxical effects noted earlier on items with high initial consistency, namely, for these motivation variables to reduce turnover, thus reduce gain of consistency, and thus often reduce net change? Let us express the effect of partisanship and environment on the parameters as follows. Such motivation biases make for the formal differences: $+ \Delta A > + \Delta p_1 > \pm \Delta p_2$. This is, environment and partisanship were found to make all the parameters higher, but the *initial* ones, A and p_1, more so (and Δp_2 sometimes minus).

Next, let these changes be the denominators in $\Delta T / p_1$, for example, the "difference in turnover with a difference in p_1" (whose limit, the partial derivative $\delta T / \delta p$, also happens to be the same as the functions below, which apply to any differencing interval). Partial differences in turnover, ΔT, that result from anything that makes a difference in parameters are:

(6)
$$\frac{\Delta T}{\Delta A} = 0$$

(7)
$$\frac{\Delta T}{\Delta p_1} = 1 - 2p_2 \qquad (\text{e.g.,} -.72)$$

(8)
$$\frac{\Delta T}{\Delta p_2} = 1 - 2p_1 \qquad (\text{e.g.,} -.56)$$

where examples on the right may be explained as follows.

For issues where there is already high initial consistency—the situation with which we are dealing here—note in the tables that p_1, and especially p_2, are found to be large, p_2 approaching 1. Therefore, Expression (7), for example, will be a large *negative* number, the examples on the right above using the average p_1 and p_2 for favorable motivational conditions in Tables 4-6 and 4-7. This means there will be a sharp *decrement* in turnover as a result of any substantive condition that makes for a positive increment—as partisanship and favorable environment do—in these p values when they are already high.

It can be shown, however, that on items in which the initial consistency was *low,* often below 50 per cent, these p values would also have to be low (unless it were entirely due to low A, which the data do not suggest). If the p values generally start low, then Expressions (7) and (8) predict a paradoxical reversing of effect of the same substantive condition. In that event, there would be no reduction and possibly a positive increase in turnover. With turnover *not* reduced, we can now see that the prospects for gains in consistency are good, as they were in the raw data.

For example, the difference that any substantive variable that changes the parameters makes in *net* trends to consistency, ΔN, is as follows:

$$(9) \qquad\qquad \frac{\Delta N}{\Delta A} = 2(p_2 - p_1)$$

$$(10) \qquad\qquad \frac{\Delta N}{\Delta p_1} = 1 - 2A$$

$$(11) \qquad\qquad \frac{\Delta N}{\Delta p_2} = 2A - 1$$

Now, let us repeat that *low* consistency requires that A be low or p_1 low, all evidence being that both are. We will consider first the lowest initial consistency, that is, with either or both A and p_1 less than .5. Low p_1 sets up the potential for a volatile change, p_1 to p_2, which primarily affects net trend to consistency. Now, Expression (9) above reveals that this volatile possibility is as if *doubled* by anything that simultaneously makes a difference in A, as partisanship and favorable environment do. Thus, a low p_1 at the start makes for a *positive* effect on net gain in consistency from any substantive condition that makes a difference in A; which is precisely the condition in which favorable motivation makes most difference—being a potential adherent of the party line in the first place.

An opposite case can be imagined in which low initial consistency was due to low A, favorable motivation then having affected only p_1, as it does. Then, Expression (10) shows the complement. If A is in a region less than .5, then anything that makes for a difference in p_1 now has a positive effect on net—contrary to the effect of raising p_1 when consistency was already high. Thus, low A makes for a positive net contribution of Δp_1, low p_1 for a positive contribution from ΔA, and so, with a low initial consistency, these are reinforcing effects for *gain* in consistency.

Next, increase the starting region for both and note the changing relationship between the two. With high p_1, the difference $p_2 - p_1$ will be slight or even turn negative, "defeating" the effect of ΔA on net consistency in Expression (9). But the complement is particularly important. As A rises substantially above .5, as it does in the case of high initial consistency, the effect of Δp_1 becomes sharply *negative* in its consequence for net consistency in Expression (10). So, high values of these parameters defeat each other. And with that the uniform effect of variables like partisanship and favorable environment, to make an increment in the initial conditions A and p_1, now has opposite consequences on turnover and net gain in consistency.

It is important to know that the same motivational force in the same direction will have opposite effects on observed turnover depending on the initial degree of consistency. Otherwise, we could not be certain that the underlying effect of substantive variables is the same for issues initially low in consistency as for those initially high. The reason is that solutions from empirical data for this particular model are indeterminate when initial consistency is near 50 per cent (the rest contrary or no opinions), as most "low" consistency items were. Visualize surfaces generated by the model whose heights are the turnover magnitudes under different conditions; the shape is like that of saddles, having a flat "seat" in the center near 50 per cent initial skew where a number of different solutions would fit.[9] Indeed, the paradoxical reversing effects of the same substantive condition in manifest data are due to the fact that these surfaces of turnover *are* saddle shaped. So, the same direction of force has effects "up" on one side, "down" on the other (as a boost up a saddle applied when one's weight is already on the top is a boost down on the other side).

Once this formal fact is appreciated, the "mystery" of why motivational conditions in these data do not have uniform short-run effects on change of consistency is unraveled. It is because such

---

9. Put another way, for example, a 10 per cent change in parameters can have almost no effect in observed turnover data. One needs more information, which Wiggins' models obtain from a third interview wave and Lazarsfeld's from additional items.

short-run *changes,* depending on accidents of initial marginals are really tangential to the substance of what our motivational variables do. They reflect, instead, long-run processes that govern the *initial* conditions, such as partisans learning what the party line is and people in a favorable environment insulating each other from what is not the party line. That is, such forces apparently keep people from getting inconsistent in the *first* place.

Effect on the Parameters of Attention Variables

Suspicion thus narrows to salience and interest—that is, changes in attentiveness to the topic—as the "dynamic" variables in the sense of making short-run *changes* from inconsistent to consistent opinion.

We may recall that the chief mystery in the effects of these variables on observed data was the paradoxical interaction between a negative condition of one of the attention variables (for example, absence of interest) and a positive effect of the other (for example, presence of salience) on net gain in consistency. Unfortunately, this occurrence of one attention variable (salience) without the other (interest) was often infrequent on these issues. So, the odd combinations occur in too small samples among the already limited sample of nonpartisans (non–straight ticket voters), to get enough stable solutions to compare with each other in a material fashion. But we can get a full set of comparative solutions for the numerically common and psychologically more important situation, when partisanship is positive. These solutions are given in Table 4-8. Since we are now interested in the simultaneous effects of different *combinations* of interest and salience, Table 4-8 has a different format to bring that out. It reports the parameter in question, A, p_1, or p_2, for each of the four combinations of salience and interest (with partisanship and initial skew controlled for all).

Table 4-8—Parameters under Different Conditions of Interest and Salience (Partisanship +, Initial Consistency High)

	Sal. +	Sal. −		Sal. +	Sal. −		Sal. +	Sal. −		Sal. +	Sal. −
				SOLUTIONS FOR						Change	
	A			p_1			p_2			$p_2 - p_1$	
Interest +	.88	.76	+	.76	.71	+	.94	.83	+	+.18	+.12
Interest −	.75	.82	−	.70	.86	−	.85	.74	−	+.15	−.12

In marked contrast to the complex "interactions" in the original observed data, the pattern of these underlying variables is remarkably simple. Under the surface flux or turnover, salience and interest do *not* have opposite effects depending on the other being negative or positive as they did in observed data. Instead, each attention variable exerts uniform effects regardless of the other, and each has identical effects. Namely, when both are positive, all parameters are higher, but when one alone is positive, the parameters are lower. Both together have greater dynamic effect ($p_2 - p_1$ on the right) than either alone, and either alone has greater dynamic effect than when neither is positive. (The only perplexing thing is a minor variation for which we have no explanation. Lack of either kind of attention is associated with temporarily higher initial conditions, which then, understandably, erode badly by Time 2.) Otherwise, attention seems to have a uniform effect: to increase the validity or reliability, p, with which responses on the issues manifests the underlying party disposition, and especially to increase the "jump" from p_1 to p_2 that affects *change* toward consistency.

Why, then, the peculiar pattern found earlier in observed turnover, where the net trend to consistency was greatest in the combination of one attention variable positive, the other negative? First, the reason why this at least half-favorable condition makes for more net trend than the negative extreme of both variables unfavorable—complete inattention—is obvious above from the erosion, p_1 to p_2, in the completely negative case. "Out of mind, out of consistency."

The other extreme, where both interest and salience were positive, *did* show net trend toward consistency in the raw data; it simply showed less net trend than the intermediate cases. This was because the turnover category in observed data earlier called *gain* was sharply reduced in the extremely favorable case. To see why, consider the effect of anything that makes a difference in parameters, for example, Δp_2 on this category of gain in consistency, ΔG:

$$(12) \qquad \frac{\Delta G}{\Delta A} = p_2 - p_1 \qquad (\text{e.g.} = +.14)$$

$$(13) \qquad \frac{\Delta G}{\Delta p_1} = 1 - p_2 - A \qquad (\text{e.g.} = -.60)$$

$$(14) \qquad \frac{\Delta G}{\Delta p_2} = A - p_1 \qquad (\text{e.g.} = +.06)$$

At the right, illustrations are again given for some sample values of these functions (here for the intermediate level where either, but not both, interest or salience is positive). It is immediately obvious that the second row, that is, Expression (13), is the one of the three that yields the rate of change that is large in magnitude. And it is *negative,* a decrement in gain in consistency, as a result of anything that makes for a positive increment in p_1. Anything raising initial conditions such as p_1, like the combination of both interest and salience (see Table 4-8), thus has a negative effect on further gain. So, the "paradox" that a negative condition of one of the variables made for greater net trend to consistency than its positive state, when the other variable was positive, is revealed as something like a ceiling effect, a purely formal aspect of turnover, when underlying it there was the *same* direction of causal forces.

It would be a mistake to confuse that with "regression" artifacts, however. Precisely what positive states of these attention variables do is reduce that kind of erosion. The expressions for difference in loss of consistency, ΔL, with differences in these parameters are:

$$(15) \qquad \frac{\Delta L}{\Delta A} = p_1 - p_2 \qquad (\text{c.g.} = -.13)$$

$$(16) \qquad \frac{\Delta L}{\Delta p_1} = A - p_2 \qquad (\text{e.g.} = -.08)$$

$$(17) \qquad \frac{\Delta L}{\Delta p_2} = 1 - p_1 - A \qquad (\text{e.g.} = -.46)$$

On the right are sample values for these expressions (for the samples of intermediate attention, $+ -$ or $- +$ in attention). All are negative, especially the last for p_2. They would be even more negative in the high attention situation $(++)$. Therefore, anything that makes for positive increments in the p's, especially in p_2 as salience or interest do, sharply reduces losses of previously consistent opinions. This is the well-know effect of interest in reducing turnover noted earlier.[10]

10. It remains to explain why the net gain toward consistency in raw data induced by these attention variables was not affected by "ceiling effects" (which prevented the motivation variables from having any net effect when initial consistency was already high). The reason is that, unlike the motivation variables, the attention variables affect p_2 and also the increase from p_1 to p_2. The effect of either parameter change on net trend to consistency in observed data is the same, namely:

To sum up, it seems clear that the general *kind* of model proposed—in spite of all the difficulties of this particular "make-do" version of it—can account for anomalies in these data that, we know from experience, are not otherwise easy to explain. Indeed, numerical solutions might be worked out for the trouble spots in this model that would fit in all cases.[11] But we prefer to put that effort into a more "explanatory" kind of theory that, while it adds nothing inconsistent with the above simple model, interprets the main diagnosis implied by it.

The diagnosis suggests that, in field data outside the laboratory, internal motivation and being externally surrounded by others similarly motivated effect long-term processes. They prevent people from long retaining inconsistent beliefs or learning them in the first place. Rather, dynamic potentials for abrupt *change* of opinion from inconsistency to consistency with basic dispositions—and thus, a change to consistency of opinions with each other—seem to be in the effect of changing people's *attention* to a topic.

III. AN EXPLANATORY MODEL

WHAT HAPPENS when public attention is called to something? We begin developing a simple theory of that problem by asking a contrasting question: What happens when the public is asked to react to something that has *not* been the center of attention, not yet prominent in the news, not well-defined politically, not clarified by discussion—in a word, not yet a matter of "public" opinion?

$$(11a) \qquad \frac{\Delta N}{\Delta p_2} = \frac{\Delta N}{\Delta (p_2 - p_1)} = 2A - 1$$

The condition of high initial consistency—where the motivation variables ran into "ceiling effects" preventing further net gain—requires that A be large. But by Expression (11a) just above, the larger A gets, the *more* positive effect on net trend to consistency there will be from anything that affects p_2 or affects the change from p_1 to p_2, as the attention variables do. Where the latter would show no effect on net is where $A < .5$, the case where the majority of the party supported the opposite of its official position. Attention would then "backfire."

11. However, without a third wave of data there is not enough information "left over" (degrees of freedom) to test fit. This is less so for the tests of fit of the model in the following section where additional items provide at least minor surplus information for a test.

Idiosyncratic Variation

First of all, if people give a "private" reaction we may all expect one thing. For example, Sherif's investigation of private reactions before group norms are established, or Kinsey's studies of private sex behavior in the absence of publicized norms fulfilled the expectation that, if people act independently of one another, individual differences assert themselves. This is formally manifested in pooled data, over many individuals, by wide *dispersions*. The standard deviations of measured rates and the heterogeneity of qualitative contents are markedly larger when individuals are "on their own."

Secondly, if public discussion has not clarified the meaning of an issue and the individual himself has not been paying attention to it, ambiguity is maximum. But that means properties of the stimulus content, which would be *common* to everyone, have minimum effect on response; rather, properties of the individual, which would be *different* for each individual, have maximum effect on response. This again means emphasis on individual differences and thus heterogeneity in pooled data.

As a third example, if the sheer mechanical uniformities induced by the circulation of common definitions by the mass media have not yet been operative, one individual may be perfectly clear on what he is talking about, another on what he himself is saying, but the two statements will not be the same. Again, this means heterogeneity in pooled data.

Let us call this kind of dispersion (one of two kinds of individual differences of opinion to be considered) the "idiosyncratic" variation. The reader should not take this to mean "random" or "error" as in the loose discussion of measurement models. The exact idea is expressed literally by *idio,* one's own, personal ideas that are perfectly determinate and sensible to oneself. They only appear to observers as examples of random error because they are seen syncratically, "mixed together" with other people's responses to their different perceptions judged from different experiences. For example, in the Elmira study of the 1948 election, a Republican woman was for Wallace. A check of this "error" found that it was because she had family members behind the Iron Curtain and judged Wallace to be the best chance for East-West conciliation. That personally rational view only seemed peculiar when thrown together with others in a scale of systematic variation, "Republicanism."

A way of formally representing this idiosyncratic source of variation in opinion, by *distribution* concepts called "perceptual dispersions," is implicit in recent work adapting the voting model reported in this volume to accept "live" data as input (McPhee, 1961). Distributions of perceptions of real issues in surveys are used to characterize what are called "stimulus distributions" in that model. If we had measured such perceptual dispersions for the present 1950 data, Figure 4-2 illustrates what the data might look like. Specifically, suppose we had made an on-the-spot clinical investigation, as was done with the Republican Wallace voter above, and suppose we and the respondent carefully graded on a "scale of cogency" how compelling his perception was of, say the Democratic side of each issue or argument, as he experienced it while answering. This scale by the cogency of perceptions of an argument is the horizontal or x-axis in Figure 4-2, the more compelling or positive side being to the right. Then the vertical curves represent what the "density" of perceptions falling at each such level of cogency might be, if we had carried out this scaling of perceived cogency for a large sample of people.

For example, there is evidence from several sources that the following "Democratic" argument in the 1950 survey, "We need strict price controls and excess profits taxes immediately," probably struck people in very *different* ways: some found it an "obviously needed" wartime move in the Korean emergency (the intent), many others as "perhaps" merited by the rising prices generally, but some as a "foolish" restatement of the quarrels over controls after World War II, some as a Republican argument "against" President Truman (for letting prices go up), and finally there is direct evidence that answers were very different depending on whether "prices" or "profits" were salient as the things to be controlled.[12] Figure 4-2 illustrates that if we plotted people's perceptions of the cogency or compellingness of such an ambiguous argument as this price-profit-controls one, the resulting dispersion by cogency would probably be very large in comparison to other arguments.

While Figure 4-2 does not portray direct measurements, of course,

---

12. In Washington (data from which are not used here) the question of price controls and that of excess profits taxes were asked separately. An analysis showed they were only moderately correlated (personal communication from Joseph Bachelder).

it is not an imaginary illustration either, but a representation of indirectly inferred distributions satisfying a simple model, which we will now develop. Let x be the cogency or compellingness of the perception to which a single individual is "exposed"—that is, the cogency of the argument as *he* gets it or experiences it—when a large number of people are exposed to some over-all argument like "we need price and profit controls." For example, $x = x_i$ would mean the individual perceived this argument at about the i'th level of attractiveness, where in the present version i can be anything from $+\infty$ to $-\infty$.

Heterogenous causes are at work determining x for different individuals; over many people, x would tend toward a normal distribution, which we call $f(x)$. It would disperse around a mean level of attractiveness characteristic of the over-all issue, $\bar{x}$, with a

4-2—Idiosyncratic Differences

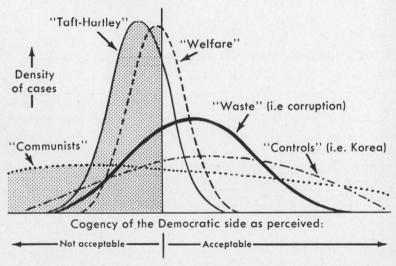

Cogency of the Democratic side as perceived:

◄——— Not acceptable ——— | ——— Acceptable ———►

Communists: Disagree or DK that "The Democrats have been too easy on Communists."

Controls: Agree that (due to Korea) "We need strict price controls and excess profits taxes immediately."

Waste: Disagree or DK that: "The Republicans would cut down waste and bureaucracy in government."

Welfare: Agree that "We should go even farther with government welfare benefits such as housing, medical care, and farm price supports."

Taft-Hartley: Agree that "The Taft-Hartley law is unfair to working people."

standard deviation characteristic of the amount of individual disagreement about all this, σ_x.

Next, assume the individual has a kind of "private rationality." If x is low or negative for him, that is, if *he* experiences the argument as indifferent or actually unattractive, then he does not say "yes" just because, for example, it would be consistent with his party choice. Rather, the argument has to strike him as at least barely acceptable enough to warrant going along with. Next, we give the meaning to "barely acceptable" of $x = b$. Thus, the chances he will "go along" by answering yes to the argument, are $P(x > b)$ or the probability that x is more compelling than the minimum acceptable, b.

Let us suppose that no one accepts unattractive and no one rejects attractive perceptions by his own lights, that is, x varies but b is the same for everyone. If so, the probability of a yes answer over many people would be, simply,

$$(18) \qquad P(x > b) = \int_{x=b}^{+\infty} f(x)dx$$

If $f(x)$ is the normal density curve, this is simply the area beyond some point in its cumulative version, sometimes called its ogive but here called its distribution function. The point b was illustrated by the vertical line in Figure 4-2.

It is clear from Figure 4-2 that over-all issues can be characterized in two ways, not only by the mean $\bar{x}$ or how likely the perceptions of the argument are to be acceptable, the "over-all appeal" of the argument; but also by σ_x or the dispersion by individual differences. The latter dispersion by x will be the formal meaning given to the "idiosyncratic" source of variation in response.

Systematic Variation

Next, relax the assumption that b or the barely acceptable point is the same for everyone, since the "bias" in these perceptions (for example, whereby strong Democrats see Democratic arguments in a favorable light) is notorious (Berelson, *et al.,* 1954). Instead, let b now represent this bias itself, by *varying* b for different people as in Figure 4-3. There we again show the inferred density of perceptions of the Democratic position on the issue, but now with the vertical lines showing how b, or acceptability of a Democratic argument, would vary from strong Democrats to the weakest Democrats (strong Republicans).

4-3—Systematic Differences

Verticals are density
distributions of perceptions:

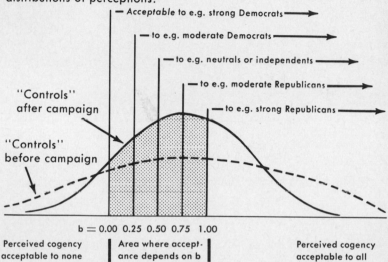

— Acceptable to e.g. strong Democrats ⟶

— to e.g. moderate Democrats ⟶

— to e.g. neutrals or independents ⟶

— to e.g. moderate Republicans ⟶

"Controls"
after campaign

— to e.g. strong Republicans ⟶

"Controls"
before campaign

$b = 0.00 \quad 0.25 \quad 0.50 \quad 0.75 \quad 1.00$

| Perceived cogency acceptable to none | Area where acceptance depends on b | Perceived cogency acceptable to all |

The metric we give to b (for example, the "maximum distance" in bias between strongest Democrats and strongest Republicans) is in a sense arbitrary; so let it vary from 0 to 1. If so, recall that, in our example of a Democratic argument, the higher the Democratic bias, and thus the higher the probability of answering Democratic on any and all issues, then the *lower* would be the point $x = b$ where such Democratic arguments would be barely acceptable. So, $b = 0$ would correspond to $p = 1$ where p was, say, some index or probability of voting Democratic. And similarly $b = 1$ or the maximum attractiveness required before even a grudging answer is given, would correspond to $p = 0$ for voting Democratic, or an absolute Republican. So, it is a natural metric to assume that

$$(19) \qquad\qquad b = 1 - p$$

where p is some point, on a scale from 0 to 1 of general disposition to favor this cause. Then we can rewrite the earlier Expression (18) now to let b vary with $1 - p$:

$$(20) \qquad P(x > b) = \int_{x=1-p}^{+\infty} f(x)dx$$

And this, while we have not yet discussed measurement of these things, brings the problem into a form that *is* familiar in measurement. Namely, suppose we know the distributions of the perceptions, as in Figure 4-3; we can express the probability of a "yes" answer as a function of a disposition scale, $p = 1 - b$, as in Figure 4-4.

4-4—Response as a Function of Systematic Bias
(Argument Is "Controls" Perceived as in Figure 4-3)

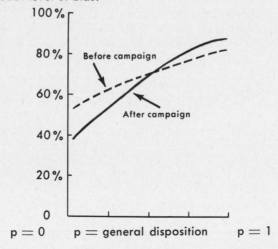

Per cent who say "yes" at each level of bias:

Figure 4-4 uses the same illustrative data as Figure 4-3, price-and-profit controls at Time 1 and Time 2. The difference is that now the sums to the right of the acceptable points, b, are cumulated as conveyed by the integral in Expression (20). Where in Figure 4-3 it was graphically convenient to show only four points by b, now located for reference at the bottom of Figure 4-4, this is of course a continuous function over the whole range of $p = 1 - b$. It is what

Lazarsfeld calls a "trace line" in latent structure analysis, that is, response as a function of an underlying disposition, p. Call this response curve $f(p)$, where that is shorthand for Expression (20) above.

We now note something essential in Figures 4-3 and 4-4. In the first we showed the density of perceptions to be somewhat *less dispersed* by x, or cogency (that is, with smaller standard deviation, σ_x) in the interview after the campaign than in the first before the campaign. The smaller dispersion had the effect in Figure 4-3 of making more of the perceptions fall within the region of x where their acceptability depends on b. But since $b = .1 - p$ that means p now plays a larger role in determining whether one answers "yes" or not. Hence, the response curve $f(p)$ shown in Figure 4-4 for the second interview wave is a somewhat "steeper" function of the disposition scale than it was in the interview only a month before.

This curve becomes very steep indeed for some issues, for example "Taft-Hartley" and "welfare" benefits. For, the reader can see by referring back to the original Figure 4-2 estimates, these issues had very narrow dispersions, that is, small σ_x. This has the effect of making answers depend on $b = 1 - p$ and again this makes the response a "steep" function of p. Thus, the correlation of the particular response with the general disposition is *inverse* to σ_x. This is illustrated in Figure 4-5.

If we are given some opinion question's marginals, that is, the total "yes" answers, in this model these can be satisfied by any one of a family of response curves $f(p)$ differing only in how "steep" a function of p each is. The correct one of these would be very steep if, for example, the original dispersion σ of perceptions was small. Since this steepness represents the systematic bias of response due to the *general* disposition, for example party bias, we call it the "systematic" variation in response.

The Effect of Attention

Since σ represented the "idiosyncratic" variation in opinion, and now the "systematic" source of variation in opinion depends on the inverse of σ, anything that reduces the idiosyncratic heterogeneity *automatically* increases the role of the systematic dimension, p. (It is, however, true there is an important class of exceptions that are not relevant here, namely, when perceptions converge around a mean, $\bar{x}$, which is acceptable to *everyone* or to *no one,* in which case the model portrays the consensus that results from "clearing up the confusion" before.) Otherwise, however, when the mean $\bar{x}$ is somewhere in the "debatable" range where response depends on p, anything that reduces the heterogeneity of idiosyncratic meanings, σ, causes perceptions to converge in this debatable range. Then, the chief remaining source of variation is the systematic one, $f(p)$. And this—reducing the "private" opinion due to individual idiosyncracy in favor of the more common perceptions of "public" opinion—is precisely what we believe public *attention* does.

For example, Table 4-10 gives the estimated σ, or the inferred dispersion of idiosyncratic perceptions, for the people who were paying most attention versus those paying least attention to the 1950 campaign. The index of attention used combines interest and salience, but because the method of obtaining these solutions discussed below is cumbersome, we had to use salience of price controls or profit controls as a surrogate for the ability to name specific issues

4-5—Illustrative Family of (Normal-Distribution) Functions Satisfying Marginals (e.g., Here 50% "Yes")

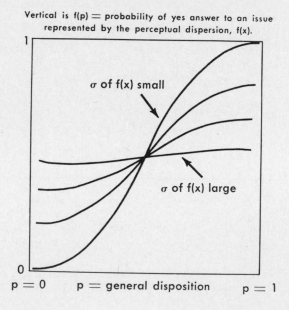

Vertical is $f(p) =$ probability of yes answer to an issue represented by the perceptual dispersion, $f(x)$.

σ of $f(x)$ small

σ of $f(x)$ large

$p = 0 \qquad p =$ general disposition $\qquad p = 1$

as salient in the campaign generally.[13] The index is more than
adequate, however, to illustrate our main point: on the left, attentive
people show narrow dispersions, small σ; on the right, inattentive
people show large dispersions, or much idiosyncratic response.

**Table 4-10—Estimated Standard Deviations (σ) of
"Perceptional Dispersions"**

	ATTENTIVE Interested and "Controls" Salient	MIXED Interested or "Controls" Salient	INATTENTIVE Not Interested and "Controls" Not Salient
Communists			
Time 1:	2.50*	3.33	5.00
Time 2:	.91	1.67	5.00
Controls			
Time 1:	1.11	.83	1.43
Time 2:	.67	.44	1.00
Waste			
Time 1:	.67	.91	2.50
Time 2:	.30	.31	.50
Taft-Hartley			
Time 1:	.33	.39	.77
Time 2:	.40	.53	.77
Welfare			
Time 1:	.31	.46	.53
Time 2:	.29	.53	.59

* The table entry is the standard deviation of normal curves whose distribution function, as illustrated in Figures 4-3 and 4-4, satisfies the item's marginals and, of the family of functions that do so, best approximates the correlations of the item with the other four. See subsequent text and the Technical Note.

Reading down by the topics of the issues also illustrates the
theory. The *new* issues in 1950, Communists and the Korean version
of wartime controls, and to some degree the Republican charges of
"waste" in the Truman administration, roughly like the "Communism, Korea, and Corruption" issues of two years later in 1952,
turn out in inferences by this model to have the widest idiosyncratic

13. It is interesting to note in Table 4-10, however, that "Controls" is the
only issue on which the standard deviation is smallest among the intermediate
cases called "mixed attention." These cases chiefly consisted of people who
were interested but did *not* name Controls as a salient issue.

It may be that *general* interest operates as shown in Table 4-10, but salience
of the *specific* issue has some disturbing effect (hence, maximum consistency
does not require salience). This was not noticeable in the solutions available
for the diagnostic model but will be investigated with the present model when
a less cumbersome solution for it is available.

dispersion. ("Communism" especially does, an issue that, for all its later party connotations, was just starting in 1950 in states other than sampled here.) Whereas, the *older* issues, the Taft-Hartley quarrel from 1947 to 1949 and the New Deal kind of issue, "welfare" programs, show the least idiosyncratic variation and thus the most systematic disagreement.

Finally, the table illustrates inferences that, comparing Time 1 with Time 2, the issues having previously had wide idiosyncratic dispersions, the first three, narrowed sharply during the campaign. By interpretation, the campaign forced more common perceptions. Indeed, the "waste" issue reaches the state of the old issues by Time 2, which is evidently as little idiosyncratic variance and as much systematic variance as one can get with data of this reliability (since these old issues do not change). There is no difference in such change by interest or salience shown here, but since the model's solutions requires that it be consistent with the earlier data, we know that if the proper controls of all variables and indexing of salience had been used and solutions worked out for every such combination, wherever there was a net gain in consistency of opinion shown earlier, it would *necessarily* be represented here by a *reduction* in σ.

For, consider what it means if public attention to the topic reduces the dispersion of perceptions, σ. That has the necessary effect in the model of making response, the $f(p)$ curve, a steeper function of the systematic disposition, p. But whereas σ is peculiar to *each* issue, p is common to *many* issues (here, all issues that evoke in some degree political-party biases and related liberal-conservative dispositions). Now, note that a political campaign calls attention to a number of such issues, explicitly or implicitly. A number are therefore becoming steeper functions $f(p)$, that is becoming more correlated with p. But if each is becoming a steeper function of the same thing, then all become more correlated with *each other*.

The apparent "interaction" of such opinions becoming more correlated with each other, however, is spurious. We show this by now making explicit the method of inferring the distributions in the charts and tables for these five issues. The method's major assumption, which we take over from latent structure and use intact as part of this model as well, is that the opinions are *independent* of one another. Their observed correlation arises, instead, because and only because they are each functions of the same general disposition, p, for example, here party bias. The appended Technical Note shows what this assumption means in more detail; but if we simplify by sup-

posing that people are about equally distributed over all points along
p, then the joint probability of a "yes" answer to issues j and k,
call it p_{jk}, is assumed to be:

$$(21) \qquad P_{jk} = \int_{p=0}^{p=1} f_j(p)f_k(p)\,dp$$

where on the right we mean the independent probabilities of "yes"
to j and to k at each point along p are simply multiplied to obtain
their joint occurrence. They are "locally independent." But since at
low p both will usually be "no" answers and at high p both will have
a high likelihood of "yes" answers, the responses of people of
different p are correlated in observed data. For example, Table 4-11
shows how the present theory reproduces the correlations in observed
data from these assumptions of (local) independence.

We said throughout, however, that the tables and charts "illustrated" the theory, for it cannot be tested seriously with these

**Table 4-11—Actual and Theoretical Data on the Number of
Other Opinions That Are Consistent with
"Controls" Opinion**

	PROPORTION OF PEOPLE AMONG THOSE WHO ARE					
	ATTENTIVE		MIXED		INATTENTIVE	
Other Items Consistent with "Controls" Item:	Interested and "Controls" Salient		Interested or "Controls" Salient		Not Interested, "Controls" Not Salient	
	Actual	Theory	Actual	Theory	Actual	Theory
All Four:						
Time 1:	.12	.11	.10	.10	.06	.06
Time 2:	.18	.18	.16	.15	.09	.08
Three Out of Four:						
Time 1:	.24	.25	.26	.25	.24	.26
Time 2:	.26	.26	.24	.27	.25	.27
Two Out of Four:						
Time 1:	.29	.28	.33	.32	.42	.39
Time 2:	.26	.25	.32	.29	.40	.36
One Out of Four:						
Time 1:	.24	.24	.22	.25	.24	.24
Time 2:	.19	.19	.20	.20	.22	.23
None Out of Four:						
Time 1:	.12	.11	.10	.09	.05	.05
Time 2:	.12	.13	.08	.09	.05	.06
n	(206)		(457)		(282)	

data. The reason is that the method of solution for parameters like σ is tautological, as most such methods are. Namely, we have to use precisely *what* the theory is explaining in observed data, *correlation* and thus "consistency" of opinion, in order to infer the unobserved parameters with which the theory does the explaining. Briefly sketching what the Technical Note expands, the solution is by iterative methods (at this stage) in a computer, in two steps.

1. From a table of areas beyond points in a normal curve, *all* significantly different $f(p)$ given by Expression (20) that satisfy the marginals of each item are found. These are functions varying in "steepness" as in Figure 4-5, this being inverse to the variable σ in the normal curve.

2. Then another computer program chooses which one of such a family of $f(p)$ functions, varying in steepness, is a steep enough functions of p to reproduce the correlation of item j with item k by Expression (21) above. This is done simultaneously for five families of functions for five issue items each playing the role of k and j for each other, until the $f(p)$ function for each is found that best reproduces the correlation with all others.

This solution method uses only correlations of *pairs* of items, so there is some data "left over" for a minor test of fit. It is data on the joint occurrence of each of thirty-two patterns of "yes" and "no" answers on *all* five items simultaneously. This fit is good and in summarized in the aspect relevant here in Table 4-11.

To summarize: the independent effect of public attention to each issue in

1. Reducing the heterogeneity of perceptions of particular issues, σ, and thus the idiosyncratic variance peculiar to each issue

2. Thereby leaves as the chief source of variance the systematic bias, p, common to many issues

3. And as this makes response to each, $f(p)$, a steeper function of p, the greater correlation of each issue with the same disposition makes all items appear, in observed data, more correlated with each other.

Tests of all this with measurement independent of the theory itself, for example, by directly measuring the perceptual dispersions $f(x)$ rather than inferring them tautologically from correlations in responses, are the needed next steps.

TECHNICAL NOTE

The following is in two sections: (1) the first gives brief algebraic solutions for the "diagnostic" model used in the middle part of the text, (2) the second gives the method of approximate solution of the "explanatory model" of perceptual distribution in the last section of the text.

1. Diagnostic Model

To recall, A is the proportion of "adherents" to their party's position on this issue, and $1 - A$ the rest of that party's voters who do *not* support it on this particular issue. Then p_1 and p_2 are the probabilities at Times 1 and 2 that these people will actually express *their* basic positions in the specific circumstances (p is the same for adherents who say "yes" and others who say "no"). What in observed data we think of as "consistency," however, is consistency with the *party's* view (or adherent's position). Then the defining equations are:

(1) Initial Consistency $\quad I = p_1A + (1 - p_1)(1 - A)$

(3) Gain $\quad\quad\quad\quad\quad G = p_2(1 - p_1)A + (1 - p_2)p_1(1 - A)$

(4) Loss $\quad\quad\quad\quad\quad L = (1 - p_2)p_1A + p_2(1 - p_1)(1 - A)$

(2) Turnover $\quad\quad\quad\quad T = G + L$

(5) Net $\quad\quad\quad\quad\quad\quad N = G - L$

These simplify to the expression numbered correspondingly in the text. The latter then lead to the partial derivatives of the text in the usual manner.

For a straightforward but cumbersome solution, Expressions (3) and (4) can be rewritten:

(3a) $\quad\quad\quad\quad\quad G = p_2(A - p_1) - Ap_1 + p_1$

(4a) $\quad\quad\quad\quad\quad L = p_2(1 - p_1 - A) + Ap_1$

Multiplying and subtracting to eliminate p_2 the result can then be rewritten as the first of the two rows below:

(3a — 4a) $G = A(2p_1{}^2 - 2p_1 + G + L)$
$$+ p_1(- p_1 + 1 + G - L)$$

(1a) $I = A(2p_1 - 1) - p_1 + 1$

where the second row is Expression (1) above rewritten so that we can subtract these to eliminate A. Recalling in this that $G + L = T$ or turnover and $G - L = N$ or net, the result finally comes down to a quadratic equation for p_1. In its solution:

$$p_1 = \frac{-b \pm \sqrt{b^2 - 4ac}}{2a}$$

The definitions in observed data come out to be:

$$a = 2N + 2I - 1$$
$$b = 1 - 2N - 2I$$
$$c = IT - L$$

The higher p_1 would normally be the one to make sense. Substituting the solution for that in equation (1a) above, one can get A as:

(1b) $$A = \frac{I + p_1 - 1}{2p_1 - 1}$$

Then p_2 follows, for example, from Expression (3a) above:

(3b) $$p_2 = \frac{G + p_1(A - 1)}{A - p_1}$$

This handy little model is suitable when (a) the data can be dichotomized, (b) such that I or initial consistency is unambiguously above, say, about 60 per cent, and (c) the time interval between waves is sufficient for the assumption of independence of responses in time to be more nearly valid—the failure of all three conditions exactly to be met in the original empirical analysis of this text accounting for the subsequent troubles in getting solutions. The reader is referred to Kendall (1953, Appendix) for use of such a model as an empirical indexing method in the study of turnover; to Lazarsfeld (in Stouffer, 1951) for analogous "latent turnover" models; and especially to Wiggins (1955, and in Lazarsfeld, 1962) for the use of more adequately flexible models than this as important substantive theories.

2. The "Explanatory" Model of Perceptual Distributions

This theory has two origins and two corresponding methods of measurement. It first arose from efforts to supply "live" input to the stimulation process of the voting model (McPhee, 1961 a, b). There, what one measures empirically is the distributions of perceptions in the first place, the model then converting these into theoretical responses. In the present problem, however, we have the observed *responses* and use a model to get back to the theoretical (unobserved) perceptual distributions.

In the latter form, what we have technically is a theory of the function involved when we say responses are a function of a disposition continuum. These functions are the "trace lines" in Lazarsfeld's latent-continuum models. No substantive theory has been developed to rationalize trace lines; instead, some function (such as linear or exponential) is assumed as convenient and then its reasonableness tested by the fit. The present model complements latent structure, then, by offering an explicit theory of the trace lines (response functions); otherwise, it adopts the latent structure logic intact as part of its theory and of its solution. This solution is the following (let us hope temporary) numerical expedients.[14]

First, we do not attempt the theoretically possible but difficult problem of simultaneously solving for both (1) the response function of p, the trace line, and (2) the distribution of the population along p, the number of people at each point. Instead, assume that the latter population distribution is given empirically; for example as in the classification of the 1956 Roper sample in the paper in this volume, "Political Immunization." Since these classifications are likely to be discrete, assume that we know the approximate proportion of the population falling at each of n equally spaced points along the disposition continuum (where we use $n = 10$, with the points

---

14. In our brief work on this as a deductive sociological (aggregate) theory, we failed to notice earlier progress in psychometrics on solutions for formally similar models, notably by Frederich Ford (1953). These are introduced and the technical literature cited in Torgerson (1960, pp. 385-395). With today's computers, these efficient but difficult solutions may prove to be as easy as our numerical expedients, which accordingly we do not develop in detail here.

$p = .05, p = .10, p = .15, \ldots, p = .95$ to approximate the continuous case in the present calculations).[15]

If we call the proportion of the population at some such point where $p = i$ the "volume" of people there, V_i, then let the conditional probability that people at this point say "yes" to the particular item be p_i'. Then, the "yes" answers originating at that point are simply:

$$p_i' V_i$$

and the·sum of similar "yes" answers over all n points would represent the marginals of the item, call it P_j, where the subscript means the marginals of the j'th item or issue. That is,

$$(22) \qquad P_j = p_1' V_1 + p_2' V_2 + \ldots + p_n' V_n$$

Now, by the theory presented in the next, corresponding to each point, $p = i,$ there is some level of cogency of the stimulus, call it $x_i,$ which is just barely acceptable but everything above it elicits a "yes" answer. That is,

$$p_i' = \int_{x_i}^{+\infty} f(x)\,dx$$

which we can substitute for p_i' in Expression (22) to get

$$(23) \qquad P_j = V_1 \int_{x_1}^{+\infty} f(x)\,dx + V_2 \int_{x_2}^{+\infty} f(x)\,dx + \ldots + V_n \int_{x_n}^{+\infty} f(x)\,dx$$

This would be a double integral if V were continuous; but nothing is gained here by assuming that, because the definite integrals of $f(x)$ referred to above are areas above a certain point in the normal curve, for which no explicit integral exists. Instead, one uses tables of the area beyond discrete points, namely the cumulative version called the normal distribution function. Now, the points, $p = i$ where i is $1, 2, \ldots, n$ above, were assumed to be equally spaced along p (as best that could be approximated in estimating V_i for n points between $p = 0$ and $p = 1$). And that means equally spaced, not by the area under the normal curve, but by what corresponds to the fixed scale

15. A difficulty in solving explicitly for these population distributions is illustrated here. The fit seems equally good with "tracelines" not fundamentally different, when we use bi-modal distributions realistic for politics versus rectangular distribution (the latter were used for the text illustrations).

on which such a curve is plotted, namely its standard deviation in units of x, call it σ_x. So, the problem posed by Expression (23) above, in which we know the marginals P_j and have estimated the V's or population distribution, is this: find in a normal distribution table of areas beyond any point, areas beyond n successive points equally spaced by σ_x that together satisfy (23).

In the brief work to date, no attempt has been to find an algebraic shortcut for this, but it is simple to handle in a computer as follows: compute the right side of (23) for *all* significantly different sets, $x_1, x_2, \ldots, x_n$ equally spaced by σ_x, and print out those that satisfy (23) above (and the others as a separate "library" for future use arranged by the marginals they satisfy). Those that do satisfy (23) are a family of functions differing in the "steepness" by which p' is a function of p, as in Figure 4-5 of the main text of this paper. Since all satisfy the marginals, the choice between them now requires additional data as follows.

Let $p_i^{(j)}$ be the same as p_i', but now making explicit that this p_i' is a member of a set of p's satisfying marginals for the j'th item. And let $p_i^{(k)}$ be a corresponding member of a set satisfying the marginals for the k'th item. Then make the latent-structure assumption of "local independence," namely that

$$V_i p_i^{(j)} p_i^{(k)}$$

is the joint occurrence of yes answers to both items originating among people at the i'th level of the disposition p. What the multiplication of p's implies is that the observed correlation between answers to items j and k is due to the fact that each is a function of p, and thus when we hold this common bias *constant*, at the i'th level of p, the answers to the two items are not otherwise connected (indeed, this disappearance of their correlation when p is held constant is what a survey analyst means by p "explaining" their correlation). So, if we let the observed joint occurrence of yes answers to items j and k be P_{jk}, it is for the whole population:

$$(24) \quad P_{jk} = V_1 p_1^{(j)} p_1^{(k)} + V_2 p_2^{(j)} p_2^{(k)} + \ldots + V_n p_n^{(j)} p_n^{(k)}$$

Now, the correct one of the family of all trace lines satisfying the marginals for item j, and the correct one of the family satisfying the marginals for item k, would be the ones that together satisfied (24). That is, each would be a "steep" enough function of the same systematic disposition for that disposition to account for each item's correlations with the *other* in observed data.

So, define an error between P_{jk} as calculated from (202) and the actually observed proportion of "yes" answers to both, P^*_{jk}, namely $P_{jk} - P^*_{jk}$. One can then calculate this error in a computer, for each of m different issues playing the role of item k in (24). If the algebraic sum of these errors,

$$(25) \qquad \sum_{k=1}^{m} (P_{jk} - P^*_{jk})$$

is negative, then the set of $p^{(1)}$ used is not a steep enough function of the disposition, p. So, the iterative program is to take the next steeper function for the next trial calculation (or conversely, if the error is the opposite). Soon (25) goes to zero. Simultaneously, the same is being done for each of the m other issues. While we cannot explicitly prove these simultaneously changing functions always converge on a unique best set of them, in practice this is what happens.

Of course, Expression (25) might be minimized by canceling errors. So, taking as the best function for each of the m items the one above that satisfied their correlation in *pairs,* the machine program tests their fit, by an expression analogous to (24) to the 2^m combinations of the joint occurrence of "yes" and "no" answers to *all* m issues simultaneously. This fit for $m = 5$ has been very good in about a dozen independent trials made, with no error over .03 and the average always under .01. The table shown in the main text summarizes that the remaining error is random-like and the systematic correlation of all five items is exhausted this way.

II

SYNTHETIC

AGGREGATION

5

A MODEL FOR ANALYZING
VOTING SYSTEMS

By William N. McPhee and Robert B. Smith

I. INTRODUCTION

*T*his paper describes the initial version of a model that
promises to be a convenient instrument for solving an old difficulty,
as follows: Assume one is already given detailed research knowledge
about the individual behavior involved in some mass situation, for
example, as is certainly the case with professional research knowledge
on how people vote in Western democracies. Now, how does one
proceed from such knowledge about discrete units at the microscopic
level to some "macroscopic" picture of how, when it is all put

The substantive work leading to design of this model in 1957-1958 was
facilitated by a grant to the senior author for basic research on mass
phenomena by the Behavioral Sciences Division of the Ford Foundation and
prior to that from free funds of the Bureau of Applied Social Research,
granted by the Loeb Foundation. Its computer work was made possible by
facilities and time generously provided by the Watson Scientific Computing
Laboratory, jointly operated by International Business Machines, Inc. and
Columbia University; and was especially implemented by the 1958 summer conference on the Simulation of Cognitive Behavior, sponsored by the Social
Science Research Council and conducted by Herbert Simon of the Carnegie
Institute of Technology and Allen Newell and Clifford Shaw of the RAND
Corporation, to whom thanks are due individually.

together, the aggregate system works? For example, how do significant properties of electoral systems emerge from various combinations of individual processes and different institutional arrangements?

The Problem of Aggregation

As an example of one such aggregate property, the American electoral system displays remarkable capacities of re-equilibration after disturbance, having oscillated back and forth around a 50-50 division between the two parties for more than a century. The precise reasons for this are not made apparent, however, by mere projection up to the requisite magnitudes from a sample of what we know about individual voters, politicians, and laws—even though the whole is the consequence of these parts in some complex sense. The complexity is the problem. Many mass phenomena—not only in voting but in fields ranging from communications and mass culture to mobility and class structure—involve unknown problems in *compounding* the known facts about individuals and their interaction (which are therefore not additive as in the census). Yet this is necessary to reach the socially significant implications in the aggregate. These problems may turn out to be as complicated as those encountered in modern economic theory.

The difficulty in certain social fields is curiously upside-down, however, from the relations between observation and theory in most science. What is required is not the usual "downward" penetration— that is, given easy observation of the total behavior of a system at the molar level, the breaking down of this whole analytically to infer unobservables at the microscopic level. Rather, we are given analytic knowledge from convenient observation directly at the level of the micro units, for example, from the many interview studies among individual voters. We wish to proceed "upward" to unobservables at the system level. It is a putting-together, or synthetic problem. Yet since the aggregate syntheses would be nothing but consequences of what is known from direct observation, this is not so much an empirical as a logical problem. It is a problem in "social logic," that is, combining large numbers of small units in long sequences of interacting processes to determine their aggregate and cumulative consequences. The dynamic behavior of the latter aggregates is the unknown in the problem, even though it consists of logical consequences of what is known or assumed about individuals.

With such problems in mind, a simple model of individual voting behavior has been constructed. It lends itself to rapid logical manipulation of sizable numbers of units ("voters") arranged in complicated structures ("communities") through long sequences of processes ("eras" or "generations"). These manipulations are intended to help analyze problems in electoral dynamics of a complexity too great to be easily understood—at first, and without such aids—by more conventional verbal and mathematical methods.

Computer Simulation

While the present instrument was created as an entirely substantive project, prior to knowledge of machinery for manipulating it, it deals with large problems whose implications are difficult to discover without an automatic computer. Therefore, the version to be described here is written in the language of a simple and widely available machine, the IBM 650. (An IBM 709 version is not materially different.) Subparts of the model and their implications, once appreciated, can be formalized parsimoniously. Yet the model in total will probably continue to be more convenient, as a working instrument, in machine language capable of handling its full complexity.

No knowledge of these machines is assumed below, nor of "computing" in connection with mathematical models, nor the topic here. It is true, the present machine program does have certain arithmetical features in which multiplication or division are performed as short cuts that do not correspond directly to the behavioral processes that accomplish equivalent results. Nevertheless, it is a "model" in a much more concrete sense than what is meant by mathematical model. In this respect, it is intermediate between two polarities in current work.

In much work called computer simulation—for example, the representation of a firm's market performance in so-called business gaming—a mathematical model has actually been constructed independent of the computer. The latter plays only the subsidiary role of fast calculator. For, since the equations are usually numerous, and general solutions difficult, a machine is needed to carry out the calculations and arrive at numerical answers appropriate for the specific cases. The model itself is quantitative and abstract, however. Nowhere in it will any concrete "customer" be found, for example, making any specific purchase.

The opposite polarity arises in certain recent work, especially that of Newell, Shaw, and Simon on psychological problems. Their model is wholly nonnumerical.[1] An individual is represented in a very detailed way in machine storage, for example, by symbols for the things he knows, subprograms for the habitual procedures he uses, and so on. When the person (the machine program) acts, in this case to solve a problem, there are no equations. The processes and mechanisms are carried out quite literally. For example, an "associational" process actually carries out an act of cross-referring from one symbol to find another in memory (storage). The theory is correspondingly nonnumerical. It is expressed in a language of comparing, sorting, classifying, conditional changes, self-modification, and the like, which is native to computer work itself (and more likely resembles everyday intuitive logic than formal mathematics).

The present model resembles the latter type in that it has no abstract equations but rather models events in a very *literal* sense. Hundreds (thousands in a 709) of concrete voters are represented, and each carries out the processes of the model in detail. For example, its social-discussion process might be represented more elegantly by probability equations summarizing their effect. But here, voters influencing one another actually *do* come into a central place in the machine. Their specific preferences (symbols) are concretely compared. Each may go through detailed processes representing a form of social influence of the other on him.

Since a computer is serial (can do only one thing at a time), however, it has the inconvenience for simulation of *social* processes that the rest of the voting community must "wait" while each person acts. If extremely detailed processes like those of Newell, Shaw, and Simon were involved here for every individual voter, it would be a long wait, to say the least, to process a sample community over a generation with presently available equipment.[2] So, it is a fortunate accident of the history of this particular model, which was originally designed without knowledge of nonnumerical work, that its processes are close to mathematical ideas in their simplicity and often use numerical short cuts. In this intermediate character,

---

1. See, for example, Newell (1957). Published versions of these authors are widely scattered and are best located by bibliographies obtainable from the authors at Carnegie Institute of Technology, Pittsburgh.
2. This is only a temporary problem in principle. But in practice, large, high-speed equipment capable of handling detailed psychological processes in a social problem involving *many* individuals over *long* time spans may not be accessible on the average campus for many years yet.

the present work resembles that of Hoggatt and Balderston (1959). They simulate directly in computer operations a market with each of almost two hundred wholesalers, retailers, and suppliers concretely making decisions, actually communicating with one another, and so on. The complexity is far greater than could be handled mathematically, but of necessity it is much simplified from what would be possible in representing *one* such decision-maker. In the same spirit, we require a very simple voter here in order to deal with complex aggregates of them.

The General Plan

It is useful to begin the explanation of the present scheme by asking: What are the most important findings to come out of modern studies about voting decisions during election campaigns?[3] Ironically, perhaps the crucial discovery is that most votes are *not* really fresh decisions made during the given election campaign. In established party systems found in the Western world today, votes are clearly fashioned over many elections. Starting from youth, there is a gradual process of political socialization or "politicization," whose eventual product typically is a more or less habitual allegiance to one party (Hyman, 1959).

The individual's enduring partisanship is then implemented in the given election when he chooses—in effect, if not always consciously—whether to continue that party preference or to make an exception this time. The model utilizes this now familiar knowledge in the problem formulation itself, choosing as the most significant subject matter the *long-term* process of political socialization rather than the single campaign or "election prediction."[4]

In this elongation, there is a resemblance to learning models, as if on a massive scale with political communities as subjects. Suc-

3. Reference here is chiefly to the so-called panel studies initiated by Lazarsfeld and Berelson in 1940 and elaborated by others in now more than a dozen election studies in this country, the British Commonwealth and Western European elections. The present model was the direct result of trying to find processes that would reproduce the inventory of findings through 1954 compiled by Berelson (1954, Appendix A) and reproduced in part in the paper by Glaser and Kadushin elsewhere in this book.
4. A short-term or campaign version of the model, adapted for television demonstration in 1960, interprets the years and decades of the present model as weeks and months in a campaign. It uses the same program (logic) but requires extensive reinterpretation, discussed elsewhere (McPhee, 1961).

cessive elections here are like successive learning "trials." Like the learning theorists, we are primarily interested not in the single trial but in the *cumulative* effect, say, over a political era or generation. We are interested in sufficiently long and complex sequences of processes to modify the system's capacities and propensities in significant ways not obvious in the elementary processes at one time. The events of each election are probably more adequately represented than are the detailed psychological processes of rats on each trial in a learning model. Yet since the psychological processes of single rats on single learning trials are conveniently unknown, but those of voting communities in an election well-known, the oversimplification here of the latter will be, not more brutal, but more evident.

Three processes are represented in the voting model: (1) response to external political stimuli, (2) mutual influence of individuals within the immediate social environment of one another, for example, the influence of family and friends on each other, (3) the "learning" over time of the habit of partisanship is acquired. How these act to produce successive modifications in the voter is diagrammed in highly simplified form in Figure 5-1.

First, the model takes from the input hopper an injection of "political stimuli" for the period since the last election. These are used in a stimulation process. Each voter, equipped with certain predispositions and other relevant characteristics, is "stimulated." By methods to be detailed later, the machine assigns particular stimuli to particular voters. Each then emerges with an "initial preference" of greater or lesser degree for one party as against the other in the current campaign. This preference is something like a "leaning" or "first impression," the kind we get from casual reading of the newspapers prior to serious thought and discussion.

In short, the stimulation process takes external stimuli and the political predisposition of the voter as input, and produces as output an initial preference.

Later, most voters enter the subroutine in the middle of the diagram, labeled "discussion process." Here each voter encounters another voter, a spouse or friend, with whom he "exchanges views." If his friend's impressions match his own, his initial preference will tend to be strengthened into a conviction or decision, which will become his vote. If his friend disagrees, the voter will return to the stimulation process for further exposure to external stimuli, which may then either confirm or alter his initial preference in reaching the decision he will express in a vote.

In sum: the discussion process takes initial preferences as input, and produces as output the conviction or decision (vote this time).

This decision now becomes the input to the subroutine labeled "learning process." This process resembles, not a conventional learning theory, but a simpler model used elsewhere to represent the progressive development of disease and similar self-intensifying phenomena. What is growing here, over many elections, is the

5-1—Flow Chart of the Model

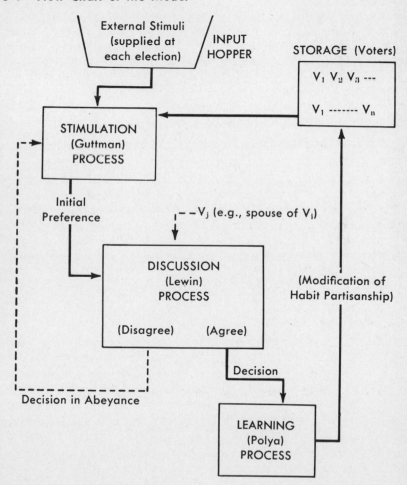

partisan bias that makes most people eventually habitual Republicans or Democrats.

What the learning process does in any single election is to take the conviction reached in that election as input, and produce as output progressive modifications of the party dispositions with which the voter will enter the next election period.

As for the data produced, output for the observer to examine can be voluminous and highly varied. For, this is a "completely observable system." Any combination of the hundreds of thousands of operations per problem can be monitored, in principle, whenever that seems worth the effort. A companion paper gives illustrations of output data that have been found useful. Here only a few examples will be included, chiefly in the form of footnotes for the technical reader, the chief concern now being to explain the internal programming representing the simple theory and its mechanical implementation.

II. THE DETAILS

THE STORAGE DRUM of the computer used here consists of cells each of which comprises 10 digits and is therefore capable of storing 10 items of information (10 columns of an IBM card). In current work, 20 items, stored in two adjacent cells, are employed to represent each voter, for example, 400 cells in storage being occupied if one uses 200 hypothetical voters to constitute the miniature electorate. The arrangement of the first cell is diagrammed in Figure 5-2, that of the second, later.

5-2—First Ten-Digit Cell for One Voter

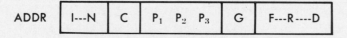

ADDR | I---N | C | P_1 P_2 P_3 | G | F---R----D

(ADDR = Address; i.e., cell number, of this voter in storage)
I---N = Interest at present time
C = Choice of party at present time
P_1, P_2, P_3 = Partisanship for each of three parties
G = Grouping or strata category
F---R----D = Friend's or spouse's or parent's address

In the following exposition, these variable properties of the voters will be introduced as they come into play, as input or output, in the processes of the model. The discussion is organized around those processes, stimulation, discussion, and learning.

The Stimulation Process

P or Partisanship. What we call "party loyalty," "partisanship," and the like is represented in this scheme by three index numbers, each single digits. In most uses, these are interpreted as if they represented *probabilities* of voting for the parties, say, Democrat, Republican, and Third Party, respectively, or simply P_1, P_2, P_3 (in a three-party model).

These two or three P dispositions are defined for a given election from the outcome of past ones, in a simple development process to be described later. But they must be set to some initial state for the first election so that the system may be started externally. For two parties, values of this partisanship index vary from 0.1 to 0.9. The value 0.0 for any party and also of 1.0 for the other are barred; otherwise they would work to exclude the always-present possibilities both of nonvoting and of voting for a nonpreferred party due to idiosyncratic reasons not covered by these processes. In the two-party version, for example, if an individual has the partisanship values .2, .6 at a particular time, he then has a 20 per cent chance of voting for one major party, a 60 per cent chance of voting for its opposite, and a 20 per cent chance of nonvoting.[5]

As in the real world, each individual's partisanship values may increase or decrease over time. In fact, the *time-paths* of development of these partisan dispositions are a central concern in much current work. The third party is intended for future comparative analyses of European systems; it can be shut off by fiat from an American user.

G or Grouping. In the real world, each voter may be classified in certain groupings or stratifications in the population to which poli-

---

5. After each election the two-party model punches out ten tables of cross-tabulations of partisanship, for different subgroups. In these tables the P probabilities are trichotomized into High, Medium, and Low. Then cross-tabulations of these dispositions toward two parties simultaneously are punched out and/or printed. The two values can vary independently, within the restriction that their sum not exceed 1.00.

ticians make differential appeals. Consequently, a necessary property of each voter is a *G* symbol (digit here), representing his type in a stratification of the test sample of voters into different categories, established by the analyst at the start. A given *G* category in the model may be interpreted as workers, or southerners, or some more abstract type, as the analyst's problem dictates. Indeed, it could be a personality category, if political appeals affect the type differentially.

These digit symbols operate internally in the computer to activate switches. These determine what pool of political *stimuli* the voter will be exposed to. They channel to the appropriate voters as many as eight (in this version) different sources of stimulation during the given election. This enables the theorist using the model to arrange for different "appeals" (different probable strengths of stimulation) to be made by the same party to as many as eight distinct strata or overlaps thereof in the population.

For example, the eight categories might in some problem represent the simultaneous classification of voters by three dichotomies: a major division by working versus business class, each class subdivided into subtypes by ethnic background, and each of those in turn by an urban-rural break. Separate machine runs could represent the same differentiation of individuals in successively different ecological units, South, Northeast, Midwest, and West. Any or all of these types could then receive different sequences of stimulation from the two parties in each of the successive elections during a problem. Thereby, quite concrete patterns of national pluralism could be represented. But in theoretic problems, of course, one would typically work with a more parsimonious categorization.

For the internal processes, however, they are interpreted by the user, the significant point is that the *G* categorization of blocs of voters determines *which* distribution of stimuli these voters will be exposed to from each party during the course of the problem if *G* is constant, or for successive periods when *G* is variable (as in problems involving mobility between social categories).

The Stimulation Process. With these essential ingredients in mind, we can now outline the process in which they are used. The instrument provides for flexible input of external stimuli, thus making no attempt to predict the stimulus aspect of an election (indeed, that would be to predict history). The model *is* committed, however, to carry out a definite theory of how these stimuli are responded to, even though that theory is customarily called a "method" in scaling work.

The key assumption is that the stronger the person's internal predisposition (here *P,* or partisanship) toward some class of objects (for example, candidates of a party), the weaker the external stimulation required from any such object to elicit a "yes" choice of it by this person. Conversely, the weaker the internal disposition, the stronger must be the external appeal (here strength of stimulus) in order to elicit the "yes" choice.

For example, a voter with strong *P* disposition to the Democrats, say, .7, will wish to vote Democratic even in a situation offering him only mediocre Democratic stimulation, say a symbol of strength 4, whereas another voter with weaker Democratic inclinations, say, .2, would not respond to this mediocre appeal. He would require a (better) "reason" to vote Democratic, here, unusually strong stimulation. The qualitative idea used here is similar to that in an elementary Guttman scale: For example, one implication is that the less Democratic the person, then not only the less he votes Democratic in general, but especially the less he votes for the *un*popular Democrats or for Democratic candidates under *un*favorable circumstances. The assumption's quantitative usage in the present model is quite arbitrary, merely taking the simplest form. It is most easily explained in the special case that follows:

Consider the *P* index as the simple probability of a voter's choosing the party. (Indeed, as will be shown later, it is merely a weighted frequency of voting for that party in the past.) Then assume that we wish to distribute *actual* votes to 100 concrete people who have a .7 probability of voting Democratic. If so, this is accomplished mechanically by assigning stimulus symbols numbered 1 to 10 at random to these voters. Then consider any and all of them receiving a stimulus symbol *above* 3 as sufficiently "stimulated" to vote Democratic. This would result in 70 "yes" votes (symbols number 4 to number 10) and 30 "no" votes, or .70 frequency.

The stimulus numbers of 3 and below which did *not* qualify the person to say "yes," even though he is usually Democratic, are thereby given the implicit definition of "weak" stimuli. For not even persons of .7 chance of voting Democratic "responded" when allocated a stimulus so defined.

Similarly, suppose we were dealing with 100 people of .3 probability of voting Democratic. We can designate those receiving stimulus symbols above 7, from a random draw of symbols between 1 and 10, as the 30 of the 100 to be Democrats. Implicitly, symbols 8, 9, and 10 are thus defined as "strong stimuli." For they elicited Democratic votes from persons of only weak dispositions in that direction.

Thus, *interpretation* is given to the usually arbitrary symbols (dice, numbers, black balls, and so on) used in Monte Carlo procedures, here the symbols 1, 2, . . . , 10 drawn at random to determine which persons out of those of a given probability of voting Democratic will actually do so in a given election. The interpretation is that the symbols vary in "strength" as stimuli. One "greater" than minimum (that is, $1 - P$) evokes a response.

A distribution of different gradations of such stimuli is represented in the machine by a table. This permits convenient sampling thereof in order to assign one to a given voter. An array of the stimulus gradations is shown in the right-hand column below. The probability that any one will be drawn is shown at far left. If we cumulate these probabilities, as shown, the chance of each one's being drawn is proportionate to the *interval* each occupies between 0 and 1.00 in the cumulative column. The distribution looks like this in the special case of *equal* probabilities (equal intervals) for all symbols:

Probability (of Each Occurring)	Interval (Cumulative Probability)	Symbol (Stimulus Strength)
.10	.00................) .09................)	1 (Weakest)
.10	.10................) .19................)	2
.10	.20................) .29................)	3
.	.	.
.	.	.
.	.	.
.10	.90................) .99................)	10 (Strongest)

Given such a table of the probabilities that stimuli of different strength will be drawn, the computer generates a random number between .00 and .99. By "table-lookup" operations explained in any machine manual, the machine finds the interval (between cumulative probabilities) containing the random number. The corresponding stimulus symbol (strength) is thus designated for the given voter. For example, suppose the machine generates the random number .97; the table-lookup operation notes that .97 falls between .90 and .99, and the machine then selects the corresponding stimulation symbol "10." The interpretation of this 10 is that, in the play of chance events, the particular voter received a very high strength of stimulation from the given party.

As the external stimulus at a given moment, this symbol number is matched against the voter's internal partisanship by the rule mentioned earlier. For example, a strong stimulus, here, "10," is sufficient to elicit a "yes" vote intention from those of the weakest partisanship.

At first, these sampling mechanics seem a cumbersome way to implement a familiar scaling assumption that could be stated in a simple equation. But the procedure has a crucial practical advantage which enables the model to reproduce quite complex processes of differential party appeal to people of different predispositions toward it.

To explain, the above example has in common with many of the discussions of random devices the simple assumption that every stimulus strength has an *equal* chance of being drawn. If this were always so in the model, it would produce vote frequencies that simply manifested internal partisan probabilities at all times. We know, however, that in real life people who are strong Democrats do not always manifest that inner probability in the same external frequencies. Rather, there is, in addition to the inner disposition, the influence of external events. One often wishes to simulate an external situation that causes people of high internal pro-Democratic "probabilities" of .7 to manifest a frequency of, say, only 50 to 60 votes for that party per 100 people. How would that be accomplished?

It is easily done by the well-known sampling technique of altering the "intervals" in the cumulative probabilities on the left side of the preceding table. That is, one makes the stimulus strengths available in a table for a given group of voters occupy *unequal* intervals and thus have unequal chances in the lot-drawing process of the machine. For example, if we made the first interval 00 to 49, the stimulus symbol of strength 1 would have 50 per cent chance of being drawn.

This intervention from outside—to alter the chances of different symbols and cause voters to display actual frequencies correspondingly different from their internal partisan probabilities—is accomplished mechanically as follows. At the beginning of the given election, at the appropriate point in some problem involving many elections, the machine revises these tables by information taken from new "stimulation" cards provided by the user in the input hopper. These cards contain new distributions of stimulus intervals for each party for each of the groups of voters involved. For example, a situation giving good chance of strong stimulation for Group 2, but chances of weak stimulation for Group 8, might look like this:

Comments

Probability for	.00 . . . 1 (Weak) < .00 . . . 1 (Weak)
"Weak" Stimulation	.04 . . . 1 (Weak) < .14 . . . 1 (Weak)
	. .
	. .
	. .
Probability for	.85 . . . 10 (Strong) > .95 . . . 10 (Strong)
"Strong" Siimulation	.99 . . . 10 (Strong) > .99 . . . 10 (Strong)

Now the reader is in a position to see the significance of the G property earlier assigned to each voter as his grouping category. It determines *which* of these tables—by interpretation, which distribution of probabilities of different grades of stimulation from the given party in the given election—the particular type of G voter will be exposed to in the switching of the machine.

In addition to being able to set these G configurations as he wishes, the user of the model has the flexibility of setting up any time-path of stimulation probabilities through successive elections for any such group. For example, one group may receive a stable sequence of "continuing appeal" from one party, while another group receives an oscillating pattern of first strong and then weak stimuli. All this is done by preparing input cards giving for each party in each election the distribution of probabilities of different strengths of stimulation for each G grouping in the given election. For simplicity, the present version of the model uses only five (2, 4, 6, 8, 10) symbols, these going together on one card per party per election. The machine takes them automatically from the hopper when needed; so, little internal storage space is used. Ways of setting these distributions of stimulation in order to reproduce data from elections which occurred in American history are under development.

All this concrete interpretation, however, is quite unnecessary. The stimulation process is chiefly a mechanical arrangement designed to permit maximum flexibility of use of the model in connection with inputs to G groups of stimulus patterns. Every user of the model can give his own substantive interpretation to these mechanical patterns.[6] Interpretations need conform only to the basic idea of the internal machine processes: that distributions of stronger or weaker stimuli set externally by the user will operate such that the weaker the voter's internal disposition for the party, the stronger will be the external stimulus needed to yield a choice. Thus "fair-weather friends," people whose weak partisanship requires strong stimuli, will swell the party's voting ranks in good time. And only the "core of die-hards," strong partisans who vote even with weak stimuli, will stay with it in bad situations, as set by the user's input of "course of events" (stimulation probabilities in successive elections of the run).

"Interest." It is useful now to explain an additional variable and another qualitative attribute that are not given in data but are the output of the stimulation operations described above. Consider a voter of .7 partisanship for the Democrats who, by the above sampling in the stimulation process, receives a symbol of strength 6 as his initial strength of stimulation from the Democrats this year. With partisanship of .7 he merely needed to draw any stimulation symbol greater than 3, that is, 4 or better, by the conventions explained above, to have said "yes" to the Democratic choice. That the actual symbol drawn as the strength of the Democrats' stimulus, 6, was greater than the minimum needed by this voter would be irrelevant in ordinary Monte Carlo operations, where the particular symbol (die face, number, color of ball, and so on) has no substantive meaning.

In this case, however, the size of the symbol number *has* taken on meaning. This is because the user of the model has set up a distribution of higher or lower probabilities of "strong" stimuli (high symbol numbers) to represent a meaningful situation. For example, it might be a historic time-pattern simulating the New Deal increase in the attractiveness of Democratic offerings. This fact that high stimulus numbers have interpretative meaning implicitly defines a new concept, "excess" or "overstimulation," com-

6. However, see Chapter 4, Part III, where these mechanical-like "rectangular" distributions are being replaced in current work by normal distributions that suggest substantive meaning.

paring the strength or stimulation number received with the smaller number that would have been the *minimum* required by the person's internal disposition to elicit a just barely "yes" vote. Thus, the rather strong Democratic partisan in the example above who needed only something more than 3, but got a 6 symbol, has an "excess" of stimulation of 3.

The concept here is like the notion of an "indifference" point or curve in economic theory. A price or barter offer above it is accepted, one below not. In this model, the indifference offer or appeal is a stimulus exactly equal to $1 - P$; for example, if the probability of voting Democratic is 0.7, then the indifference stimulus is 3 or 0.3. Stimuli greater than this natural indifference point are interpreted as creating positive interest in degree proportionate to the excess.

This excess is recorded by the model and used in social discussion processes as the degree of interest in discussing one's beliefs and trying to convince others, and it is also interpreted in the learning process as the "impact" of the stimulation of this campaign on this voter for purposes of weighting this experience in his longer-term formation of partisanship. For the excess of stimulation over minimum is something like all of these things, varying positively as it does with both the strength of external stimulation intended by the user of the model (chances of higher stimulus numbers and thus greater chance of excess over minimum); and varying also with the degree of internal partisanship of individuals (hence, lower minimum stimulation required and thus greater excesses on an average).

Choice or Intention. In the mechanics, such an "interest" is produced originally for both parties, since a voter is stimulated by both. Usually, interest in one party is positive and interest in the others is a deficit below minimum, or negative. Only the relevant positive one is used. Yet under conditions set up for very strong stimulation from two parties—for example, in a major duel such as between Roosevelt and Willkie—both interests could be positive for some voter with inclinations both ways himself (significant P for both). This situation, then, is as if the person wanted to vote for both candidates. In that event, the model takes the higher of the two interests as dominant. This is entered as the voter's interest, and the party involved is recorded as the voter's *choice*.

After only the first stage of stimulation, this choice is interpreted as only a first impression or intention. Later, after other processes of the model that may or may not change it, the surviving choice when "election day" comes is recorded as the final *decision* or con-

viction. Either way and at any time, choice is simply a digit symbol
$(1, 2, \ldots)$ used qualitatively to stand for one of the parties or no
choice, and recorded in the place marked C in Figure 5-2 above.[7]
If no choice survives on election day, it means nonvoting. Interest in
this no-choice situation—where the best stimulus-disposition combination does not reach the minimum—is the deficit below that indifference point, recorded without sign.[8]

The "Learning" Process

The above "interest" (I) and "choice" (C), are the ingredients
that later, at the conclusion of this election, will go into a simple
learning-like process that, in turn, will generate as its product, the
next election's P's or partisan probabilities, discussed earlier. While
chronologically this takes place as the last of the model's three main
processes, it is discussed here while its ingredients are fresh in
mind. It will also be helpful in later explanation of a process of
political discussion and social influence among friends, which mediates
between the initial stimulation above and the final effect on learning,
now to be discussed. While those social processes may modify I
and C, let us assume that we have the final versions of I and C, as
they are "cast" officially in the election. Now the problem is, how do
interest and choice in this election modify partisanship for the *next*
election, and cumulatively thereafter?

Curiously, one of the most noncommittal assumptions that could
be made here is one a still cruder version of which was found by

---

7. After the stimulation process is completed, a series of ten turnover
tables, showing change in choice from the preceding election through the initial
stimulation process of the new election, are punched out for various subgroups. This turnover is like that in a repeated interview study between the
recalled vote in the *last* previous election, that is, 1956, and the initial preference
called "intention" in panel studies at the beginning of the new campaign, early
fall, 1958.

8. After both the stimulation process *and* the influence process, that is, at
the time of final decisions, the program punches out the average Democratic
stimulus and the average Republican stimulus received by each group over the
whole period of both stimulation and discussion processes in the election.
Among other uses, this is to keep check on chance variation, errors in stimulus-
setting instruction cards, and so on. For more substantive uses, the average
interest (for the party chosen) for each group is punched out. When none of
the interests in the parties is positive, that is, large enough to impel the person
to vote, this fact is tallied and the average nonvote (negative) interest per
group is punched out.

a Social Science Research Council Committee to have been about as accurate as are the public opinion polls on the average (Mosteller, 1949). It is a simple "persistence forecast," that is, the assumption that frequencies of voting for the parties remain constant for short historical periods, even though votes turn over. Here, a roughly equivalent assumption for individuals would be that a voter's future *probability* will be the same as his relative *frequency* of voting for that party over some recent past period—if the stimulus situation remains the same. The long-term nature of voting preferences explains why this apparently crude assumption is, in practice, a good estimating procedure. It treats votes as if they were not discrete choices of the moment but manifestations of something like the moving average of only slowly changing probabilities of an underlying sort, here partisanship. We have this not only from the voting studies made since 1940, but from historical evidence. Lee Benson (1957, 1961) has shown that, for the period from after the Civil War to the 1890's, the frequencies of voting for the two parties in almost all small election districts in a test state remained virtually unchanged.

It is useful for oversimplified exposition at first to see how one might implement in the machine this simple assumption that probability of choosing a party (P) for the next time is simply the relative frequency of doing so in some period of the recent and not-so-recent past. This would be easily accomplished by keeping for each voter a tally of how many times he votes Democratic, how many times for the third party or nonvoting, and how many times Republican, as these are determined by the political "events" and "appeals" to his group that the user of the model has set as distributions of stimuli. (Tallies like this actually are made, in appropriate places in the second ten-digit cell of the two cells that record information for each voter.) Next, if after each election the machine simply divides to find the ratio of the new total of tallies for the Democrats to the new total for all three, then a new P representing a new partisan probability for the Democrats would emerge as simply the past frequency adjusted to include the latest choice. A new Republican P could be calculated in the same way, and the total for all parties plus nonvoting (treated exactly as if a party choice) would equal 1.00.

Such an idea that probability equals frequency would seem to be a "know-nothing" assumption of a purely statistical sort. Actually, it involves major theoretic commitments. For instance, consider the case of young voters with very little accumulation of past voting experience. Concretely, let us say that they have voted once for each of the two parties and failed to vote once. So that, for simplicity, say, they carry tallies of 1, 1, 1 in the respective cumulations for each possibility (here ignoring the third party). The result for the next election is a .33 probability for each of the three alternatives. Now, suppose these young people vote Democratic in the next election. Each one's tally for that party is now 2, out of 4 elections. The probability of voting Democratic increases from ⅓ to ¾, or from .33 to .50. (Two-place probabilities are useful for exposition, although small machine versions of the model use only tenths.)

Now consider the same choice made by the same voter after he is a mature person with, say, 21 elections (42 years) gone by. If these votes had been equally divided by thirds as in the example of young voters, it would be $\frac{7}{21}$ for each party. But now a new vote for, say, the Democrats would increase the ratio from $\frac{7}{21}$ to only $\frac{8}{22}$, or only from .33 to .37. This is a minor increase of .04 in comparison to the effects of the same event at a younger age, when the increase was .17 (from .33 to .50). Thus, the assumption discussed above implies a substantive commitment, among many others, to an interpretation that the less the cumulative experience (for example, the younger the voter), the more influence any new experience will have in changing dispositions (changing P, partisanship). This result, of course, is just what we want in the case of voting, judging by all research evidence.

Consider another substantive implication of even the over-simplified assumption used for expository illustrations above. After processes of stimulation and also after those of social discussion and of personal reconsideration have taken place, as will be discussed shortly, the present assumption will operate to *increase* the chances in future elections of making the choices that survive discussion and perhaps reconsideration in the current election. For, any given tally to the credit of one party, but not the others, gives that party a higher P value when the frequencies are recalculated into new probabilities for the next election. Thus, a vote for the given party is now still more probable. And if it is therefore cast in this next election, the refiguring of the probabilities with still another tally for this party makes it still more probable in the future.

It is thus a "progressive" process, the more it happens, the more likely it is to happen (although not deterministically for an individual because of random elements in stimulation and possible changes in the stimulus situation introduced by the user). While the authors were not familiar with Polya's work at the time of writing on this process, the simplified version discussed above turns out to be logically identical with G. Polya's "urn models" worked out to represent similar progressive phenomena, say, in the self-development and contagion of infectious disease.[9] Feller (1957), Friedman (1949), and Coleman (forthcoming) report in sociology a number of other models that have much the same logical consequences as Polya's. Thus, the same consequences result from a variety of substantive interpretations. But we call it a "Polya process."

The use of such a process here, to make a vote choice at a given time *increase* the chance of repeating it further in a gradual build up of partisan bias through the years, is a summarizing interpretation of the common *consequences* of a variety of detailed findings in voting studies. (See the list of findings through 1954, in Berelson, 1954, Appendix A.) Among the detailed mechanisms that have this common consequence are: the selective exposure to arguments and perceptual distortions that follow in the wake of a commitment; the effect on oneself of rationalizing one's preference to others; the social rewards that in real life (and in this model, as we will see) reinforce most such choices; the voter's increasing antagonism to the opposite party as a consequence of its attacks on the candidates that are his own considered choices; and so on. Such mechanisms are not incorporated directly, of course, nor is there any actual "learning" process spelled out in this nonpsychological model. It is merely that their usual or statistical consequences are all in the same direction, the progressive one simulated here as in Polya's models by the simple operation of letting each choice increase the chances of its own repetition by adding it to a cumulating frequency that is the probability for the next choice.

Weight by Interest. Numerical quantities used in any such process are arbitrary until experience is available on how the process behaves in relation to real data, but important modifications of the simplified account above remove some of the arbitrariness and improve realism. First, instead of keeping a tally of one unit for each choice and assuming that new probabilities are the frequency of all past choices

---

9. For concreteness, Polya visualizes sampling with replacement from an urn of different colored balls. Each time a color is chosen, an additional ball of that color is added to the urn. The consequences are discussed in a number of contexts in Feller (1957).

weighted equally, it is better to give the tally unit a variable weight. A good weight for this is the excess of stimulation over minimum required, previously interpreted as "interest." Thus, instead of the simplified example of equally weighted elections above, the actual model tallies the voter's final *interest* in the cumulative total for the party he chose. The probability for the next time, then, is the past frequency of voting for each party weighted by the degree of interest (conviction, and so on) at that time.

Interest varies sensitively, it will be recalled, with the strength of external stimulation (chances of high-numbered stimulus symbols). So, the weight given this election in dispositions in future elections will be in proportion to something like the "impact" (excess stimulation over minimum threshholds) of the campaign stimuli in the given election. Thus, presidential elections, with the substantially stronger stimuli required to produce their high turnout in this model, will have most weight on future partisanship. And as will become apparent in this model's social processes, an especially strong appeal aimed at particular groups (high stimulus symbols for specific G's, by interpretation events especially affecting that group's self-interest), will have weighty effects on that group's learning of greater partisanship for the future. For, even if some individual does not receive strong impact, due to random elements, his fellow group members have received it, and their influence on him or his children will be correspondingly greater for the party involved in the long run.

Also implied is that votes in special or random circumstances for the other, habitually *not*-preferred party, have typically less weight on long-term learning. For, interest, that is, the excess stimulation, is seldom high where P is low and even strong stimuli produce little excess. This low weighting of unusual choices for the "unnatural" party, along with other features of the model, results in reproducing the empirically real tendency for voters to fall back into older patterns after temporarily successful disturbances, for example, Democrats' choices of Eisenhower in 1952. Appeals must be *sustained* over a number of elections, for example, as Democratic stimuli were sustained in the New Deal–Fair Deal era, to accomplish significant switching of underlying partisanship (as opposed to turnover in manifest votes). Since for nonvoters the negative interest (deficit below minimum for either party) is tallied analogously, without sign, as the weight for nonvoting, apathy also is self-reinforcing, unless social forces intervene.

Forgetting. A second modification of the earlier example of equal tallies for each past vote also makes the model more realistic. It is an arithmetical short cut used in place of a "forgetting process." (A direct simulation could be incorporated, but would require too much space to store its components for each voter in this particular machine, the IBM 650.) If there were no "forgetting" in long problems, indeed, if there were none in real political systems over many decades, the older voters would be basing their judgments on so much accumulated experience that events of the current era would have almost no weight. The assumption, which is approximated, is the following: "Forgetting" of an election choice or its unconscious loss of effect on current partisanship is proportionate to the number of elections *since* then. The impact of a past election in computing new partisan probabilities for each new election diminishes in proportion to "the water over the dam" since then. The short-cut way the computation is performed is to multiply the summed tallies of votes (weighted by interest) by a constant less than 1, for example, .85 at each election. Since an "old" election choice has been reduced many times this way, it is of less current weight.

These cumulative tallies amounting to the past history of voting are kept in the second of the two main cells in storage for each voter. In this cell again, qualitatively different information is packed into the same ten-digit "number." Inside the machine, the second cell looks like Figure 5-3.

5-3—Second Cell for Each Voter

A	D D	N N	R R	T T	O

DD $= \Sigma$ of past Democratic votes weighted by interest
NN $= \Sigma$ of past nonvotes weighted by interest (the deficit without sign)
RR $= \Sigma$ of past Republican votes weighted by interest
TT $= \Sigma$ of past third-party votes weighted by interests
A $=$ Age in decades, for example, 1 $=$ teenager, 2 $=$ twenties, and so on
O $=$ Old—previous—choice for computing turnover

The separate components must be "unpacked" into temporary work cells, of course, before arithmetical operations are performed on them. The arithmetic is then simply

$$\frac{\Sigma D}{\Sigma D + \Sigma R + \Sigma T + \Sigma N} = P_d$$

(Democratic probability). It is, of course, analogous for the other probabilities including that of nonvoting.[10]

The Discussion Process

Finally, what was skipped, the middle process chronologically of the three main routines that the machine goes through for each voter in each election, can now be presented. It is best explained in connection with Figure 5-4.

The discussion process and its consequence of possible social influence, now to be explained, can be seen in the center of the diagram. We see that social influence is a type of switching operation that changes the *articulation* between the other processes, depending on agreement or disagreement (or no discussion) with one's associates.

Let us explain the mechanics first while the diagram is at hand. The model is seen from the standpoint of only one person ("Ego"), for simplicity. A second person ("Alter," for example, a spouse or friend) will here be considered only in his role of recipient, not initiator, of influence (although he will in his turn play that role, also). Who the Alter is for this voter, that is, the sociometric tie that connects these two rather than some other pair, is determined by the user at input. The address of the Alter is punched in the right-hand digits of Ego's first ten-column word of information (next to *G* in Figure 5-1). Sociometric ties thus take the form of cross-references, as to different places in the file. Given one voter being processed, his digits identifying the friend's address in storage can be put into a machine instruction that, when executed, supplies the friend.

Assume both voters have been initially stimulated (Step 1 in the diagram). Ego is now being put through the discussion process (Step 2 in the diagram). Here the machine brings in Alter, say the friend, from storage to the processing unit (Step 3). The program now examines the interest of both Alter and Ego to determine whether they are jointly interested enough in this election to discuss it. Close or daily contact is assumed between them; the sociometric net does not include, by definition, casual acquaintanceships. But whether they talk *politics* or not depends on their joint interest. Rather arbitrarily,

---

10. After the learning process, ten turnover tables for various subgroups are punched out. These show the turnover in *final* choices or "official" votes cast (as opposed to the preliminary intentions discussed earlier) between the last election and this election.

the model lets discussion take place if the *average* of the two interests is above the indifference point or minimum to vote, discussed earlier. This summation represents, in effect, an assumption that either could bring up the topic. If both are interested, it is likely, if neither, unlikely, to come up. But a much interested person can talk politics to a slightly uninterested nonvoter.

If the two do talk politics, their initial intentions are assumed to become apparent to one another. The choices are compared to determine agreement, and the switching action mentioned above is set in

5-4—Two Persons Going Through the Model

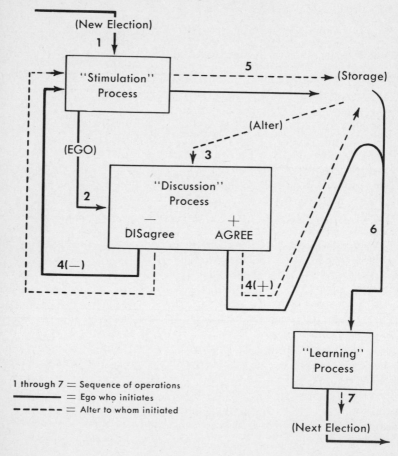

(New Election)

1

"Stimulation" Process

5

(Storage)

(Alter)

(EGO)

3

"Discussion" Process

2

— DISagree   + AGREE

6

4(—)

4(+)

"Learning" Process

7

(Next Election)

1 through 7 = Sequence of operations

———— = Ego who initiates

– – – – – = Alter to whom initiated

A Model for Analyzing Voting Systems   147

motion. Assume they disagree. Both are sent back to the *stimulation* process (Step 4 — at left in diagram). There they may, in repeating that process, develop new choices and new degrees of interest—although the new intention will often reaffirm (be the same as) the old. The new choices, upon restimulation, depend on the voter's own internal dispositions and on the external stimuli his group is being exposed to—exactly as before in the initial stimulation of both. Then both return to storage (Step 5) with this new provisional choice. (Later, the influence may be further complicated, since some other voter might initiate to Ego and start it all over again. And Alter, the friend, at his turn, will initiate to someone else. But Figure 5-1 ignores these complications in following only Ego in this one episode.)

If the two voters had agreed, the existing initial choices would have been *retained* (and the two voters returned without further stimulation to storage, via Step 4+ in the diagram). The socially supported choice, then, is not subjected to the possibly upsetting process of new stimulation. And thus supported, the choice will tend to survive to become the decision as of election day. In mature stages of problem runs, sociometric cliques tend toward homogeneity and the voter *is* likely to be agreed with all along and thus his initial preference survive until election day unchanged.

The mechanics were given above for those interested in how each case is handled in what, in high speed running, is a mass of reciprocal social influences happening "simultaneously." But these mechanics disguise simple and attractive substantive ideas, which can be interpreted as a "reinforcement" theory in the case of agreement, a "social-validity testing" theory in the case of disagreement.

As for the former, the *learning* of a person who is "confirmed" and "rewarded" on the wisdom of his choice by associates who agree with his initial choice will be affected by that particular preference. For, this choice will be the surviving one on and after election day, permanently entering into calculation of all future dispositions. In effect, then, friends and associates act to "reinforce" in the learning sense of *selecting,* among what would otherwise be much more randomly generated preferences, the behavior they wish to encourage. We will see shortly, in the case of children, that by this process stable dispositions will be learned out of what can at first be random responses. So, if we interpret the process as a reinforcement theory, social intimates are the agents selecting *what* is to be reinforced and learned. Influence is selection from stochastic outputs.

When there is disagreement, however, no "punishment" is administered here (for, after all, politics is not that important). Rather, all that happens when a voter is not confirmed or reinforced as above because there is disagreement with his associate is further exposure to stimulation (repeating the stimulation process). This, in effect, holds the final decision "in abeyance." During that time, we interpret voters as "uncrystallized," a half-conscious counterpart of giving "further consideration" to the matter in more consciously rational realms of decision-making.

The theory in this case is a variant of Kurt Lewin's "social reality" ideas. Unsure of the correct choice (objective reality) in the new situation, voters test their preferences against friends' impressions (social reality). But if that does not confirm the decision and the social validity of their own and friends' impressions disagree ambiguously, they again check with objective reality (the stimulation process). It is a cross-checking of objective by social *and* social by objective stimuli.

This process was chosen because its consequences include many known empirically. For example, whether effective influence takes place, that is, whether a *changed* choice emerges in place of the first one, will depend on the strength of the person's convictions on this topic. For, to make him continue (repeat) the stimulation process brings his P partisanships back into play. And if his partisanships are strong for the party of his initial choice, the odds are he will simply repeat that choice again. Because of the random aspects of the stimulation process, however, a person of weak dispositions toward the party he had originally chosen will be unlikely to come up with the same choice. In accord with empirical evidence from voting studies, influence here works on (changes the votes of) those of *weak* dispositions in the given area.[11]

As another example, the flavor of "social determinism" that has accompanied research emphasis on social influence in politics is here remedied. For, *if* objective (external) stimuli from the political world are strongly favorable to the party of original choice, the person now repeating the stimulation process will simply come up

---

11. Logically, a third turnover table, in addition to those mentioned in Footnotes 7 and 10, is required to describe the changes completely. It is the turnover from intention to final vote. As yet unsolved problems of providing space in records for each voter have temporarily ruled this out. Instead, the current running version gives the turnover resulting from all *disagreements*. (This may count the same voter several times. But those who encounter no disagreement, or no discussion, and therefore do not change, are omitted.)

again, on an average, with that same party choice. The other person who attempted to influence him, in fact, is more likely to be the victim. Thus, the reality of external events "strengthens the hand" of one side or the other in this social-influence process. All of which means that the political stimuli the user has chosen as inputs to represent some external historical situation have ramifications throughout the social and psychological processes internal to the model.

An attractive feature of the discussion and influence process, on at least intuitive grounds, is that the voter makes up his *own* mind. Nothing material is transferred from one voter to the other, as in "diffusion" ideas taken from chemistry, and no "forces" are exerted, as in notation taken from physics. Indeed, no decision is reached that is not convincing to the voter himself. For, in cases of agreement he retains a decision he made himself; in disagreement he makes up his own mind again, and if that represents a change, his *own* new impressions confirm the prior judgment of his intimates.

If this is so, then what is the effect of the influence? To see it simply, consider a situation in which two alternatives are chosen at random with equal chance. But assume one of these will be, if drawn as the choice, unacceptable to a significant person whose judgment one trusts. So, if that choice turns up, let it be "rechecked" by "taking another look," namely, drawing another sample of the stimuli. Then let that be retained, whatever.

The advisor's choice already had a 50 per cent chance, randomly, and now it gets a ½ chance of replacing the other alternative on the second draw in the other 50 per cent of the original cases. The odds are therefore .50 plus ½ times .50 or .75 that the advisor's choice will win out on a "50-50" proposition. Figure 5-5 below shows how the frequencies are affected with one such advisor or influencer for different probabilities of voting for a party.

The straight diagonal gives vote frequencies expected (vertical) for people with different internal probabilities for the given party (horizontal). Then, the lower frequency is that manifested in the face of influence *against* this party: the upper frequency that manifested when influence is *for* this party. Contrary influence is most effective when dispositions are weak; favorable influence when dispositions are moderate.[12]

---

12. After the turnover tables mentioned in Footnote 11, in the present version, output consists of tables that tally for the various groups information

5-5—Voting Probabilities Conditional on Social Influence

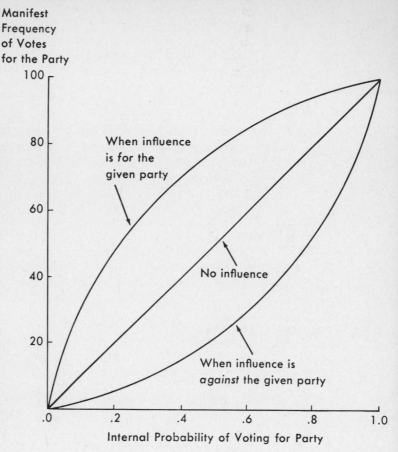

Manifest
Frequency
of Votes
for the Party

Internal Probability of Voting for Party

Decision Rule. When all voters are processed, and thus no further initiation of discussions can occur, what is cast as a final vote and learned for purposes of future partisanship is the *surviving* choice of each voter. In the simple example above, it would be the

---

about interaction and influence. These give the number of persons in a given subgroup who do and do not discuss their preferences, and then of the latter, the number who agree or disagree. Data come out first in raw numbers and then in percentages.

outcome for both voters of the second passage through the stimulation process; in practice it might involve still more discussion, if the two are highly interested, because of the action of others on these voters.

Here, the model has the simplicity of classic democratic theory and the arbitrariness of its modern implementation in elections. The former depended on "discussion" to crystallize the alternative viewpoints and their free competition to determine the surviving decision. The latter elections set an arbitrary date for cloture, however, often before ordinary people will have had very much discussion among themselves. Then in the model as in the real world, we count as "official" votes the preferences surviving at that moment, in the present model version, the point at which everyone has had his opportunity to talk and further discussion would be duplicative.

Data Conventions

Children. The model will "raise" its own future voters. While not crucial for adult problems, social influence will be most significant in problems involving inputs of future voters introduced into the system before legal age. One reason is that data representing the young will not have built up the strong partisan dispositions of later experience. So, when influenced to reconsider (be restimulated), the young are less likely to come up with the *same* choices again. The parent or other influencer can easily get new choices to select among, in reinforcement, by merely causing the younger voters to reconsider. More important, consider that for the young, the accumulations of past voting records, from which partisan probabilities are computed, are small. Then, the recording of a socially encouraged choice in the record for future elections makes a significant increment in the P or partisanship calculation. This, in turn, makes more likely the individual's adoption of that choice for the next election.

With a decade or so of this kind of selective encouragement of choices, that is, reinforcement of one out of several random possibilities, the encouraged choice becomes *internally* self-maintaining. For, by the learning process, each choice makes its own repetition more likely and in due time a durable bias is built up that maintains itself. Social influences (such as parents) may now be removed from the individual's experience, but his voting choice persists in a gyroscopelike manner. However, peers, random factors, and strong objective stimulation against the fortunes of the parents' party can make children in this model as contrary as real ones.

At what age children are introduced to the system, with what sociometric relations to parents and peers, and with what initial states of partisanship, and so on, are to a considerable degree flexible independent variables at the discretion of the model's user. (A note describes the writers' conventions for introducing children to simulate contemporary American customs.)[13] All that the model proper assumes is that whoever is in the machine with whatever recorded information will be processed the same as everyone else. (Indeed, operator mistakes occasionally send the machine into the "hash" of old numbers left over from someone else's computations. The program then makes voters out of the hash by processes exactly the same as those by which it makes voters out of children with originally unpredictable tendencies.) The model is very sensitive to these initial conditions, however, and experience is as yet unavailable on how widely they can be made to vary in different problems without violating the spirit of other internal processes.

Sociometric Nets. Similarly, arrangements for sociometric configurations are left outside the theory proper, although later versions could include an optional program forming sociometric ties by random choice within some framework of probabilities of contact between *G* categories, supplied by the model's user. The reason for leaving this matter outside the present model, in common with

---

13. Inputs of voters representing children are given very small nonzero numbers in the positions in the second cell where there will be accumulated later choices weighted by interest in order to calculate subsequent partisanships. For example, 2, 2, 2, 2. Or random numbers are assigned as the original "state of nature." These are used to calculate partisanships for the first election and thereafter accumulate with real choices. In the first decade, the address of the parent is used in the position used for "friend" in later adult life. Then, the children are simply entered into the system a decade or so *before* voting age.

They are allowed to make choices "like everybody else," they are influenced by their parents by the same reconsideration process by which adults influence each other, and they learn as do adults according to the succession of events. Indeed, all processes work as well for socializing as for adult decision-making, and the model can thus be used to "grow its own voters." After a decade or so of such incubation, say, representing the teens, the children are taken out of the machine and their sociometric ties are changed from parents to peers (for example, friends and spouses). Then, with all other information intact, as accumulated in their teens, they are reintroduced into the machine as "first" (twenty-one-year-old) voters for use in adult problems.

most other questions of social configurations, is simply that these are precisely the variables and structural situations the analyst is likely to want to manipulate independently.

At present, the scheme provides space for only one associate to be listed on the input card and thus in the internal cell of each voter. This is dictated in part by space and time limitations of the original machine used (IBM 650). But even in a larger IBM 709 version, we have hesitated to go beyond this. For already each voter carries some other voter's address location, and these addresses are usually chosen by some sampling plan that makes it unlikely that sociometric choices will be duplicated reciprocally. Then each voter is, on an average, tied into *two* relatively independent net segments— one, the net of the Alter recorded in his cell, and the other, the net of one or more Egos who have this voter's address recorded in their cells. The given voter is thus "grounded" socially in at least one, on an average two networks; and by either random or deliberate concentrations of choices on "popular" persons, some are grounded in many different net segments. Since the internal operations of the model treat these relationships as if they were intimate, continuous associations capable of real political influence, it is doubtful that a much larger number of such ties would be realistic.

Moreover, beyond two such independent ties to very different segments of a structure of informal association, it is unlikely that further ties would or should be *independent* of these. Thereafter, the voter's further friends would more likely be the "friends of his friends." Provision for the latter is planned as an optional feature in later versions, which will generate additional possibilities of social influence from the friends of friends, without designation of these persons on input data and space for them in storage.[14]

Real Data. Since the above, progress has been made in determining all these input problems empirically, in effect, by making the re-

---

14. A similar issue, again not part of the internal theory proper, is how systematic all these factors are to be in *time*. The writers' own conventions are to break the problems down into decade units of five elections each. At the end of a decade, the machine is relinquished to others, and manual operations are used to rearrange the sociometric nets, to change the *G* groupings to allow for mobility, to arrange for births and deaths, and the like. Much like the Census Bureau does, it is practically convenient to assume that everything "holds still" for a decade, and then suddenly everything changes with the new Census. Different uses would dictate different conventions, including the user's programming his own subprocesses to change many of these things automatically every election.

spondents of a national or state or community sample survey the "electorate."[15] This has been done, for example, with the 1956 electorate. With these real voters in place, most of what would be the initial conditions and parameters of a mathematical model are empirically fixed. It then proves possible to make serious estimates of the remaining unknown, the stimulus distributions necessary to reproduce real situations. Progress will be reported (e.g., McPhee, 1961), but it has already made clear that there is no serious obstacle to bringing this model to bear on reality—and vice versa.

The flexibilities discussed in these concluding pages are a fitting summary of the spirit of the scheme. Namely, it is a *working* instrument, capable of endless experiments involving varied inputs of stimuli, voters, sociometric structures, *G* groupings, time changes, and all combinations thereof over time. If this seems an excessive number of parameters for a theory, that simply emphasizes the purposes stated in the beginning. To repeat, it is *not* intended to be, or at least to be interesting as, a theory of individual behavior. It is instead an instrument, virtually a method, for applying simple assumptions to highly flexible input materials. This is in order to examine their developing consequences over time in large social aggregates; what one might call the "dynamics" of electorates.

15. This work is a collaborative venture kindly supported and carried out by a staff group of International Business Machines, Inc., headed by Eugene Lindstrom. The 709 Model used was programmed by Charles Stevenson and Gladys Garabedian, with adaptation for live data by Frank Scalora and Albert Morton.

6

POLITICAL IMMUNIZATION

By William N. McPhee and Jack Ferguson

By "immunization" in politics we mean not a metaphor, but the literal logic of the immunity idea: Resistance to disturbances is built up by disturbances; lack of resistance to disturbances is due to lack of disturbances. This paper illustrates why we should expect this kind of resistance to strong political stimuli to develop in modern electorates, whether it actually does, and what conditions govern its degree.

The possibility of immunization is important in politics for the same reason it is in medicine. There is only so much that can be done to protect a political system by explicit prohibition, in advance, or by intervention after the fact. For example, explicit legal guarantees tend to be overwhelmed by the same disturbances they were intended to protect again. So, it is important to understand any implicit process by which the system develops its own natural resistance, in the hope of fostering more of such a process. This is especially true

Initial work on this problem was supported by a 1957 grant to the senior author by the Behavioral Sciences Division of the Ford Foundation. Its completion was supported by a 1960 grant from the Social Sciences Division of the National Science Foundation, NSF G #13045. Computing time was freely supplied by the Watson Scientific Computing Laboratory at Columbia University.

We are especially indebted to Robert Smith for substantive suggestions in the early work.

when the immunization that is possible, "in theory," is being realized only in moderate degree in practical or empirical data, as we will find to be the case for the recent American situation. For then, as an example from the Weimar Republic will illustrate, the theory may not be wrong, but the contrary practice dangerous.

The reasons to expect immunization to take place are discussed in detail later, but for now the major reason is obvious: strong political stimuli would create among electoral groups and individual voters *commitment* to parties, bias for one party and against the other. If so, this would leave subsequent votes much less dependent on, and more resistant to changes in, *current* stimuli.

The originally strong stimuli that would accomplish this commitment would have to be real historical appeals, however. Therefore, unlike immunity experiments in medicine and biology, one cannot experiment "over the dead bodies" of socially significant systems. Moreover, the few historical cases that come to grief naturally, such as the Weimar Republic, are always complex configurations including other variables. So, to analyze political immunization per se, a greater resort to theory is inescapable. For this purpose, we use the computer model described in a companion paper in this volume. In fact, this is precisely the kind of aggregate or macroscopic problem it was designed to investigate. For, we wish to experiment, not on individuals, but as if on an electoral system.

THE MODEL EXPERIMENTS

SUCH EXPERIMENTS on a computer must be done in particular circumstances at first, analytic solutions being unavailable although we will outline the general argument later. The particular experiments that suggest the immunization idea are:

1. A hypothetical electorate is used as input to the model, but is intended to represent "a new generation" typical of known distributions of *young* or new voters. Briefly, this experimental population includes all combinations of a small amount of political experience distributed systematically so that, while some are, the majority of these new voters are not, at the start, irreversibly polarized into mutually exclusive camps.[1]

---

1. Referring to the characteristics of voters described in the companion paper in this volume, the initial state of the test population is:

Political Immunization 157

2. In subsequent elections over a period of, in America, the equivalent of a decade, this new generation or age band is subjected to appeals by a "Dynamic" party and an "Opposition" party. The "Dynamic" party makes a dramatic appeal to the nation early in the period and as a result wins power. But then it suffers a decline back to normal, followed by dramatic reversal that throws it out of power. Finally, it returns to where it started at the end of the experimental decade.

Specifically, the "Dynamic" party's "stimulus distributions" (see the companion paper) are set as follows in the first decade:[2]

Election or Period	Stimulus Distributions	Interpretation
1	Balanced (Rectangular)	Normal
2	Strong (Skewed +)	Dramatic Appeal
3	Balanced (Rectangular)	Decline to Normal
4	Weak (Skewed —)	Dramatic Reversal
5	Balanced (Rectangular)	Recovery to Normal

In contrast, the "Opposition" party has a defensive posture throughout the era, namely, (a) *constant* stimuli equivalent to normal above, except (b) *biased* to appeal to certain population groups more and other groups less than average, at all times.[3]

3. The above sequence is a not uncommon introduction to politics for some generations in America for example, the 1930's and early 1940's. But, to see its effect, we now examine what would never

---

a. Initial *P,* or probability of voting for a party, is *rectangularly* distributed, equal frequencies of each possibility, with each party's distribution independent of the other so all combinations occur at the individual level.

b. The initial Σ's or sums of previous experience are *small,* averaging 3.4, 3.4, 2.4, respectively for each party and nonvoting.

c. Sociometric nets are random choices by each voter of another within his *own* one of eight groups used in the experiment (each receiving different stimuli noted below).

2. "Strong" stimuli mean a distribution set so as to reproduce the 1936 situation among young people. For the above population, it is a distribution in which the strongest stimuli occur with probability .40, the next strongest with .30, middle .20, weaker .10, and weakest .00.

3. In the note above, call the "strong" distribution a "plus 20" skew— the strongest fifth of the stimuli occurring with probability .40 instead of the usual .20. Then, the opposition party's appeals (distributions) are set for each of eight groups in the model as +. 15, + .05, + .05, + .05, — .05, — .05, — .05, — .15. It's over-all appeal averages out, then, to the balanced or "normal" situation.

happen so exactly in history—namely, to *repeat* a precisely comparable sequence of appeals (same stimuli) by each party in the corresponding years of a *second* decade. The only change is that the previously newer electorate has now been through a comparable experience before, for example, it is now in its 30's.

The above distributions of stimuli are set so that initial responses of the young to the "Dynamic" party's fortunes and misfortunes are roughly comparable to the real swings by younger voters in the period 1928-1940 (with the reversal like a much intensified 1938, worse than 1946). The obvious purpose of the sequel in the last paragraph above, where the experiment is repeated as if to have another New Deal immediately after the first one, is to see whether the responses to comparably strong appeals in the second decade or era are substantially *less*. This is what we mean by the theoretic expectation that such voters would have been immunized by the previous experience.

Figure 6-1 gives average results typical of experience with model populations to date.

In Figure 6-1, the familiar practice is adopted of connecting what are actually discrete vote divisions at distinct times by continuous lines, as if they were a rising and falling tide of opinion. Thus, the "Dynamic" party's initial gain labeled A is not literally the diagonal shown but its vertical elevation or change from previous vote. But it is clear we can compare the vertical gain involved in A with that in A', the corresponding response to comparable appeals in the second decade. For example, A involves an increase of 33 per cent in the "Dynamic" party's vote, while A' is 23 per cent. Similarly, the drops at B and B' are comparable, 24 per cent and 19 per cent, and so on through any other change in either party's vote. For example, the disaster for the "Dynamic" party between third and fourth election costs them 24 per cent of this age group in the population, while the corresponding drop in the second decade was 21 per cent.

Absolute magnitudes are not precisely meaningful, of course, (although Figure 6-1 gives the average of five independent runs, each run following the full "case histories" of 200 different young voters, each one of them in turn starting from initial predilections systematically varied through all combinations).[4] We will later look at

---

4. This summarizes earlier experience to the same effect with different inputs, stimuli, and so on. Steps are being taken in current work to get beyond

6-1—Vote over Two Decades When Stimuli for One Party Are Oscillating

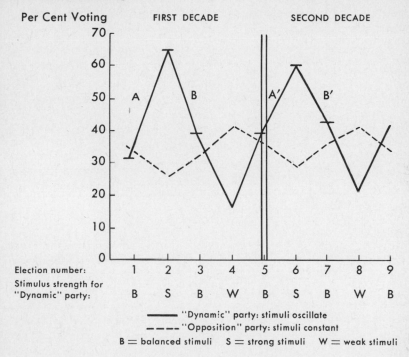

Per Cent Voting   FIRST DECADE   SECOND DECADE

Election number: 1 2 3 4 5 6 7 8 9

Stimulus strength for "Dynamic" party: B S B W B S B W B

——— "Dynamic" party: stimuli oscillate
– – – – "Opposition" party: stimuli constant

B = balanced stimuli   S = strong stimuli   W = weak stimuli

more precise comparisons, but for now Figure 6-1 illustrates the gist of all experience here and earlier on the problem. Namely, (1) there *is* an immunization effect in the model, a "damping" of the oscillatory swings in response to the same stimuli in successive decades, as would be expected of the model's theory for reasons given in detail later; but (2) the degree of such damping of response is *small* in any one decade's time (or *slow* if we consider many decades). The latter results had not been expected of the intuitive theory and are contrary to the impression given by voting research, namely, that party loyalties rapidly "rigidify" with maturity. If they do not rigidify

these "experiments" into systematic exploration of all combinations of parameters and starting conditions with large samples, but this taxes even a large machine, much less the IBM 650 on which the above work was done.

quickly, however, and the effect of previous experience in damping out new responsiveness is no more than roughly that above, in the real American circumstances today, then the immunization effect would be of only academic interest, and insufficient for any real protection.

II. AMERICAN DATA

BEFORE PURSUING the theory further, then, we pause to examine the actual degree of this effect in real American data. A procedure is required that will be illustrated in Table 6-1. It tabulates, from a Gallup poll made just before the 1940 election, the vote for Roosevelt by different age groups as recalled for 1936 and as planned for 1940. It is well-known that the young had swung more for Roosevelt in 1936, as the figures show, for reasons that probably go beyond the fact that the same result would be expected here because of the young's lack of previous commitments from prior experience.

Table 6-1—Change in Democrat Vote for Different Age Groups in 1940 as a Percentage of Average Change for the Whole National Sample*

	PER CENT (TWO PARTY) FOR ROOSEVELT		PER CENT CHANGE $= 100 \times \dfrac{\text{Change in Age Group}}{\text{Change in Total Sample}}$
	1936 Recall	1940 Intent	
20-29	75%	58%	135%
30-39	68	53	114
40-49	64	51	102
50-59	62	49	103
60-69	58	49	71
70 and Over	65	55	83

* Roper Public Opinion Research Center tabulation of AIPO survey #221.

† This index is computed for the 20-29 age group, for example, by dividing the change in Democrat voting frequency between 1936 and 1940 = .171, by the average change in voting frequency for all age groups during the same period = .127. This is 1.35, or 135 per cent of average change.

The present theory makes, however, the further and less obvious prediction that the young would *abandon* Roosevelt faster when his current appeal waned and a new hero—Willkie—arrived. Table 6-1 suggests that inexperienced voters did just that in 1940. The per cent for Roosevelt (of the two parties) among young voters declined from 75 per cent to 58 per cent, a drop of 17 points. The average drop in the whole sample was only about 12 to 13 points. So, the young changed about 17/13 or 135 per cent of the average swing. The next older group changed 114 per cent of average, and so on to the most experienced, who showed only 70-80 per cent of the average swing.[5]

So much for illustration. In a similar fashion, every significant swing from 1936 to 1958 has been studied by comparing the two-party division in the recalled previous vote with this division in the current vote, or intention. The difference for the whole sample is the average change. Then the corresponding change in each age group is expressed as a per cent of that average change (that is, average "swing" equals 100 per cent). Table 6-2 shows such results by age generations. The youngest legal voters at the time are always shown on the left, the oldest at the time on the right. A damping or immunization effect would be manifested by greater change on the left, less on the right, whether the change was toward the Democrats, as it was in 1956-1958, or toward the Republicans, as in 1948-1952. This overresponse by the inexperienced and damped response by the experienced, to the same appeals in the same election, was indeed the case for all instances studied, with one exception. It is a para-doxical exception not capable of explanation in this volume—our friend, 1950! No doubt Korea was involved, but if so, it struck the age groups differently than the European war in 1940 and 1942. (Rather, 1950 more resembles 1954, that is, the McCarthy era.)

To see the different ages in a single period like this, the table is read *across*. To follow a single generation for many elections, for example, those whose first full decade of politics was the 1930's, the table is read *down*. The latter attempt to reconstruct generations from the variable age classifications of separate surveys, however, was less successful. For example, those whose first decade of voting was in the 1920's can be found in a 1940 survey not only in the 40-49 age group—those who were in their late twenties in the 1920's —but some are also in the survey's 30-39 age classification—those who were in the early twenties in the 1920's. We can only reconstruct "the generation of the 1920's" as they voted in 1940, then, by

---

5. In raw data, the young people have a typical bias to the Democrats. This bias is accentuated when the Democrats are strong, but disappears when the Republicans are strong, leaving a "flat" distribution by age.

averaging the two age categories in the survey, with weights .6 and .4 respectively to reflect which age category in the 1940 survey contains more of the 1920's generation. Analogous weighting of the votes of different age groups were used to reconstruct the generations in each survey. But we see from the blurred differences down the table versus the sharper ones across it, that generational results are thereby attenuated.

No matter; the conclusion is the same whatever way the table is read. Namely, the immunizing effects of prior experience are clearly visible but, as in the model runs, are too *small* to promise practical protection. Note that the index of relative change in Table 6-1 and 6-2 is sensitive. It would be zero if an older generation did not respond at all, negative if mature voters were repelled by a new political wind that was attracting young people innocent of previous commitments. This does happen among individuals in particular groups, but for the aggregate of any whole age band across the nation, enough people respond at all times for all generations always to move in the *same* direction (no minus index numbers) in surprisingly

Table 6-2—Change in Two-Party Vote for Different Age Groups As a Percentage of Average Change for the Total Sample: Generations (by First Full Decade in the Electorate)†

	1960's	1950's	1940's	1930's	1920's	1910's	1900's	1890's	1880's
Roosevelt Era									
1936-1938			118*	110	101	103	92	89	94
1936-1940			135	122	107	103	84	78	83
1940-1942			128	82	106	130	80	59	57
Truman Era									
1944-1946		116	114	106	95	99	105	81	
1944-1948 (June)		116	109	100	109	83	91	72	
1948-1950		98	79	91	82	92	134	151	
Eisenhower Era									
1948-1952		120	113	97	101	103	98	96	
1952-1954	118	116	104	87	100	98	121	125	
1956-1958	137	126	101	98	96	76	77		

* The table entry is: $\dfrac{\text{change in age group's vote}}{\text{change in total sample}} \times 100$ (see Table 6-1, right column).

† The text explains weighting of age-group tabulations, supplied by The Roper Public Opinion Research Center of AIPO surveys 136, 221, 283K, 283T, 383, 420, 467K, 506, 539K, 606. The fact that an age band whose first full decade was in "the 1960s" means that the youngest age band then will partly complete its decade in the 1960s and partly (is also weighted into) in the 1950s.

Data for the 1960 election were not yet available.

similar degree (none show less than 50 per cent of the average trend). Contrary to the popular image of older and younger generations pulling in opposite directions, the rule seems to be "as any generation goes, so goes the nation."

For those concerned with progress, this is fine. But from the present standpoint of protecting the system against too much "progress," all at *once,* the above data are not reassuring, as Figure 6-2 illustrates. It shows how the response might be to the political winds blowing at the moment, in increased votes by age generations with 1, 2, 3, and 4 decades of previous experience. On the right are responses by age like those found in the model runs and in the above data for American elections, that is, response when previous experience creates only a small damping of subsequent response. How response to a disturbance would look when there *had* been effective previous immunization is shown on the left. Then, disturbances would be handled like "rolling recessions" in economics. Each generation responds when its first time comes, and then it resists later, while still newer generations "go overboard" in newer disturbances. But with four or five such age bands in the same electorate, not everybody and indeed only a minority would go overboard at the *same* time.

6-2—Response to a New Appeal by Age

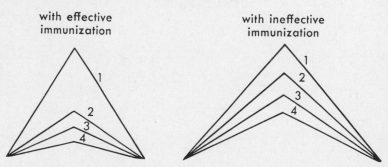

with effective immunization

with ineffective immunization

1, 2, 3, 4 = age in decades of experience

Economists call these "rolling" phenomena because the disturbances, response to which is essential to keep the system correcting itself, strike different sectors of the economy at different times. The over-all picture is one of rolling adaptively with a succession of blows rather than crashing under simultaneous ones. The logic is not different in immunology where, for example, polio would have been sufficient to overwhelm the nation in one giant disaster had we not been taking the blows successively in each incoming generation while the previously matured adult population always remained on its feet. Perhaps the American electorate could similarly remain on its feet by a comparable "division of fervor" by generations. It is a hope tantalizingly visible in Table 6-2. But it would seem too little and too late in life for a minority of elders to save the rest of us from succumbing, "too simultaneously," when some 1936 turns into a 1984.

III. REASONS TO EXPECT DAMPING OF RESPONSIVENESS

IT IS USEFUL to return to the theory, then, and examine two questions more closely: (a) whether a potential really *is* being missed here, that is, why one would expect *more* immunization effects in the sense of much more sharply damped response to new political appeals as a result of previous experience; and (b) if there is such a theoretic potential, why it is *not* sufficiently realized in practice, apparently not in real American data nor in model runs with any imput resembling American circumstances. We take up the former promise in this section, the latter difficulty in the next. The former theoretic potential lies in two kinds of political bias that develop, in individual dispositions and in group distributions.

Dispositions

First, consider what makes for variability of response with changing appeals. It is having a disposition, or predilection, of a moderate down to a marginal degree toward the party offering those changing appeals. This is for the reason the marginal consumer in economics accounts for change in consumption with change in price: he can go elsewhere. In politics, for example, with a sudden increase in conservative appeals, it is not the already conservatives (nor the committed liberals), but the "half-conservatives" who *change* their response.

Why this is so in the particular model is implicit in discussions of the theory of its "stimulation process," in the companion paper (and in elaborations of that process in Part III of the paper on "Attitude Consistency" in this volume, and explicitly in McPhee, 1961). But that detail is quite unnecessary for present purposes. Figure 6-3 illustrates a qualitative reason, independent of any particular model, that is sufficient and obvious.

6-3—Per Cent Voting for "Dynamic" Party under Different Average Strengths of Stimuli

Per Cent Vote for "Dynamic" Party

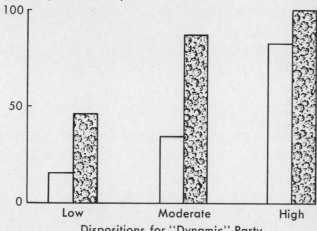

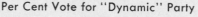

First, those already for a party or cause in very high degree cannot, with still more attractive stimuli, become "more than 100 per cent" for it. The change with changing stimuli must come from where there is potential for increase. But those with low dispositions toward this party have, with an important exception discussed later, a mostly low attraction toward this cause, too, because they are already committed *elsewhere* (in such a high degree that changes in this party's appeal tend to be, by comparison, irrelevant). So, it leaves as the greatest practical potential in a competitive situation those "in the middle," of course. Indeed, what we mean by intermediate or moderate dispositions is that the probability is not near one nor zero precisely because the response *is* variable.

Figure 6-4 shows what happens to the sheer number of such voters with moderate or variable dispositions during the hypothetical model runs reported earlier in Figure 6-1. The input populations used to represent young people happened to have about 60 per cent of such voters in the range classed as moderate probabilities of voting for any given party (probability of turnout multiplied by the probability of choosing this party = .3 to .6). As Figure 6-4 shows for the average of actual runs reported earlier, these intermediate or "moderate" voters rapidly decline in numbers.

Exact numbers are not necessary to the argument, however, nor are the particular assumptions in the model's learning process that

6-4—Decline of Moderate Dispositions for "Dynamic" Party over Nine Elections

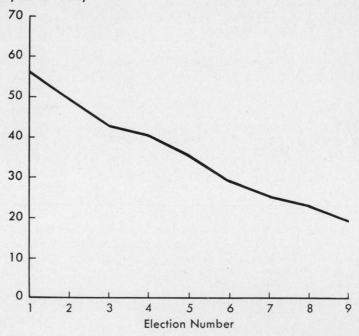

Per Cent Moderate Dispositions for "Dynamic" Party

accomplish the result in the example. For that result simply illustrates that young voters, exposed to vigorous political stimuli, develop party *commitments,* that is, high probability of voting for one party, low for the other. Any one of a variety of learning processes, teamed with the political stimuli and social reinforcements of this or any other reasonable model, would accomplish the same.

Indeed, any model would *have* to have this consequence or it could not parallel the results found in real data for mature populations. The consequence is first illustrated in Figure 6-5, which shows what this particular model's learning process tends toward. If we start with a rectangular distribution of equal numbers of people at all disposition levels, the learning process tends toward "scooping out" the middle of the distribution. On the one pole, it commits the maturing people toward the given party (on the right in Figure 6-5) or on the other pole toward the other party or toward nonvoting, which together become those not disposed to respond to this party (on the left in Figure 6-5).

6-5—Typical Change in Distribution of Dispositions for "Dynamic" Party after Nine Elections

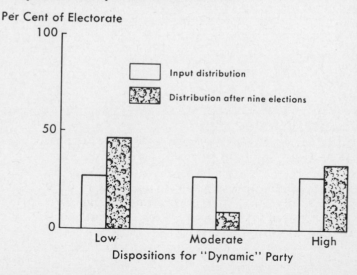

For the illustrative instance of the problem shown earlier in Figure 6-1, average figures for the two parties were:

DISTRIBUTION BY PROBABILITY OF VOTING FOR (AVERAGE) PARTY				
After Election No.	Low (p ≤ 0.2)	Moderate	High (p ≥ 0.6)	
1	27%	55%	18%	= 100%
9	46	17	37	= 100%

Real data for a national cross-section of matured adults will be shown later. These data have the same kind of bimodal or "hollowed out" distribution as in the second row (and in anticipation of the chief interest in those data, the reader might note now that even with the violent events set in motion for the above model runs, more cases pile up at the lower polarity combining not only opposition but indifference to the given party). So, any model that would generate real data would require some process whereby, so to speak, moderation does not last long.

Therefore, the first main reason we expect an immunity to changing stimuli to develop, is:

a. *Variability* of response to changing stimuli depends on moderate dispositions toward the given party or cause.

b. But moderate dispositions are precisely what *decline* with strong stimuli favoring commitment, weak stimuli favoring apathy, and contrary stimuli favoring commitment elsewhere.

We turn now to the second reason, an analogous development in groups.

Group anchoring. The other main reason to expect damped responsiveness with increased experience, that is, immunization due to that experience, is the effect of "collective experience." If a *group's* vote division becomes one-sided, that will reduce responsiveness, just as the development of one-sidedness in individual dispositions does.

We need not bother to show empirical data on what is commonplace knowledge: that while individuals therein show continuous change, one-sided bloc alignments in American politics have remained remarkably resistant to change since the Civil War (Negroes being one of the few real group changes). This remoteness of historical origins makes · the process whereby a group develops resistance to opposite political appeals especially hard to study, however, and the model is helpful to clarify the logic of such a process.

We choose for illustration of the complex group interactions in the model, a simple one especially relevant to immunization. Figure 6-6 shows, as the vertical in both charts, the per cent of (initially random) voters who come later to "reinforce" one another's choices. Reinforce means that both become interested enough to discuss politics *and* then discover they agree and thus confirm each other's choices.

In Figure 6-6, the results for the second decade are plotted above the first. With the systematically randomized populations with which we started, the occurrence of both mutual interest and the same choice, necessary for reinforcement, is low in the first decade. But it is building up by the second and, if we plotted successive decades, the group in the left figure would go toward a very high asynptote. But that means mutual reinforcement of *existing* choices and thus a bloc "anchored" against the attractions of newly changing appeals of any contrary part.

These machine data are, as usual, from the experiment described

6-6—Per Cent Who Reinforce Each Other's Choice (Discuss and Agree) in Two Demographic Groups Receiving Different Strengths of "Opposition" Party's Stimuli

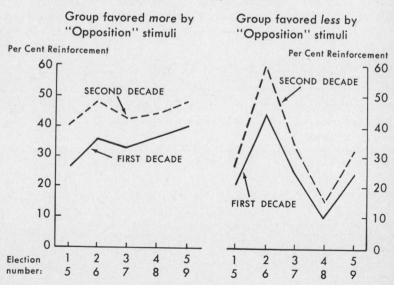

earlier in connection with Figure 6-1. The reader will recall that there the "Opposition" Party had a defensive posture much like the Republicans during the 1930's. Namely, it had a constant appeal biased toward a more than average favoring of certain groups, for example, the middle-class townspeople. Data for these groups are shown on the left in Figure 6-6. But the "Opposition" party correspondingly neglected the interests of other groups, for example, the urban masses. These show the saw-toothed pattern of reinforcement on the right.

Now the latter blocs, unorganized by the "Opposition," are like atomized individuals who only get strong stimuli when the party-of-the-moment's ("Dynamic" party's) nationwide appeals are strong to everyone. In that event, these people strongly reinforce one another's "swing" to that party, accentuating that swing. But, having no particular involvement with any permanent party looking out for their interests through thick and thin, when the "Dynamic" hero-of-the-moment falters and the "Opposition's" destiny arrives, these groups do not resist that change. Rather, they lose interest (hence, show less discussion) or fall into idiosyncratic choices (hence, show less agreement), and thus fall into a state of mutual discouragement, by omission and commission. All of which means that, just as on the upswing they stimulated one another and intensified the swing, on the downswing they fail to check one another and thus intensify the collapse. So, if large groups of the electorate were left without a "natural" or permanent party, like the individuals the "Opposition" party leaves uncultivated, illustrated on the right in Figure 6-6, social processes would not check but *intensify* political swings.

In marked contrast, the left chart in Figure 6-6 shows a situation more typical when interest-group politics and bloc tradition are prevalent. Namely, it plots reinforcing discussion among groups persistently cultivated by the "Opposition" party. Not only is reinforcement building up more solidly in the second decade; but especially note that the reinforcement of votes, contrary to the "Dynamic" party's appeals, is almost *impervious* to changes in those contrary appeals. The latter otherwise would cause the intensifying pattern illustrated on the right, whereas the actual pattern on the left of organized blocs shows little disruption by the changing stimuli. It does not intensify, but *resists* oscillation.

The point, illustrated on the left side of Figure 6-1, is this: we may expect damping out of responsiveness to fluctuating appeals not only because individuals become one-sided, biased to one party and impervious to changes in the other's appeal, but because the same one-sidedness will arise in groups. The essential condition is only that appeals not be randomly distributed but concentrated socially and continued over time in certain blocs. When this is so, the social "density" of a certain political bias will become so great in such groups that this choice will receive constant reinforcement, the contrary view, constant discouragment. Then, the new hero or demagogue faces not just the problem of converting the individual, but groups: to keep that individual persuaded, *simultaneously* converting his family, friends, and group leadership.

That this cannot be done simultaneously, yesterday's heritage of bloc traditions and group interests be reversed altogether and at once by the new hero (or demagogue), means that the social processes involved in perpetuating the former blocs today are immunizing processes against the latter heros tomorrow.

IV. LACK OF EFFECTIVE IMMUNITY

WE EXPECT immunization, then, because the two main consequences of strong political stimuli today, (1) increasing individual commitment, and (2) increasing group bias, would have as their consequences, in turn, the damping down of further responsiveness to such strong political stimuli. But this is paradoxical. The developments required to keep swings in the aggregate electoral system within *moderate* bounds, oscillating near enough to 50-50 to preserve checks on the majority, are that individuals and groups become *immoderate*: themselves hopelessly one-sided.

Therefore, when we now take up the question of why there is not a more substantial degree of this immunization, apparently, in America today, suspicion clearly focuses on lack of commitment among too many individuals and lack of one-sidedness in too many groups. Figure 6-7 shows how intimately lack of commitment is associated with instability, "overoscillation," in the model. These again are data drawn from our illustrative experiments when the "Dynamic" party's stimuli and thus its votes are widely oscillating. Figure 6-7 shows in an especially simple way why the oscillations are not damped out: not primarily because of exchanges between the "Dynamic" party and individuals and groups cultivated by the "Opposition" party, but mainly by exchanges between the "Dynamic" party and those who, in the absence of strong stimuli for it, fail to vote for *either* party.

6-7—Comparison between Per Cent Voting for "Opposition" Party and Nonvoting

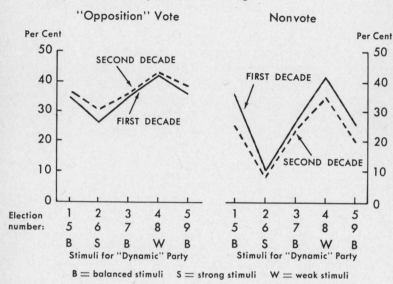

B = balanced stimuli   S = strong stimuli   W = weak stimuli

That is, the exchanges that keep the system from damping out are between the "Dynamic" party and a pool of marginally *indifferent* people who, not cultivated by the "Opposition" and only voting for the "Dynamic" party's heroes in their heroic period, never become permanently committed. Being noncommitted they remain a pool of potential votes for the next hero, wherever he comes from. And this pool remains large enough again to destroy the balance between the committed partisans who, without these marginal people, would hold each other in check after the first decade or so. It is not, then, that the involved persons fail to be immunized against *each other;* it is that neither is protected against a *third group* where, so to speak, the initial vaccinating experience "didn't take."

The fact that there exists in the United States a comparable pool of people with marginal commitment to either party, and thus marginal *resistance* to the other party or to some new hero from a third source, is illustrated by Figure 6-8. It is a classification of respondents in a Roper national sample in 1956, by crude but for our purposes sufficient estimates of their probabilities of voting for each party at that time.[6] The sample was so classified in order to serve as input for the present model, and when used as such (for purposes otherwise irrelevant to this paper) the model would not damp out response to strong stimuli even after many cycles on a large machine. The reason is obvious. Along the horizontal toward the right are only a minority of cases dependably committed to the Democrats and who therefore will not respond to changing Republican appeals. And along the left margin is only another minority, i.e., Republicans, similarly removed from any significant probability of responding to a new Democratic hero. But neither is a proper safeguard against the other when we see the large collection of cases clustered at the upper left, with moderate to low probabilities of voting for either party.

Many of us have tacitly assumed for years that these indifferent people were a constant bloc, "the" nonvoter. But Glaser, in this volume ("Fluctuations in Turnout"), and Campbell, with other data (1960), show that these marginally indifferent participants are actually in and out of the electorate and play a role like marginal buyers in economics. They already are crucial in putting the winning party, for whom they vote disproportionately, into power now. But when the truly strong stimuli of a violent disturbance come, sufficient for most or all of them to vote, if the present model is correct these people with no commitment to an opposition party would tend to go unrestrainedly for the winning (strong) appeal. In that event, as the reader can see by adding a major block of these cases in Figure 6-8 to either party, it would be not just defeat, but it would virtually rule out the other party as an effective opposition competitor in the newly expanded electorate.

---

6. We do not report procedures in detail because it is proving possible in current work to get more justifiable (but not greatly different) estimates by latent-structure methods. But briefly, each individual in the September, 1956, Roper sample was first classified by all available items indicating his past turnout and current intentions to vote. Then (past) frequency equals (current) probability. Next, each was characterized in direction, by party, on the basis of recent past voting and current opinions, again with frequency equaling probability. Then, the two probabilities, turnout and direction, were multiplied to get the final figure for the party shown. The Republican figures are inflated somewhat by Eisenhower items.

Apathy prevents that from happening now, of course. But precisely the eventuality we wish to be protected against is not routine political stimuli, which are easy to be apathetic about today, but extraordinarily strong political stimuli difficult to resist tomorrow. Then, the only real guarantee of resistance would not be apathy, because that dangerous situation is not conducive to apathy, but

6-8—Distribution of Cases in a National Sample Polled in 1956 by Estimated Probabilities of Voting Democratic and Republican

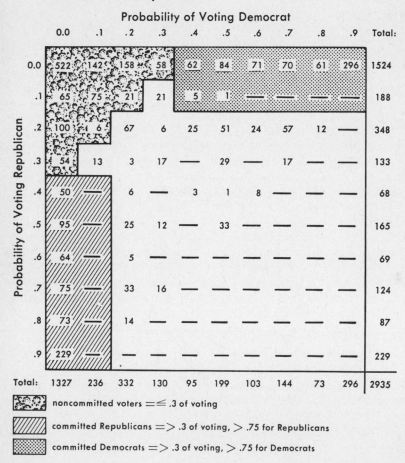

		Probability of Voting Democrat									
	0.0	.1	.2	.3	.4	.5	.6	.7	.8	.9	Total:
0.0	522	142	158	58	62	84	71	70	61	296	1524
.1	65	75	21	21	5	1	—	—	—	—	188
.2	100	6	67	6	25	51	24	57	12	—	348
.3	54	13	3	17	—	29	—	17	—	—	133
.4	50	—	6	—	3	1	8	—	—	—	68
.5	95	—	25	12	—	33	—	—	—	—	165
.6	64	—	5	—	—	—	—	—	—	—	69
.7	75	—	33	16	—	—	—	—	—	—	124
.8	73	—	14	—	—	—	—	—	—	—	87
.9	229	—	—	—	—	—	—	—	—	—	229
Total:	1327	236	332	130	95	199	103	144	73	296	2935

(Row labels 0.0–.9 = Probability of Voting Republican)

noncommitted voters $=\leqslant .3$ of voting

committed Republicans $=> .3$ of voting, $> .75$ for Republicans

committed Democrats $=> .3$ of voting, $> .75$ for Democrats only *antagonism*. But since that must be antagonism to what then will be exciting and popular, in defense of something then unpopular, it would have to come from previous commitment to the latter now. This "antagonistic immunity" is what America's indifferent voters do not have.

Americans have never seen the consequences, after a previous balance between what are actually both minority parties, of stimulating every man, woman, and youth in the population to enter the struggle. Then the previous balance or checkmate may prove to have been illusory, as Figure 6-9 illustrates.

6-9—Per Cent of Those Eligible Voting and Nonvoting in Reichstag Elections from 1928 to 1932

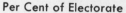

Per Cent of Electorate

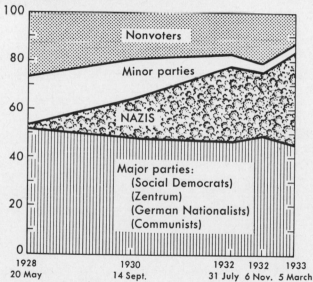

Adapted from Dittmann (1945).

This figure shows the vote in the German elections during the Weimar Republic that brought the new Nazi party from a negligible to a dominant plurality in the short period from 1928 to 1933. The vote is percentaged differently from usual, however—namely, on the basis of the full adult population including nonvoters and followers of minor splinter parties that had not been effectively committed to the previous major parties in the struggle. The results seen in this light certainly suggest (although do not prove, of course) that the Nazis drew much of their sudden strength from those previously not committed to the major-party struggle. This way of examining the German vote was suggested by the need to illustrate the model implication above, but we find students of the actual historical problem have reached the same conclusion from purely empirical considerations:

> In September 1930 the Nazis appear to have drawn most of their gain from the ranks of the former non-voters. . . . The established major parties together more than held their own.

> On July 31, 1932, the major parties again held their own. . . . But the 1932 gain of the Nazis came primarily from the minor parties. (Simon, 1958, p. 288-9)

> . . . the most plausible interpretation of this evidence is to suggest that the increase of Nazi votes resulted from a radicalization of members of the nationalist [that is, mostly smaller] parties of the Right and from the sudden participation of about 4,200,000 non-voters and young people. (Bendix, 1953, p. 605)

Another way to make the same interpretation is to assert that the politics of the earlier Weimar Republic in the 1920s was not yet *vigorous* enough, as American politics is not today, to commit more than about half the population to the major antagonists, which means nearly half not committed to the "checkmating processes" whereby the supporters of each major position are the enemies of each others' and newcomers' ambitions. Of course, German politics *had* become sufficiently vigorous by 1932-1933, to say the least, so that if the Republic had survived it probably would have shown little further response to the Nazis. But this is like saying, about a population dealt too crippling a blow by too sudden an epidemic, that it would have been immune thereafter if it had survived. Obviously, the immunization processes must be continuous, the political vigor sustained at all times, in order not to overwhelm the system simultaneously at any one time.

To illustrate the effect of even very slight increases of political vigor in ordinary times on damping subsequent response to disturbance, we repeat the model experiments shown earlier in Figure 6-1. Now, however, two variants are designed to show the consequences of even very small increments in daily political vigor. The two variants introduce more vigor of two kinds (a) slightly *stronger* average appeal to all individuals, (b) no stronger appeal, but more *bias* in appeals to groups. In these variants, the original experiment's oscillating boom and disaster for the "Dynamic" party will remain exactly the same, as well as the constant but biased (to certain groups) defensive strategy of the "Opposition" party. The only changes will be that:

1. In a "more-stimulated" variant, the normal stimulus distributions are redefined to be very slightly skewed toward strong (by the "Opposition" party at all times and the "Dynamic" party when its appeal is normal, that is, in elections 1, 3, 5, 7, and 9). The degree is slight: the vote for each party at such a time is increased by about five per cent points of the total population.[7]

2. In a "more-biased" variant of the original experiment, the "Opposition" party remains as in the original and also the "Dynamic" party's booms and disasters remain the same. But when the "Dynamic" party is at normal (elections 1, 3, 5, 7, and 9), it does not appeal equally to all groups, but has a biased appeal that is the mirror opposite of the "Opposition" party's, that is, those groups the latter neglects, it favors, and vice versa.[8]

Table 6-3 shows the results. They are given in index form, like the earlier results from real American electoral swings in Table 3-2. Namely, we show the per cent of average change displayed by model electorates that are in their first decade of experience versus those who are in their second (here, second decade means having been through the identical "Dynamic" party's gyrations before, as in the original experiment).

---

7. Technically, the strongest fifth of stimuli in the "normal" (rectangular) situation are now made to have probability .25 of occurring, the weakest fifth probability .15, with the others graded linearly in between. This is about the *slightest* change in stimulus distributions that can be made with any noticeable effect.

8. That is, normal for the "Dynamic" party is the reverse of the situation in Note 4. Notice again how *slight* this bias is for most groups.

Table 6-3—Per Cent of Average Change During a Swing and
Return by Electorates in Their First
Versus Second Decade

	PER CENT OF AVERAGE CHANGE OF BOTH AGE BANDS (= 100%) AMONG	
	Those in Their First Decade	Those in Their Second Decade
Original Model Experiments (See Fig. 6-1)	114%*	86%
"More Stimulated" Variation on Original Experiment	123	77
"More Biased" Variation on Original Experiment	123	77
Real First and Second Decade Voters, 1936-1958, Repercentaged from Table 6-2, to Be Comparable to Above	106†	94

* The table entry is the vertical change involved in A and B in Figure 6-1 as a per cent of the average vertical change in A and A' and B and B'.

† The table entry gives the two youngest age bands as a per cent of their own average change. The first-decade age group averages 120.7 of the whole population's change for all instances in the earlier Table. The second-decade age at the time averages 107.9 of average swing. For comparability with the above machine runs with a population of only two age bands, we put

$$\frac{120.7 + 107.9}{2} = 114.3 \text{ and } 120.7 \text{ is } 106 \text{ per cent of } 114.3 \text{ while } 107.9 \text{ is } 94 \text{ per cent of it.}$$

Despite the small average difference, the first decade changed more than the second in all nine instances from 1936 to 1958.

Since in the model runs the average swing is only for a population of *two* age bands, in their first and second decades, these model data are not comparable to the real United States data given earlier. For comparability, we repercentage the latter as if the real population included only the two age bands in the first two decades. In this form the data show the damping effect of only one decade, and one can see how mild it is both in real data and in the original model experiments. But in the experimental variations where we only *slightly* increase—indeed, about as slightly as is possible—the strength of political appeals to individuals, or bias to groups, the damping out of responsiveness in the second decade is noticeably increased (it happens to be the same in each variant).

In principle, by less slight (and less realistic) changes, one could increase this damping-out of response to a limiting case of an electorate that rigidifies virtually 100 per cent in its first decade's experience. For at least in theory it is clear what is required: (a) to increase the vigor of political stimuli until every individual is committed and no "pool" of previous indifferents is left for any further potential, and (b) increase the bias of the two parties' appeal toward different groups until no groups are left without high majorities and thus all individuals are "anchored" against charges contrary to the one-sided experience of a group. Strangely, this extremity would produce a perfect moderation in the *system,* a total electorate that would move gently and never stray far from 50-50. But that "system moderation" would require political quarreling so intense as to make all its *individual* parts grotesquely immoderate, blindly partisan individuals and one-sided groups.

We do not want this, of course. For example, as Jones says:

> . . . the presence of the apathetic part of the electorate . . . may . . . have a beneficial effect on the tone of political life itself. For this group is a more or less vivid reminder of the proper limitations of politics, a more or less effective counterforce to the fanatics who constitute the real danger to liberal democracy. (1954, p. 37)

He is surely right about the undesirability of fanatics for other reasons. But this happy view of moderation and indifference—in which we had previously concurred—may be a risky confusion between whether we want to avoid fanatic individuals or "fanatic systems." For, overresponsive systems, in any event, are fostered by the opposite of fanatics at the individual level: by people of moderation and, paradoxically, of indifference. They are the ones who, because not certainly *for* something, are not safely *against* anything.

7

THE CONTEXTUAL DIMENSION

IN VOTING

By Philip H. Ennis

Contemporary sociological research about American voting has been predominantly concerned with how the individual voter decides to vote in a presidential election.[1] Voting studies in this vein have produced over the past two decades substantial knowledge about how a person's social-class position, his religious affiliation, national origin, sex, and age shape his political preferences. They also have shown how the issues and appeals of the political campaign are differentially perceived and responded to by voters of various backgrounds and political tendencies. These findings have been summarized by Berelson (1954, Appendix A) and the field critically reviewed by Rossi (1959, pp. 5-54).

Yet these studies have suffered from a consistent limitation: the

This is a revised and extended version of a paper first presented at the 1952 meetings of the American Association for Public Opinion Research and subsequently included in *A Progress Report of the 1950 Congressional Voting Study* (New York: Bureau of Applied Social Research, 1952).

1. Voting studies do not, of course, exhaust political sociology. Lipset (1959) and Key (1959) point out the relative neglect of other traditions of political analysis, a neglect which only heightens the characterization of voting analyses as being untouched by sociological theory, political content, or historical perspective.

voter is cut off from his surroundings, suspended, as it were, above the political and social conditions of his community. Both the emphasis on the individual and the neglect of political and social community influences stem from the leading position of the sample survey method in the sociologist's research armamentarium. The community context[2] of voting has either been randomized as in the nationwide cross section of voters used in such studies as Campbell (1954), or the effects of community context as a variable have been eliminated by sampling voters from a single community, as in Lazarsfeld (1948) and Berelson (1954). In both cases, the systematic use of social structure as a determinant of voting takes second place to the reliance on characteristics of the individual voter.

Political science and political history, on the other hand, deal almost entirely with the organization and operation of the political system. The *political community* is the major focus of attention; voting *processes* are explained by speculations about "the mood of the electorate" or the "climate of opinion" or the "play of social forces." Because such studies seek a level of generalization above the individual, there is rarely an attempt to assess empirically what the voters were thinking about or how they made up their minds.

Clearly, a bridge between these two styles of work is needed and has, indeed, been emerging in such recent research as MacRae (1955), Campbell (1956), Miller (1956), Lipset (1956), Benson (1957, 1961), Blau (1957), Lazarsfeld (1958), Cutright (1958), Coleman (1959), Selvin (1960), and Davis (1961). In these studies, variations in the nature of high schools, union locals, colleges, and army companies—to mention just a few of the community contexts involved—were found to have important effects on individual members' behavior and thinking.

---

2. The term "community context" is but one of several terms designating a generic class of social influences upon individual behavior and attitudes. Merton (1957, pp. 52-53) has called them "structural contexts" and emphasizes the limitations in the possible range of variations in any social pattern. Blau (1957) has used the term "structural effects" to refer to the narrower idea of direct interaction among individuals, and more recently Davis (1961) has used the term "compositional effects." To oversimplify somewhat, all these concepts are concerned with how a correlation between two variables is affected by a third variable at a higher level of social aggregation. And this, of course, is part of an established sociological tradition in which Durkheim's *Suicide* is the pioneer empirical application. The works of Heberle (1945), Benson (1957, 1961), and MacRae (1960) develop ecological and quasi-ecological explanations of individual political behavior in ways that somewhat resemble the use of the foregoing contextual concepts.

The design and analysis of the Regional Panels study was one of the earliest of these attempts to create such a bridge. It was hoped that, in selecting voters from different social and political environments, the resultant *comparative* analysis of social contexts would reveal a wider range of influences affecting the individual voter and at the same time would define more precisely the conditions under which known influences operated.

COMMUNITY CONTEXT

AN ALMOST infinite variety of community differences might be relevant to political behavior. In the present four-state comparison, for instance, the stable farm-belt Iowa scene might be compared with the more rough and tumble politics of Colorado; the self-sufficient big-city politics of St. Paul and Minneapolis might be contrasted with the state-wide politics of Washington, where differences over federal control of power resources give the whole state a different political coloration.

Such conceptions of "community," though real enough for the day-to-day interpretation of current politics, are too idiosyncratic for systematic analysis. Moreover, the *state-wide* area may be too remotely connected to the individual voter to have any discernible effect on his behavior. Different aspects of the voter's political life are likely to be influenced by different levels of the "community" around him. For some attitudes, his immediate neighborhood is the important context; for others, the city or state is the relevant level.

This paper, then, is about how differing social and political contexts affect individual standards of judgment and frames of reference that in turn affect the choice of a candidate. Because of limitations in the data, the analysis is not intended as a full-dress exploration but simply as an introduction to contextual variations in voting behavior.

Three different kinds of community context have been chosen, each illustrating a particular sector of political behavior. They are demographic structure, party preponderance, and local climates of opinion.

Demographic structure. Voting is in large measure expressive behavior, expressive of sentiments keyed to life experiences whose shorthand designations include age, sex, race, social class, and religious-ethnic groupings. It is likely that such characteristics differentially influence the voter depending upon the composition and structuring of these groups in his community.

The first contextual variable, therefore, defines communities along the *nonpolitical* dimensions of its population composition. Specific community distinctions can be as simple or as complex as theory dictates and data allow. Simple aggregates of individual factors such as the proportion of Catholics, workers, or transients can order communities in terms of religion, class composition, or population stability. More complex indexes can distinguish them in terms of their homogeneity, integration, density of internal organization, and so forth.

Now, where do such community influences enter the process of political choice? Probably at every level; but, because they are pervasive social experiences, their impact can be most readily seen in party preferences rather than in final choice of candidate. The distinction here is both temporal and one of generality. Broad political standards are formed long before a person has to choose between specific candidates, and these standards have a wider reach over political thought than do the reactions to a candidate in a specific election.

Party preponderance. If the social structure of the community selectively influences the bases of party preferences, the *political structure* of the community is quite likely to influence the ways these preferences are reexpressed in the act of voting. This brings us closer to the campaign and to the language of politics—the issues, the candidate imagery, and the party rhetoric. Berelson (1954, Chap. 13) discusses this process of "implementation"—the translation of dispositions into action.

The appropriate context, therefore, is a political one, and a first-order approximation to the complexity of the community's political structure is the *relative preponderance of one party over the other*. Clearly, political life for a Democrat in a strongly Democratic area will be different from that of a Democrat in a Republican area. The strength of the *party organization* is likely to be different for a minority than for a majority party. The relations between the rank and file voter and the formal party organization are also likely to be different, and the level of interaction and mutual influence *among* the rank and file voters is likely to vary with party preponderance.

Moreover, the process by which the individual voter chooses his candidate (or decides to vote at all) is likely to be influenced by the parties' majority-minority relations.

Local climates of opinion. The final contextual variable to be described is closer to the final act of voting than the first two. It involves the political campaign itself with all its intangibles in which idiosyncratic differences in political tone and content, the immediate climate of opinion, are important determinants of the candidate choice. What is being studied here might be more accurately called the political "weather" of the community, that is, short-term influences. If given short-term characteristics persisted for a long time they would mark the community with a particular "climate of opinion." The distinction is exactly analogous to the "mood" versus "trait" problem in individual attitudes.

The problem here is to separate the effects of other contextual influences from the immediate ones under study, or at least recognize their differential impact. Thus, in the empirical example of a local opinion climate, party preponderance is inextricably involved in the analysis, as are the demographic bases of party preferences.

Each of these contextual variables is analyzed in the following three sections.

I. DEMOGRAPHIC STRUCTURE
OF THE COMMUNITY

IT IS AXIOMATIC that most voters bring to politics stable loyalties, or at least leanings toward one of the two major parties, determined by their own social position and beliefs. Social class, race, religion, and geographical location, for example, all shape political preference. To ask which of these is the most influential is not very useful, because at different elections and in different social and political contexts these characteristics have different meanings. (Being a Catholic in Massachusetts has different implications for politics from those of being a Catholic in Iowa.) More important, each of these characteristics is differentially drawn into political life depending upon the kind of community in which we live. This is the problem to be explored here: How and to what extent does the community's demographic structure determine which of the voter's own characteristics will come into play in his political preferences?

A grouping of demographic attributes at once suggests two different frames of reference for choice of party. The first is formed by *class-economic interests*. The second is a *traditional orientation* where religious-ethnic affiliation, regional-geographical interests, or, more generally, family-linked styles of life organize the political scene. Negro Republicans or well-to-do Catholic Democrats are examples, albeit oversimplified examples, of such traditional orientations. Also, the strong family inheritance of party preference among young voters is what might be termed a short-term traditionalism.

A third familiar frame of reference is the *personalization of politics,* by which the voter responds to the candidate's personal attributes—his vigor, charm, honesty, his personal achievements (for example, military record), or his embodiment of some ideal. The person rather than the party is decisive. This frame of reference differs from the first two in that it is not immediately traceable to any particular demographic characteristic. Personalized politics, in fact, draws its adherents from a variety of types, cutting across familiar social groupings, much in the same way that Eisenhower's support came from widely disparate sources.[3]

These three orientations or *frames of reference* are not mutually exclusive; people generally apply all to some extent in their political choices. Neither is any one of them a particularly stable posture. American electoral history is replete with examples of shifting priorities among them; see particularly Key (1955), Hofstadter (1955), and Meyers (1957). At any given time, however, various sectors of the population may differentially rely upon one frame of reference rather than another. The following analysis suggests that, although each voter possesses the capacity to use any of these frames of reference, the one that becomes dominant and therefore the basis of political cleavage is determined by the community context of politics.

The Class-Economic Frame of Reference

There is little doubt that communities of all sizes, even the smallest, are stamped with social-class distinctions. Nor is there much

---

3. This is not to deny that extremist movements of right or left draw their support from particular social strata. The success of such movements, however, hinges on their ability to reach beyond their "natural" constituency to wider and more varied publics. Kornhauser (1959, Chaps. 11 and 12) suggests that responsiveness to mass movements rests more on a lack of social integration in a status group than on the status position itself.

reason to doubt that these distinctions are important to politics. Yet, not much is systematically known about how the variety of stratification systems in communities of *different sizes* intersects with their political life. Not that our interest is with size per se. The size of a community is only a crude index of its structure—the larger the community, for example, the greater the social distance between class levels in everyday informal interaction, as well as in school, church, and other such organizations. By the same logic, political organization and process also reflect this class cleavage to a greater extent in larger communities. Documentation for these commonsense assumptions is spotty; clues are provided by Heberle (1945), Kornhauser (1959), Lynd (1937), Mills (1951), and Saenger (1953).

Before exploring class contexts of voting, it is useful to provide a baseline from the total state samples. Table 7-1, using occupational groupings, recalls the familiar correlation between Democratic sentiment and lower social status.

Table 7-1—Social Class Position and Political Preferences:
Per Cent Democratic* of Two-Party Vote

	BLUE COLLAR		WHITE COLLAR	
	Per Cent	Number of Cases	Per Cent	Number of Cases
Colorado	72%	(236)	50%	(236)
Washington	76	(153)	49	(241)
Minnesota	79	(275)	37	(212)
Iowa	58	(111)	44	(269)

* Based on the Index of Party Habit, described in Appendix C.

The clear class basis of political preference shown in Table 7-1 is now diffracted through the prism of community size to see if such a different structuring of class relations alters the lines of political cleavage. Table 7-2 shows for three states—the Minnesota sampling, being entirely urban, is excluded—that as community size declines, so, too, does the importance of class position in determining party preference.

The trend is quite clear in each state and fairly comparable between states: As community size declines, the *difference* in the support given by the two occupational groups to the Democrats diminishes. Social class becomes less relevant as a line of political cleavage

Table 7-2—Social Class Influences on Political Preferences as a Function of Community Size

	METROPOLITAN AREA		SMALLER TOWNS		RURAL AREAS*	
	Blue Collar	White Collar	Blue Collar	White Collar	Blue Collar	White Collar
Washington						
Democratic	86%	43%	77%	41%	70%	54%
Republican	14	57	23	59	30	46
	100%	100%	100%	100%	100%	100%
	(n = 63)	(n = 72)	(n = 43)	(n = 46)	(n = 94)	(n = 123)
Difference in Per Cent Democratic between Blue and White Collar	43 pts.		36 pts.		16 pts.	
Colorado						
Democratic	81%	41%	69%	55%	70%	54%
Republican	19	59	31	45	30	46
	100%	100%	100%	100%	100%	100%
	(n = 52)	(n = 73)	(n = 98)	(n = 74)	(n = 86)	(n = 89)
Difference in Per Cent Democratic between Blue and White Collar	40 pts.		14 pts.		16 pts.	
Iowa						
Democratic	†	†	65%	37%	47%	46%
Republican			35	63	53	54
			100%	100%	100%	100%
			(n = 66)	(n = 60)	(n = 45)	(n = 209)
Difference in Per Cent Democratic between Blue and White Collar			28 pts.		1 pt.	

* Includes rural and rural nonfarm areas in this and subsequent tables, unless otherwise specified.
† There were no Iowa respondents from communities of metropolitan size.

in smaller towns.[4] Campbell and Cooper (1956, pp. 115-116, Tables B-3 and B-4) support our finding here, as does MacRae (1955), using purely ecological correlation.

4. The results are even clearer if we use a sharper definition of class, such as the index that combines occupation, income, and educational level, and that is described in Appendix C. If we compare the proportions of lower-class persons who supported the Democrats in Colorado, for example, the magnitude of the differences declines from 49 per cent in the metropolitan centers to 23 per cent in the smaller towns to minus 8 per cent in the rural areas. In other words, the lower class was much more Democratic than the upper class in the metropolitan areas, more in the smaller towns, but less so in the rural areas.

The Traditional Frame of Reference

If a class standard of voting is less operative in smaller communities, then what orders the political scene? Probably some form of traditionalism, varying in different parts of the country from religious-ethnic ties to regional or even local loyalties. More extensive discussions of rural traditionalism are to be found in Heberle (1945), Kornhauser (1959, pp. 143-50), and Lubell (1952, Sec. 7).

Again, as a rough approximation, the voter's religious background will be used as a tracer for traditionally oriented politics. Table 7-3 shows the party differences between Catholics and Protestants (holding occupational level constant) in large and small communities. The Washington respondents are omitted because they were not asked their religion, and the Minnesota sample is again left out because it is entirely urban.

In both Colorado and Iowa, as community size declines, Catholics and Protestants show an increasing divergence in party affiliations, and, concomitantly, class differences decrease in importance. These two frames of reference, then, seem to be differentially engaged in political choice as a function of the community's structure.

Table 7-3—Class and Traditional Frames of Reference as a Function of Community Size: Per Cent Democratic

	METROPOLITAN AREAS				SMALLER TOWNS				RURAL AREAS			
	Blue Collar		White Collar		Blue Collar		White Collar		Blue Collar		White Collar	
	Per Cent	Num- ber	Per Cent	Num- ber	Per Cent	Num- ber	Per Cent	Num- ber	Per Cent	Num- ber	Per Cent	Num- ber
Colorado												
Catholics	90%	(19)	60%	(15)	95%	(20)	78%	(9)	100%	(25)	83%	(12)
Protestants	73	(30)	34	(53)	61	(74)	51	(63)	58	(55)	47	(66)
Average Differences between Catholics and Protestants*	22 pts.				31 pts.				39 pts.			
Iowa†												
Catholics					83%	(12)	67%	(12)	83%	(6)	100%	(8)
Protestants					49	(77)	28	(64)	52	(107)	40	(134)
Average Differences between Catholics and Protestants:					37 pts.				46 pts.			

* These numbers are the average Catholic-Protestant differences in Democratic party habit between blue collar and white collar groups. For example, the average difference in Colorado metropolitan areas is ½[(90 — 73) + (60 — 34)] = 22.

† In Iowa, where the population of farmers is considerable, income differences have been used to distinguish rich from poor farmers, the latter being added to the "blue-colar" groups.

The Personalization of Politics

Cross-cutting both class and traditionalist frames of reference is the conception of politics in personal terms. From such a perspective, party labels and programs recede into the background, and the qualities of the individual candidates become the salient guidelines. These personal qualities may express something about the candidate himself—his integrity, leadership, and the like. They may also shade into more general abstract ideological or value terms such as individualism or paternal social responsibility. At the extreme such a perspective approaches the *antiparty* movement of a charismatic leader. But with rare exceptions in American political life, the personalization of politics is generally set within the limits of class and traditional orientations and is therefore relatively difficult to isolate from them.[5]

Nevertheless, the logic of our previous discussion suggests that voting for the "man" should show some contextual variation and might occur most often in smaller communities where class voting is less dominant. First, then, Table 7-4 presents the over-all distribution of responses of the Iowa sample to the question, "When you vote for Senator, which is most important to you: the man himself, the stand he takes on public issues, or his political party?" The respondents are stratified by educational level, since it might be expected that the answer would be affected by the degree of sophistication of the respondent.

Table 7-4—Most Important Reason for Candidate Choice (Iowa)

	Low Education*	High Education
Man†	49%	38%
Issues	45	58
Party	6	4
	100%	100%
	(n = 206)	(n = 234)

* Low education includes those who did not complete high school. High education includes those who completed high school or higher education.

† About 10 per cent of the respondents gave joint answers, such as man and issue, or party and issues. These were assigned in the reverse order of social acceptability, that is, party, man, issues.

5. An important exception is the personal clique system of politics found in many Southern states, where, of course, the disciplining impact of a two-party contest is generally absent. See Key (1949).

Synthetic Aggregation

At the upper educational level, "issues" considerably outweigh "the man"; in the lower, "the man" is slightly ahead. (At neither level do the voters acknowledge a reliance on the party label.)

The picture changes considerably, however, when the answers of voters in large towns, smaller ones, and in the more rural areas are compared (Table 7-5). For both low and high educational groups, the reliance on "the man" is considerably greater outside the large towns, with a concomitant decrease in the use of "issues."

Table 7-5—Most Important Reason for Candidate Choice in Relation to Community Size and the "Personalization" of Politics (Iowa)*

	LOW EDUCATION			HIGH EDUCATION		
	Large Towns	Small Towns	Rural Areas	Large Towns	Small Towns	Rural Areas
Man	33%	60%	50%	23%	36%	42%
Issues	61	37	43	71	61	54
Party	6	3	7	6	3	4
	100%	100%	100%	100%	100%	100%
	(n = 36)	(n = 30)	(n = 140)	(n = 31)	(n = 59)	(n = 144)

* There is only one large town in our Iowa sample, Council Bluffs, which had 45,429 residents at the time of the Regional Panels survey in 1950. The other towns range from 2,500 to 10,000. Rural areas include rural and rural nonfarm areas.

A fuller confirmation of the view that personalization of politics occurs more often in smaller communities requires a more careful analysis than the available subsamples permit. Additional support, however, is provided from a more subtle measure, the degree to which the voters hold strong opinions about the issues in the campaigns. It is not unlikely that the more the voters are involved with the campaign issues, the less probable it is that their dominant orientation to politics is a personalistic one. We shall use here the Index of Issue Involvement that is based on the strength of feeling toward the issues of the 1950 campaign and that is described in Appendix C. Voters in large and small communities are compared with Democrats and Republicans separated because Republicans generally say they are more interested in the issues (Table 7-6).

In all three states the movement is consistent though slight: as size of community declines, so, too, does voters' involvement with issues.

To sum up: Most voters have potentially available a number of general frames of reference that can organize the political scene

Table 7-6—Community Size and Involvement in Issues
(Per Cent High Issue Involvement)

	DEMOCRATS					REPUBLICANS					
	Metropolitan Areas		Small Towns		Rural Areas		Metropolitan Areas		Small Towns		Rural Areas	
	Per Cent	Num-ber	Per Cent	Num-ber	Per Cent	Num-ber	Per Cent	Num-ber	Per Cent	Num-ber	Per Cent	Num-ber
Colorado	51	(72)	43	(108)	37	(108)	62	(53)	56	(68)	46	(68)
Washington	19	(85)	12	(52)	11	(133)	30	(50)	16	(37)	27	(84)
Iowa			26	(81)	11	(132)			32	(92)	29	(171)

for them and thus influence their voting decisions. These frames of reference, in turn, stem from the variety of social experiences shaping their lives. Which of them becomes the dominant basis of party preference depends in good measure upon the way they are differentially emphasized by the structure of the voter's community. The data suggest that where social-class cleavages are pronounced in a community, class perspectives will ramify into political choices to a greater extent than in communities less sharply polarized. It is further suggested that traditional or personalistic frames of reference are more dominant in communities where a class orientation is minimized.

II. PARTY PREPONDERANCE

THERE IS AN unpredictable rhythm in American political campaigns. Last year's vital issues are now either forgotten or fashionably rephrased beyond recognition. Beneath the shifting rhetoric, however, is the defensive posture of the "ins" and the offensive thrust of the "outs." Some elections can hardly be understood except in these terms. Insofar as the strategies of the "ins" and the "outs" reflect, respectively, majority and minority party strengths, the dimension of party preponderance in a community can be incorporated as a contextual variable to interpret the voting decisions of the individual. For, as suggested above, voters in a minority party are likely to respond to politics quite differently from those in a majority. In this brief section some of these differences are illustrated.

First, a word about the difficulties of applying the concept of party preponderance empirically. An important operational problem is the proper political unit: Is the precinct, the ward, the county, the congressional district, or the state the relevant political community by which to define the voters' majority or minority status? For most purposes, the precint seems too small to have much effect. The state level, on the other hand, may be too large, because no state is homogeneous throughout with respect to the balance of party strength. The choice of the political unit, therefore, depends on the particular situation and problem under study.[6]

The second difficulty is one of definition. By what measure is a party considered to be in the majority or in the minority? The past voting of the community is the obvious source of data by which to characterize it as Democratic, Republican, or marginal. But a community may be traditionally Democratic in national elections and Republican in state elections, or Democratic in its congressional voting but Republican in the presidential election. Equally puzzling are the situations where one party has more registered voters but the other party turns out in greater numbers and thereby wins the elections. Which should be treated as the majority and which the minority? Again, the problem under examination should dictate the definition of party preponderance.

Our four-state samples are not particularly amenable to this kind of contextual analysis. While they are indeed different in their historic preponderance—Iowa is clearly more Republican than Washington—they are too heterogeneous within themselves. There is, moreover, no single set of candidates common to all four samples; this precludes comparative analysis of the effect of the campaign on *candidate choice* in the four states.

For illustrative purposes, however, some differences between majority and minority voters can be discerned at the state level.

The first deals with the issues in the campaign. Political issues serve in part as levers of persuasion; they are at the same time modes of expressing the more diffuse sentiments discussed in the previous section. The key presumption here is that the amount of social reinforcement these sentiments receive from the community and the amount of persuasion a voter is subjected to will influence the extent to which his opinions on the issues will be in conformity with those of his party. It is not our purpose here to disentangle the separate effects of these two variables. A crude index of both their effects is the party preponderance in the community.

---

6. The difficulties in designating a realistic unit of community influence are nicely and unhappily illustrated with the standard concept in rural sociology—"the neighborhood." See Slocum and Case (1953).

The logic of the notion is familiar: the more people of like sentiments that surround a person, the more those sentiments will be mutually reinforced; similarly with persuasion: the more people of like opinions around the voter, the less likely there will be arguments from the other side to change his views on the issues. The data from the four-state samples shown in Table 7-7 support this hypothesis. The extent to which Democrats and Republicans support their party's position on all or a majority of five issues[7] is compared for each of the four states, which are arrayed from left to right in order of decreasing Democratic preponderance in the state.[8]

Table 7-7—Party Preponderance and Agreement with One's Party on All or a Majority of Issues

	DEMOCRATS				REPUBLICANS			
	Minne-sota	Wash-ington	Colo-rado	Iowa	Minne-sota	Wash-ington	Colo-rado	Iowa
Their Own Party	42%	41%	34%	22%	66%	78%	75%	86%
The Opposite Party	11	30	31	47	10	6	6	5
Mixed or No Opinion	47	29	35	21	24	16	19	9
	100%	100%	100%	100%	100%	100%	100%	100%
	(n = 269)	(n = 270)	(n = 288)	(n = 213)	(n = 223)	(n = 171)	(n = 185)	(n = 263)

Among the Democrats, the extent of substantial agreement with their party systematically declines from 42 per cent in the Democratic area of Minnesota down to 22 per cent in Republican Iowa. At the same time, substantial agreement with the opposite party is increased from 11 per cent in Minnesota to 47 per cent in Iowa. Among the Republicans, the same result is observed, although it is

7. The five issues are concerned with defense, foreign policy, domestic welfare measures, labor legislation (Taft-Hartley law), and treatment of the domestic Communist problem. The wording of the items appears in Appendix B and the Index of Issue Opinion used in our analysis is described in Appendix C.

8. Party preponderance is defined by the average of the Democratic percentages of the presidential votes for the years 1936 through 1948. By this measure, Washington was actually slightly more Democratic than Minnesota; but since our sample from Minnesota was entirely from the Twin Cities, which have been more Democratic than the rest of the state, its Democratic preponderance exceeds that of Washington state as a whole.

less marked. Republicans show much more resistance to influence from the community preponderance.

These opinions on the issues were from the first wave of the panel, and thus fairly early in the campaign. An important question that arises at this point, therefore, is the extent to which the normal *convergence* of opinions on issues and political predisposition is accelerated or retarded by the party preponderance. Questions of change in attitude during the campaign must await the more detailed analysis of the last section. It is sufficient here to suggest one pattern of change responsive to minority-majority relations. This occurs between the October intention to vote and the November final vote in the Senate race.

For this analysis, a definition of party preponderance in smaller units, *within* each state, is necessary. Each state was divided into counties or groups of counties according to their voting history in the same manner as were the states themselves. Because the original samples were not drawn for this purpose, only the Colorado and Iowa samples allowed the delineation of strongly Democratic, strongly Republican, and marginal areas.[9]

Now, what happened to majority and minority party members over the course of the campaign; are there any differences in the extent to which they supported their own party's candidate? In the following table, party labels are ignored by designating Democrats living in Democratic areas and Republicans from Republican areas as "majority" voters. Democrats living in Republican areas and Republicans from Democratic areas are conversely "minority" voters. (Results for Democrats and Republicans separately are comparable. They are combined to maximize economy of presentation and number of cases in each group.)

Majority voters show a much greater swing to their own party during the course of the campaign than do those in a minority. Total turnover, however, is not very different in the two situations. (Turnover consists of the proportion who make any change at all— from "no choice" to "own" or "opposite" party, and from a definite

9. Marginal areas were excluded from the analysis. In Iowa, however, since there were so few Democratic areas, the marginal counties were included with the Democratic ones in counterpoise to the Republican areas. The Minnesota sample is to be analyzed subsequently, and the Washington sample was discarded because no clear Republican or even unambiguously marginal area was found.

party choice to no choice.) The crucial difference is in *net result* of the shifts, that is, all the shifts toward the Republicans minus all shifts toward the Democrats. Among majority party members, changes during the campaign yielded a net increment of 18 per cent for their own party; among minority party members, the shifts cancelled themselves out with no net gain for either party. To put it still differently, 75 per cent of the changers in the majority moved in the direction of their own party, but among minority party members only 50 per cent of the shifts were toward their own party.

The same results obtain for the Iowa sample, although to a lesser extent, presumably because the contrast of Democratic areas with Republican ones has been attenuated by the inclusion of marginal areas with the former.

The fact that the majority party picks up strength during the campaign at the expense of the minority suggests a set of problems that begin to transcend the concern with the individual voter. These problems have to do with the political equilibrium of the community over time, for it is likely that up to a point the majority party gains strength cumulatively across a series of elections. V. O. Key (1956) has in fact shown that, over the past fifty years, marginal election districts have declined considerably in number, turning into areas of polarized Democratic or Republican dominance. These questions then arise: First, what are the mechanisms by which the

Table 7-8—"Majority" and "Minority" Voters and Changes in Vote, Colorado, Senate Race, in Per Cent

	"MAJORITY" VOTERS November Choices				"MINORITY" VOTERS November Choices			
	Own Party	No Choice	Opposite Party		Own Party	No Choice	Opposite Party	
October Preferences								
Own Party	57%	2%	5%	64%	62%	5%	5%	72%
No Choice	13	0	2	15%	4	4	5	13%
Opposite Party	14	0	7	21%	11	0	4	15%
	84%	2%	14%	100%	77%	9%	14%	100%
				(n = 56)				(n = 55)

Turnover = .36*
Net Trend toward "Own" Party = .18†

Turnover = .30*
Net Trend toward "Own" Party = .00†

* The total proportion of changers, all cases of the main diagonal.
† The difference between the changers above the main diagonal and those below it.

majority achieves its ascendancy; and, second, what prevents the minority from disappearing altogether? In the final section some clues to the answers are provided.

III. CLIMATES OF OPINION

WE TURN finally to a more complex kind of community context, one less objective or explicit than the others. It is the ill-defined and variously named "climate of opinion," "political atmosphere," or "political mood." It seems almost foolhardy to attempt to give such a notion empirical meaning; it is even riskier to attempt to trace its effect on the voter's decision. Yet, if a fairly simple example of a political climate is chosen, the problem is not formidable and the general analytical outline can be readily illustrated.

The first basic requirement is a *comparative* context. The influence of a "pessimistic mood" on the voters or of "witch-hunting hysteria" or of a "hero-worshiping climate of opinion" cannot be evaluated without explicit contrasts to optimistic, non-witch- and non-hero-ridden areas.

Secondly, insofar as the climate of opinion enters the political campaign, it must at some point, if only tangentially, be expressed in the language of politics, the issues. How else are the voters to identify the candidate who satisfies the implicit needs of the given climate of opinion? The issues thus can be tracers of more subtle currents of opinion. Given the undoctrinaire character of American politics, the campaign can be decisively shaped by issues having little to do with the formal party platforms. Such issues may arise from campaign events or from the background or personalities of the candidates, or they can be infused with more subtle undercurrents in the community.

Our central hypothesis is that the climate of opinion affects the voter *by changing the relative priority of his criteria for candidate choice rather than his position on any specific criterion.* Issues, in other words, will be selectively "geared" into the voting decision according to the emphasis they receive from the prevailing climate of opinion. This process of persuasion is like that in advertising "wars" where, for example, one cigarette company says, "It's the filter that counts," while its competitor, seeking to shift the frame of reference (rather than opinions about filters), counters with the slogan, "It's what's up front that counts."

The climates of opinion explored here were in two adjacent congressional districts in the cities of St. Paul and Minneapolis. Intensive qualitative reports prepared by journalism students at the University of Minnesota provide the background to the campaigns. Here are summaries of the two campaigns with a description of the social composition of the two districts.

The Two Campaigns

The Third Congressional District is a patchwork area, including six wards in Minneapolis, which are strongholds of the so-called labor vote, a portion of residential suburbs surrounding the city, and several thinly populated farming counties. Roughly 40 per cent of the vote comes from the working-class wards in the city, a third from the suburban areas, and the remainder (about 20 per cent) from the farm counties. The district as a whole is a marginal one— in the four elections prior to 1950 it returned to Congress a Republican twice and a Democrat twice—*but the city wards, where our entire sample of voters was selected, are solidly Democratic.*

The Democratic candidate (and incumbent), Roy Wier, was a veteran AFL official who had run for Congress in 1946 but had been defeated in the Republican sweep of that year. He had campaigned again in 1948 and had been elected. In the election under study, 1950, he was uncontested in the primary. Politically he was characterized as "in the middle," liberal enough to satisfy the farmer-labor element, and party minded enough to appeal to the old line Democrats.

Alfred D. Lindley, his Republican opponent, was a younger man from the liberal wing of his party. A wealthy lawyer practicing in Minneapolis, he had been elected to the State Legislature in 1940 and had served until his enlistment in the Navy following Pearl Harbor.

In the campaign each of the candidates concentrated on one issue—Wier on Lindley's wealth and social position and alleged hostility to the interests of labor, Lindley on Wier's "leftism" as demonstrated by the similarity of his voting record to that of the allegedly pro-Communist Congressman, Vito Marcantonio. The candidates disagreed on straight partisan issues as well—the Taft-Hartley Act, the Brannan plan, compulsory health insurance, and so forth, but these disagreements were subsidiary to the more generalized "issue."

In the neighboring Fifth Congressional District, a Republican stronghold, the situation was in large measure reversed. The Republican incumbent since 1940 was Walter Judd, skillful and effective campaigner, a well-known supporter of the Nationalist Chinese Government on Formosa, and vigorous opponent of the Democratic foreign policy. The Democratic candidate was Mrs. Marcella Killen, also an experienced political figure with a long record of public service. She had run against Judd in 1948 and had come as close to beating him as anyone ever had.

The central issue in the 1950 campaign stemmed from Judd's identification with Asian affairs. The Korean War had reached the stage where the Red Chinese had just entered the fight. Judd attacked Secretary of State Dean Acheson's policies, arguing that if we had supported Chiang Kai-shek our boys would not be fighting in Asia. Mrs. Killen attacked Judd's championing of the China lobby and his identification with the Nationalist Chinese leader. She also attacked Judd's opposition to such welfare measures as public housing, social security, and new minimum wage legislation, but her emphasis on domestic policies was minor, her attacks muted. She acceded, unwillingly perhaps, to the centrality of the foreign-policy question.

The Fifth District lies entirely within the city of Minneapolis and has a slightly higher average income than the rest of the city, since it contains upper- and upper-middle-class residential areas. About a third of the wards in the district house fairly low-income families. Respondents in our sample from the two districts were thus all urban dwellers.

Comparing the campaigns in the two districts, it is hard to believe that they took place at the same time in the same city, for the two political climates were almost entirely different. The Korean War, although in the headlines for both districts and probably in the minds of the voters throughout the city, did not become a political issue in the Third District. Nor did issues stemming from social-class perspectives assume any visible political significance in the Fifth District. These are conclusions, it should be borne in mind, based upon newspaper reports, informant interviews, and observations obtained during the Regional Panels study.

In addition to the different *issue climates,* the two districts had opposite minority-majority relations, urban Democrats in the Third District being a clear majority, but in the Fifth District, a definite minority. Thus, at least two contextual factors were operative at the same time, the particular issue climates and the different party preponderances. Untangling their joint effects is difficult, but, as will be suggested, not impossible.

Results of the Election

The Democratic candidate, Roy Wier, was re-elected in the Third District, though by a smaller margin than in the previous contest; and Walter Judd, the Republican incumbent, won handily in the Fifth District. In both instances the majority party was the victor.

The point of departure in analyzing the two campaign climates is to see how successful each party was in mobilizing its potential support. Table 7-9 shows the net differences between October candidate preference and November vote for Democrats and Republicans in each of the two districts.[10]

Table 7-9—Choice of Congressman, Intentions and Vote: Democrats and Republicans in the Third and Fifth Congressional Districts of Minnesota

THIRD CONGRESSIONAL DISTRICT (DEMOCRATIC MAJORITY)

	AMONG DEMOCRATS		AMONG REPUBLICANS	
	October	November	October	November
Democratic	72%	71%	2%	20%
Republican	9	15	77	74
None	19	14	21	6
	100%	100%	100%	100%
	(n = 89)		(n = 70)	

FIFTH CONGRESSIONAL DISTRICT (REPUBLICAN MAJORITY)

	October	November	October	November
Democratic	76%	55%	8%	11%
Republican	11	41	62	78
None	13	4	30	11
	100%	100%	100%	100%
	(n = 68)		(n = 56)	

The Democrats, in their Third District stronghold, managed to hold practically all of the 72 per cent intended vote for the Demo-

---

10. Only those respondents who actually voted are included. "Democrats" and "Republicans" are designated by the same Index of Party Habit used in the previous sections.

cratic Congressman. In the Fifth District the equally high initial intention (76 per cent) was sharply reduced; the final vote showed the Democrats barely supporting their own candidate (55 per cent) and giving the Republican candidate 41 per cent of their votes.

Essentially the same thing happened to the Republicans. In their own Fifth District, Republicans augmented their initial support for their party's candidate (from 62 to 78 per cent). In the Democratic Third District, however, Republican support declined and the Democratic candidate gained. Only 2 per cent of the Republicans there originally intended to vote for the Democratic candidate for Congress, but 20 per cent finally did so.

The net result, then, was that the minority party in each district suffered marked attrition of its initial strength. This is comparable to the results reported in the previous section (Table 7-8) and might simply be explained in terms of party preponderance. Our argument here, however, is that the interaction of minority position and the particular climates of opinion prevailing in the two districts was responsible.

In the *gubernatorial* vote in these districts, there was no party-preponderance effect at all. The Democratic candidate for governor, poorly supported in both districts in October, made the same small gains in both districts in November (from 46 per cent to 57 per cent in the Third District, and from 36 per cent to 48 per cent in the Fifth). Nor did the Republicans differ in their support of their candidate in the two districts; they increased from 83 per cent to 86 per cent in the Third, and decreased from 76 per cent to 75 per cent in the Fifth. It appears probable, therefore, that party preponderance alone did not account for the results of the congressional election and that differences in the congressional campaigns are the key to explaining the vote shifts in the two districts.

Issue Opinion and Issue Perception

What seems to have happened is that in both districts the majority party effectively defined the major issue on which it wanted to campaign. Insofar as the opposition candidates and voters could be drawn into *seeing and accepting* the contest in these terms, to that extent were they led to accept the strength of the majority's position, to that extent were they deprived of the arguments and sentiments bolstering their own party's candidates.

Do the panel data document this diagnosis? They do, but imperfectly. A rigorous demonstration would require an analytic framework too detailed for the number of cases available.[11] The following analysis is therefore necessarily somewhat sketchy and piecemeal. The first step is to show how the voters' opinions on the important "climate" issues were distributed in the two districts. This is necessary because a simple view of the problem would be that Democrats when surrounded by Republicans disagree more often with their own party on the decisive issues and therefore fail to support their party's candidates. This would be in accord with Table 7-7, which showed that agreement with one's party depends upon its local strength. Let us see, therefore, how the voters in the two districts reacted.

In the Third Congressional District, we recall that the Democratic incumbent campaigned on a class basis, alleging that the Republicans were the party of the rich and therefore had no interest in the people's welfare. While our respondents were not asked their opinions on an issue directly aimed at the class character of the election, one question was reasonably close; this asked their opinions on the Taft-Hartley Act and the strike threat generally. In the Fifth District, the most prominent issue, as noted before, was United States foreign policy on Korea. The nearest question in the survey was one in which the respondents were asked whether they agreed or disagreed with the statement, "Democratic administrations

---

11. For each of the two districts, eight sixteenfold tables are required. The sixteenfold table shows simultaneously the voters' *opinions* on the dominant issue (foreign policy in the Fifth Congressional District, domestic labor and class issues in the Third Congressional District) at the beginning and at the end of the campaign, as well as their voting intention and their final vote. A model explication of the sixteenfold table's use in the interaction of the two variables over time is found in Lazarsfeld and Merton (1954b, pp. 40-55). From such a table it is possible to assess how much *change* there was both in opinion and candidate choice, to what extent opinions were brought into harmony with candidate preferences, and to what extent candidate preferences were shifted to conform to issue opinions. Separate sixteenfold analyses must be carried out for those voters who *see* and *do not see* foreign policy or labor-class problems as the important issues in the two districts. Actually, the situation is more difficult than this. The sixteenfold table is really an eighty-one-fold table, since the alternatives for both candidate choice and issue opinion involve three alternatives: Democratic, "No Choice," and Republican. The sixteenfold table is modeled on a *two*-alternative choice rather than a *three*-alternative choice.

have made many bad mistakes in foreign policy." Table 7-10 shows how Republicans and Democrats in each district answered these two questions.

Table 7-10—Issue Positions in the Two Congressional Districts, in Per Cent

	Third District	Fifth District
Democrats Agreeing with Democratic Party on		
Foreign policy	52%	51%
Labor and strikes	33	40
	(n = 89)	(n = 68)
Republicans Agreeing with Republican Party on		
Foreign policy	56%	61%
Labor and strikes	52	64
	(n = 70)	(n = 56)

Among the Democrats there is hardly any difference in the extent to which they support their party's stand on the two issues in the two districts. In fact, there is, if anything, more agreement with the Democratic position on the labor issue in the Fifth District. Differences in *position* on the issues, then, cannot explain the Democrats' failure to support their Fifth District candidate. For the Republicans the situation is less clear, since there is a slight tendency for them to support their party's position more in the Republican Fifth District than in the Democratic Third. But it is unlikely that these small differences could account for the substantial shifts in their vote which we saw in Table 7-9. *The simple distribution of opinions over political issues, in other words, is unlikely to account for the minority party's poor showing.*

This does not mean that issues play no role at all. They entered into the collapse of the minority vote, it was suggested, via a selective perception of what the campaign was about. The survey data partially confirm what we already know about the candidates' dominant issues. A question all respondents were asked was:

According to your impression of the election campaign, which of these issues or questions were talked about most right here in (the respondent's area)?

A list of issues including "foreign affairs" and "labor unions and strikes" was then read to the respondents. Table 7-11 shows that foreign policy was much more generally regarded as a major issue, by both Democrats and Republicans, in the Fifth District than in the Third. In the Third District, however, there did not occur a uniformly high perception of the class issue.

Table 7-11—Issue Perception in the Two Congressional Districts, in Per Cent

	THIRD DISTRICT		FIFTH DISTRICT	
	Democrats	Republicans	Democrats	Republicans
Issue That Respondent Believed Was Talked about Most Often in the District				
Foreign Policy	45%	34%	63%	66%
Labor and Strikes	37	26	29	25
	(n = 89)	(n = 70)	(n — 68)	(n — 56)

Thus, while positions on the two issues differed little between the two districts, their relative salience differed notably. And it is the salience that was decisive. For when Democrats in the Fifth District accepted the Republican definition of the situation—that is, when they saw foreign policy as the important issue—they were on the way to succumbing to the Republican candidate. This is shown first by directly comparing the Fifth and Third Districts with respect to the shifts in candidate choice made during the campaign by those Democrats who did and those who did not see the foreign policy issue as important (Table 7-12).

A word here about the presentation of candidate choices in October and November, which are in the form of a ninefold turnover table. Gross voting shifts can be seen in the marginals, but a more sensitive measure is the "net trend," which subtracts all the changes toward the Republicans (including the shift from "Democratic" to "no choice" and from "no choice" to "Republican" as well as the complete change from "Democratic" to "Republican") from all the changes toward the Democrats. In the Fifth District almost half the Democrats who saw the foreign policy issue as an important one finally supported the Republican candidate; Democrats in that district who resisted this climate of opinion maintained their initial Democratic preferences to a greater extent. The necessary test of the hypothesis lies in the Third District where seeing or not seeing the foreign policy issue *makes almost no difference* in the vote shifts

Synthetic Aggregation 204

during the campaign. Thus, it seems likely that it was the coloration the Republican campaign gave to the foreign policy issue that made it work in their Fifth District and not the Third.

It appears, then, that *position* on the foreign policy issue—agreement or disagreement with one's party—should be "geared" into the vote more closely in the Fifth than in the Third District. This is indeed the case, as shown in Table 7-13, for the Democrats in the two districts.

The turnover tables show that Democrats in the Fifth District shifted more to the Republican candidate if they took a Republican point of view on foreign policy than if they agreed with their own party. Just the opposite was true in the Third District, but this appears to be a ceiling effect; there is more possibility of attrition among those giving near maximum support to their party. It is clear, as a whole, that the foreign policy issue worked to the Re-

Table 7-12—Perception of Foreign Policy Issue and Vote Shifts among Democrats in the Two Congressional Districts, in Per Cent

FIFTH DISTRICT

	PERCEIVE FOREIGN POLICY AS AN IMPORTANT ISSUE November Choices				DO NOT PERCEIVE FOREIGN POLICY AS AN IMPORTANT ISSUE November Choices			
	Demo-crat	None	Repub-lican		Demo-crat	None	Repub-lican	
October Preferences								
Democrat	46%	0%	30%	76%	56%	4%	12%	72%
None	0	0	7	12%	0	8	8	16%
Republican	0	0	12	12%	4	0	8	12%
	51%	0%	49%	100%	60%	12%	28%	100%
				(n = 43)				(n = 25)

Net Trend toward Republicans = .37   Net Trend toward Republicans = .20

THIRD DISTRICT

October Preferences								
Democrat	43%	10%	15%	68%	62%	6%	6%	74%
None	15	8	0	23%	10	2	4	16%
Republican	3	3	3	9%	6	0	4	10%
	61%	21%	18%	100%	78%	8%	14%	100%
				(n = 40)				(n = 49)

Net Trend toward Republicans = .04   Net Trend toward Republicans = .00

publicans' advantage much more in the Fifth, where it was made the main theme of the campaign, than in the Third, where it was not. In establishing the definition of what the election was about, the Republicans in the Fifth deprived the opposition of its strong points, since this definition was cast in terms favorable to the incumbent. Judd's characterization of the Korean War as a result of Secretary of State Acheson's mistakes made it likely that if foreign policy were dicussed, it would be to Republican advantage.[12]

Table 7-13—Position on Foreign Policy Issue and Vote Shifts among Democrats in the Two Congressional Districts, in Per Cent

FIFTH DISTRICT

	AGREE WITH OWN PARTY ON THE FOREIGN POLICY ISSUE November Choices				DISAGREE WITH OWN PARTY ON THE FOREIGN POLICY ISSUE November Choices			
	Demo-crat	None	Repub-lican		Demo-crat	None	Repub-lican	
October Preferences								
Democrat	56%	3%	23%	82%	35%	0%	30%	65%
None	3	3	6	12%	0	0	15	15%
Republican	0	0	6	6%	5	0	15	20%
	59%	6%	35%	100%	40%	0%	60%	100%
				(n = 35)				(n = 20)

Net Trend toward
Republicans = .29

Net Trend toward
Republicans = .40

THIRD DISTRICT

October Preferences								
Democrat	69%	9%	13%	91%	37%	10%	5%	52%
None	7	0	0	7%	14	5	5	24%
Republican	0	0	2	2%	19	0	5	24%
	76%	9%	15%	100%	70%	15%	15%	100%
				(n = 46)				(n = 21)

Net Trend toward
Republicans = .15

Net Trend toward
Republicans = —.13

---

12. There are several missing links to this analysis. The first is to show that holding a given position on foreign policy does *not* affect the perception of the issue's importance. The second is to show that issue opinions did not change very much in the two campaigns, and particularly did not change more in the Fifth than in the Third District. As noted above, the sixteenfold table, relating candidate choice and issue opinion during and after the campaign, is

How did the Republican voters respond to the situation? It is important to examine their voting, both to check the existence of the foreign policy climate in the Fifth District and to determine its differential consequences for the majority party. Table 7-14 indicates that recognition of the prevailing campaign climate by Republicans built support for their party's candidate. Those who failed to see the major issue show little change during the campaign, but they were already more Republican. For Third District Republicans, the foreign policy issue, instead of being "neutral" as it was for the Democrats in their district, had the effect of keeping the Repub-

Table 7-14—Perception of Foreign Policy Issue and Vote Shifts among Republicans in the Two Congressional Districts, in Per Cent

FIFTH DISTRICT

	PERCEIVE FOREIGN POLICY AS AN IMPORTANT ISSUE				DO NOT PERCEIVE FOREIGN POLICY AS AN IMPORTANT ISSUE			
	November Choices				November Choices			
	Demo-crat	None	Repub-lican		Demo-crat	None	Repub-lican	
October Preferences								
Democrat	5%	0%	3%	8%	0%	0%	5%	5%
None	8	5	19	32%	5	16	5	26%
Republican	0	0	60	60%	0	5	64	69%
	13%	5%	82%	100%	5%	21%	74%	100%
				(n = 37)				(n = 19)

Net Trend toward Republicans = .14   Net Trend toward Republicans = .00

THIRD DISTRICT

October Preferences								
Democrat	0%	0%	0%	0%	2%	2%	0%	4%
None	0	0	13	13%	9	2	15	26%
Republican	8	8	71	87%	15	2	53	70%
	8%	8%	84%	100%	26%	6%	68%	100%
				(n = 24)				(n = 46)

Net Trend toward Republicans = —.03   Net Trend toward Republicans = —.09

the proper analytical tool for this. As far as the data allow answers to these questions, neither change took place; perception of the foreign policy issue's importance was not related to position on the issue, and these positions were practically unchanged during the campaign.

licans who regarded it as important from sliding into the Democratic camp.

However, the Republican voter's position—agreement or disagreement with his party's stand—on the foreign policy issue made no difference in the level of final support to the Republican candidate in the Third District. In the Fifth District the results indicate that agreement with the party on the issue only slightly strengthened the vote for Congressman Judd, but disagreement with the issue generated even *more* support for the Republicans, although here again the ceiling effect may be operative. There was a comparable result, it will be recalled, for the Democrats in the Third District. This suggests that the majority party is better able to bring "strays" back into line over the course of the campaign than the minority. The results are seen in Table 7-15.

Table 7-15—Position on Foreign Policy Issue and Vote Shifts among Republicans in the Two Congressional Districts, in Per Cent

FIFTH DISTRICT

| October Preferences | AGREE WITH OWN PARTY ON THE FOREIGN POLICY ISSUE November Choices | | | | DISAGREE WITH OWN PARTY ON THE FOREIGN POLICY ISSUE November Choices | | | |
	Democrat	None	Republican		Democrat	None	Republican	
Democrat	3%	0%	0%	3%	0%	0%	6%	6%
None	3	3	9	15%	13	13	25	51%
Republican	0	3	79	82%	0	0	43	43%
	6%	6%	88%	100% (n = 34)	13%	13%	74%	100% (n = 16)

Net Trend toward Republicans = .03   Net Trend toward Republicans = .18

THIRD DISTRICT

October Preferences								
Democrat	0%	0%	0%	0%	0%	0%	5%	5%
None	0	0	13	13%	16	0	21	37%
Republican	10	3	74	87%	21	5	32	58%
	10%	3%	87%	100% (n = 39)	37%	5%	58%	100% (n = 19)

Net Trend toward Republicans = .00   Net Trend toward Republicans = —.16

Space forbids a comparable analysis of the class-linked political climate in the Third Congressional District. The results duplicated those presented here for the Fifth District but were less decisive, probably because there was no issue question in the questionnaire capturing the specific climate as accurately as did the foreign policy issue question.

To summarize this part of the analysis: Climates of political opinion, defined here as subtle restrictions in the *area of discourse* during the campaign, can have a powerful effect on the voters' decision processes. A climate of opinion as a *contextual determinant* does not fit the rubric of *influences,* that is, mass media, friends, the political organization. It must be discerned in a different way, in this instance by journalistic analysis of the political campaigns in their community setting. Its impact, moreover, does not seem to be in changing the voter's *position* on the issues involved, but rather in changing the *priority* or weight of the issues in the final choice of a candidate.

Thus, we might speculate that disharmonies between candidate preference and opinions on issues affected by a climate of opinion are more likely to be resolved by changing candidate choice to fit the issue position. The implied comparative context here, of course, is to another community with a different climate of opinion, where comparable disharmonies are resolved in the more typical direction of adjusting issue positions to candidate preferences.

Climates of Opinion and Party Preponderance

There is no self-evident or theoretical reason why the decisive climate of opinion in a community must necessarily be advantageous to the majority party in that community. The majority party generally has the incumbent candidate who, being more "visible" to the electorate, is better able to define the terms of the contest. Yet a vigorous (and probably extreme) minority position might also create the political climate. The McCarthy era is a case in point. In fact, the precampaign explorations of both political parties appear to be largely a search for an advantageous set of issues. Each party seeks, that is, to define the terms of the debate rather than to prepare positions on agreed-upon issues.

What is the relation, however, of a climate of opinion defined by the majority party and the response of the minority voters? How does the minority party defend itself from a majority campaign climate and thus from ultimate extinction? Some tentative clues are provided from the minority Republicans in the Minnesota Third Congressional District and the minority Democrats in the Fifth.

The first is a mechanism by which members of the minority party can resist the dominant climate of opinion. It is to respond to politics not in terms of issues, but rather in terms of party loyalty: *to ignore, in other words, the proffered frame of reference.*

This does seem to have happened, as may be seen by using voters of the minority party who ultimately voted for their own party's candidates as the tracer. Table 7-16 shows that these voters, whether Democrats in a predominantly Republican setting or Republicans in a Democratic setting, attached more importance to "party" in choosing a candidate than did those whose party was in the majority.

Table 7-16—Reasons for Voting: "Party," "Issues," or "Man" in Majority and Minority Contexts

| | AMONG DEMOCRATS WHO VOTED DEMOCRATIC | | AMONG REPUBLICANS WHO VOTED REPUBLICAN | |
	In Democratic Third District	In Republican Fifth District	In Democratic Third District	In Republican Fifth District
Party	55%	81%	35%	14%
Issues	26	13	28	41
Man	19	6	37	45
	100%	100%	100%	100%
	(n = 62)*	(n = 32)	(n = 51)	(n = 66)

* The numbers refer to reasons, not to voters, since a voter could mention more than one reason. This did not occur very often.

The implication, that minority voters have maintained support for their party's candidates by rallying about the symbol of the party, suggests that over time they become more *partisan* than their counterparts in a majority context. Partisanship in this sense does not mean political hyperactivity but rather a tenacious attachment to the major symbols of one's party, in contrast to the more labile, issue-centered politics of voters in a majority setting who can afford the luxury of disagreeing with the party on political issues. There is no direct test for this notion but only this hint from the political histories of our minority and majority voters. Respondents were asked whether they considered themselves mainly Democrats, Republicans, or neither, and whether they had supported their party's presidential candidate in the previous election. We call a "party regular" the voter who *both* affirmed an affiliation with one of the parties and said he had voted that party's national ticket, and an "irregular" one who failed in either of these qualifications; in our data, we shall use the Index of Party Habit described in Appendix C. Table 7-17 shows quite nicely that minority voters, Republicans and Democrats alike, were more likely to be regulars, while those in the majority tended to be irregulars.

Table 7-17—Party Regularity in Majority and Minority Contexts*

	DEMOCRATS		REPUBLICANS	
	Third District	Fifth District	Third District	Fifth District
Party "Regulars"	44%	62%	59%	43%
Party "Irregulars"	56	38	41	57
	100%	100%	100%	100%
	(n = 108)	(n = 81)	(n = 85)	(n = 68)

* The number of cases is larger than in previous tables, since the whole sample was used here. Panel mortality was excluded from most of the other tables.

Here, obviously, is a partial answer to the problem of how a minority party manages to survive the corroding pressures of the majority. As the minority party gradually loses strength to the majority, the proportion of rigid partisans in its ranks increases. It is, therefore, increasingly difficult for the majority party to win over each succeeding convert. Within the minority party, to carry these speculations one step further, there is likely to be a process of dissolution that will even further encapsulate the minority. V. O. Key (1956, p. 195) suggests that as the real locus of political decision in a community shifts from the minority to the majority party (by virtue of increased primary electoral activity), the minority loses its function of opposition and its leadership atrophies. Together, these two processes constitute a downward spiral wherein a declining minority loses its ability to attract and hold superior leaders and candidates and at the same time generates in its membership a defensive posture of rigid partisanship. The spiral "bottoms out" stably at some point determined by the tenacity of the hard core and the effort (increasingly expensive) of the majority to eliminate it.

SUMMARY

THE SURVEY approach to political behavior has concerned itself largely with the processes by which the single voter comes to make up his mind about candidates. The political science tradition, on the other hand, has been oriented to political institutions and processes above the level of the individual. One bridge connecting these two approaches has been the increasing sophistication of the survey method itself by incorporating within its sample design and analytical apparatus systematic data about the social environment of individual political choice.

Three types of environmental context have been elaborated, each one of which has been shown to affect the behavior of the individual. The first is a *social* context, the demographic composition of the voters' community. The familiar relations between such individual characteristics as class position or religious background and identification with a particular party were shown to vary systematically depending upon how these characteristics were mirrored in the community's social structure.

A second contextual determinant was *political,* the relative preponderance of the two parties in a community. Some empirical leads were provided for the general proposition that individual voting processes differed depending on whether or not the voter found himself in a majority or a minority political environment.

The third contextual level was contained in the rather imprecise term *"climate of opinion."* Here, the way that differential emphasis placed on campaign issues by the candidates affected the voters in two communities was the focus of attack.

8

THE POLITICAL INFLUENCE

OF VOLUNTARY ASSOCIATIONS

By Howard E. Freeman and Morris Showel

The political activities of voluntary associations can take many forms. Not only do they embrace the application of pressure *directly* upon the instruments of government (be they executive, legislative, or judicial), but they increasingly include attempts to influence public policy *indirectly* via influencing the attitudes and beliefs of the electorate. This necessarily includes attempts to influence the attitudes and beliefs of nonmembers as well as of members, for few associations have so large a membership base that they can afford to neglect that mass of the electorate that is not within their ranks.

While many associations seek to influence the electorate, the effectiveness of their influence varies considerably. Moreover, this effectiveness varies not only from association to association, but will also vary between members and nonmembers. In some instances, associations exert *positive* influence; that is, they influence the electorate, be it made up of members and/or nonmembers, to follow the policies advocated by the associations. In other instances, associations exert a *negative* influence; that is, they influence the electorate, be it

Reproduced in part from *The Public Opinion Quarterly,* 15 (Winter, 1951-1952), 703-714.

made up of members and/or nonmembers, to follow a path contrary to that advanced by the association.

Few studies have attempted to measure the relative effectiveness of the political activities of voluntary associations. What data there are, however, suggest the following working hypotheses:

1. Associations will vary in the extent to which the public looks to them for leadership in the political sphere.

2. The membership of an association will be more likely to look to that association for leadership than will individuals who do not belong to the association.

3. Associations will vary in the extent to which they are able to influence individuals who do not belong to the association.

4. Associations specifically organized to provide leadership in the political sphere will be less influential than associations whose activities in the political sphere are coincidental to their other activities.

5. The larger an association is in terms of size of membership, the greater will be its positive influence.

The study here reported was designed to throw some light on these preliminary formulations, and, more broadly, to develop useful data in this relatively unexplored area.

METHODOLOGY OF THE STUDY

A PORTION of the pre-election survey in Washington was designed to "get at" the relative political influence of a large number of associations recognized for their activities in public affairs. In the course of the interview, respondents were handed a list of some thirty-five voluntary associations and then asked the following three questions:

QUESTION 74. Are there any organizations (on this list) to which you or your (husband/wife) belong and take an active interest?

QUESTION 80. If you were not well informed about the candidates or issues in the forthcoming election, which three organizations' advice would you most likely take?

QUESTION 86. Which three organizations' advice would you least likely take?

Thirteen of the thirty-five associations listed were selected for intensive analysis on the basis of their having received at least fifty choices in response to at least one of the three questions. The tabulation of responses to the three questions is set forth in Table 8-1.

THE FINDINGS:
RELATIVE NET POLITICAL INFLUENCE

To OBTAIN a ranking of the associations in terms of their net political influence, each of the associations was assigned a numerical weight on the basis of the following formula:

$$\text{Net Political Influence} = \frac{\begin{array}{c}\text{Number of Individuals}\\\text{Most Likely to Take}\\\text{Its Advice}\end{array} - \begin{array}{c}\text{Number of Individuals}\\\text{Least Likely to Take}\\\text{Its Advice}\end{array}}{\begin{array}{c}\text{Number of Individuals}\\\text{Most Likely to Take}\\\text{Its Advice}\end{array} + \begin{array}{c}\text{Number of Individuals}\\\text{Least Likely to Take}\\\text{Its Advice}\end{array}}$$

Net political influence scores reflect the relative position of the various associations only among those respondents who indicated that these associations had some impact upon their political behavior. It does not reflect the net political influence of the association in the total population.

Three separate rankings of the thirteen associations along a net-political-influence continuum were calculated: (1) a ranking based on the responses of both members and nonmembers; (2) a ranking based on the responses of the associations' members only; and (3) a ranking based on the responses of nonmembers only.

Of the thirteen associations listed, eight had *positive* scores. This indicates that the net balance of their influence in the political sphere was in a positive direction. Five associations had *negative* influence scores. It is interesting to note that the influence of a group in the political sphere is not dependent upon the specific "interest complex" for which it may have been organized.

The avowedly political-interest associations, the political parties, both rank relatively low on the influence scale. On the other hand, associations whose interests might be termed only secondarily politi-

Table 8-1—Frequency Distribution of Responses to the Three Questions

	Q. 74. No. Members* (1)	Q. 80. No. Positively Influenced			Q. 80. No. Negatively Influenced			Mentioned + or — (8)
		Total (2)	Members (3)	Nonmembers (4)	Total (5)	Members (6)	Nonmembers (7)	
Protestant Church	152	(74)	51	23	(29)	3	26	103
American Federation of Labor	134	(67)	58	9	(68)	5	3	135
Parent Teachers Association	54	(47)	20	27	(12)	4	8	59
Congress of Industrial Organizations	46	(14)	13	1	(59)	1	58	73
American Legion	34	(54)	14	40	(7)	—	7	61
Grange	29	(60)	18	42	(10)	—	10	70
Democratic Party	28	(77)	14	63	(54)	1	53	131
Republican Party	27	(50)	12	38	(68)	2	66	118
Catholic Church	27	(11)	7	4	(57)	—	57	68
Veterans of Foreign Wars	21	(53)	11	42	(6)	—	6	59
Chamber of Commerce	11	(59)	5	54	(28)	—	28	87
Better Business Bureau	4	(54)	1	53	(10)	—	10	64
Pension Union	3	(12)	1	11	(49)	—	49	61

* An individual respondent could indicate membership in more than one association as well as indicate a positive or negative choice to more than one organization.

**Table 8-2—Relative Net Political Influence of
Thirteen Organizations**

		Influence Score
1.	Veterans of Foreign Wars	77
2.	American Legion	77
3.	Grange	71
4.	Better Business Bureau	68
5.	Parent-Teacher Association	59
6.	Protestant Church	43
7.	Chamber of Commerce	36
8.	Democratic Party	17
9.	American Federation of Labor	—7
10.	Republican Party	—15
11.	Pension Union	—60
12.	Congress of Industrial Organizations	—61
13.	Catholic Church	—67

cal rank high on the influence scale. The relatively high position occupied by both veterans' associations may reflect the large number of veterans in the population, the large number of individuals having near kin who are veterans, and the nationalistic and militaristic tenor of our times.[1] The high rank of the Grange probably reflects the unusually active position the Grange has in the state of Washington with its large rural population. Farm and business associations both scored higher than the two labor associations. This is striking in view of the relative size of the memberships of the business and labor associations. (See Table 8-1.) While the two labor associations have a far larger membership than the two business associations, they scored lower on the influence scale than did either of the business associations. This suggests that the strength of the business associations lies outside the ranks of their membership.[2]

---

1. See Warner (1941, p. 120) for another rationale for the influence of veterans' organizations.

2. A ranking of the associations in terms of their gross political influence (ignoring the direction of the influence) can be seen in Table 8-1, Column 8. This ranking was based on the frequency with which each association was mentioned either in response to the positive (Q. 80) or the negative (Q. 86) question. The AFL for example was mentioned a total of 135 times, 67 in response to the positive question, 68 in response to the negative question. The ranking indicated in Table 8-1, Column 8, may be considered an indication of the relative total impact each of the associations had upon the political thinking of the adult population. While it did suggest that total impact might be a function of the size of membership, a rank order correlation between these two variables yielded a value of but 0.32.

Relative Net Political Influence among Members

The ranking of the thirteen associations along the membership net-influence continuum can be seen in Table 8-3. When ranked on the basis of the evaluation of their memberships only, all thirteen associations scored on the positive end of the influence continuum. This suggests that, regardless of the particular interests for which an association is organized, members are likely to follow its lead when seeking direction in a political contest. This may reflect the influence exerted by the association upon individuals once they have joined and/or be a reflection of the manner in which associations attract to themselves individuals with like political orientation.

Table 8-3—Relative Net Political Influence of Associations among Their Membership

Rank on Total Net Influence (Table 8-2)			Membership Influence Score
1.	1.	Veterans of Foreign Wars	100
2.	2.	American Legion	100
3.	3.	Grange	100
4.	4.	Better Business Bureau	100
7.	5.	Chamber of Commerce	100
11.	6.	Pension Union	100
12.	7.	Congress of Industrial Organizations	92
6.	8.	Protestant Church	88
8.	9.	Democratic Party	86
13.	10.	Catholic Church	85
9.	11.	American Federation of Labor	83
10.	12.	Republican Party	82
5.	13.	Parent-Teacher Association	79

The shift in the relative position of some of the associations should be noted. Leaders with reference to the total influence evaluation, the veterans' groups and the Grange, retain their high position when their ranking is a reflection of the evaluation of their members alone. On the other hand, if we confine our attention to shifts in rank of three or more positions, the CIO., the Pension Union, and the Catholic Church rise considerably on the influence scale when their position is considered a function of their respective memberships. The Parent-Teacher Association, however, drops when its position is determined solely by the evaluation of its membership.[3] A further indication of the relative contribution of members alone to an association's position on the net-influence continuum is shown in Table 8-4.

Table 8-4—Per Cent of an Association's Positive Influence Contributed by the Responses of Members Only

		Per Cent
1.	Congress of Industrial Organizations	93%
2.	American Federation of Labor	86
3.	Protestant Church	69
4.	Catholic Church	64
5.	Parent-Teacher Association	42
6.	Grange	30
7.	Veterans of Foreign Wars	28
8.	American Legion	26
9.	Republican Party	24
10.	Democratic Party	18
11.	Chamber of Commerce	8
12.	Pension Union	8
13.	Better Business Bureau	2

The bulk of the favorable evaluation secured by the labor and church associations clearly comes from their respective memberships, while the bulk of the favorable evaluation secured by business, veterans, and political associations is clearly derived from the evaluation of individuals who do not belong to these associations. This in part reflects the small size of the membership in the business associations. Thus, it is clear that certain associations (veterans, business, political) exert positive political influence beyond the confines of their own membership, while others (labor and church) exert positive political influence only among their own membership.

When the evaluation of members is considered in terms of negative influence, the results shown in Table 8-5 are obtained. It is evident from Table 8-5 that where negative evaluation is forthcoming, it seldom if ever is given by the membership of an association. On the contrary, negative evaluation seems to arise primarily from the ranks of nonmembers. This may be due to the selective nature of the associations as well as to the tendency for those opposed to the association's political policies to give up their membership in it.

---

3. The reader is cautioned when interpreting this and other tables that the *N*'s that can be observed in Table 8-1, Columns 1-8, are sometimes quite small.

Table 8-5—Per Cent of an Association's Negative Influence
Contributed by the Responses of Members Only

		Per Cent
1.	Parent-Teacher Association	33%
2.	Protestant Church	10
3.	American Federation of Labor	7
4.	Republican Party	3
5.	Congress of Industrial Organizations	2
6.	Democratic Party	2
7.	American Legion	—
8.	Better Business Bureau	—
9.	Catholic Church	—
10.	Chamber of Commerce	—
11.	Grange	—
12.	Pension Union	—
13.	Veterans of Foreign Wars	—

Relative Net Political Influence among Nonmembers

The ranking of the thirteen associations along the nonmember net-political-influence continuum is seen in Table 8-6. The similarity between the rankings on the total net-influence continuum and on the nonmember net-influence continuum is clear, and re-

Table 8-6—Relative Net Political Influence of Thirteen Associations
among Nonmembers

Rank on Total Net Influence (Table 8-2)	Rank on Membership Net Influence (Table 8-3)			Nonmember Influence Score
1.	1.	1.	Veterans of Foreign Wars	75
2.	2.	2.	American Legion	70
4.	4.	3.	Better Business Bureau	68
3.	3.	4.	Grange	61
5.	13.	5.	Parent-Teacher Association	54
7.	5.	6.	Chamber of Commerce	32
6.	8.	7.	Protestant Church	—6
10.	12.	8.	Republican Party	—27
11.	6.	9.	Pension Union	—63
9.	11.	10.	American Federation of Labor	—74
8.	9.	11.	Democratic Party	—85
13.	10.	12.	Catholic Church	—86
12.	7.	13.	Congress of Industrial Organizations	—96

flects the fact that an association's position on the total net-influence continuum was in large part a reflection of its evaluation by nonmembers. The rank-order correlation of .93 obtained between these two rankings is thus spuriously high.

A comparison of the rankings on the membership net-influence continuum and on the nonmember net-influence continuum yields a rank-order correlation between these two rankings of .53. This suggests a similarity between an association's evaluation by both its members and nonmembers. Some striking shifts in position are evident, however. The veterans, farm, and business groups retain their high position among members as well as nonmembers. The CIO, however, sharply drops in its position when its evaluation is made by nonmembers only, while the P.T.A. makes an even more striking rise on the influence continuum. Evidently, the CIO's influence is greatest among its members, while the P.T.A.'s influence is greatest among those who do not belong to the P.T.A. When shifts of three or more positions alone are considered, it can be noted that the CIO and the Pension Union are more influential among their members than among nonmembers.

Size of Membership as a Determinant of Political Influence

One possible determinant of an association's political influence that suggests itself is the size of the association's membership (Hypothesis 5 below). When the thirteen associations were ranked according to the size of their respective membership (see Table 8-1, Column 1) and this ranking compared with the rankings obtained on the three net-political-influence continua, the following values of rank order correlation were obtained: with rank on the total-net-influence continuum, .06; with rank on the membership net-influence continuum, —.35; with rank on the nonmember net-influence continuum —.18. The value of —.35 suggests that the larger an association's membership, the smaller is its political influence among that membership.

CONCLUSIONS

To WHAT EXTENT do the data support each of the original hypotheses? The following conclusions seem justified:

Hypothesis 1. The thirteen associations vary widely as to the extent of their net political influence. This variation holds true when the ranking is based upon a combination of members and nonmembers, as well as when the ranking is based on separate evaluations of these two classes of respondents.

Hypothesis 2. The associations do not vary widely in their ability to influence positively their own membership in the political sphere. In all cases an association's net-political-influence score among its members was positive. In no instance did a sizable proportion of an association's membership indicate a negative evaluation of that association.

Hypothesis 3. The associations vary widely in their ability to influence positively adults who are not of their membership. Some associations appear to be able to influence positively nonmembers as well as members. For others, positive influence is confined to their membership. This pattern was clearly evident in Table 8-4. Business, political, and veterans associations appear to exert the widest positive political influence; labor and church associations the narrowest positive influence.

Hypothesis 4. The most influential associations in the political sphere do not appear to be those which have for their specific objective the influencing of the electorate. Veterans groups, the Grange, and business associations appear to be far more influential in this area than are either of the political parties. Labor unions and the Catholic Church appear to be the least influential of all.

Hypothesis 5. The only important relationship between net influence and size is between size and rank on the *membership* net-influence continuum. This value is negative and may indicate that there is an inverse relationship between membership net influence and size of membership.

III

SUBSTANTIVE

PREDICTION

9

INTENTION AND TURNOUT

By *William A. Glaser*

Panel methods permit the study of attitude change, decision-making, and action over time. By reinterviewing the same respondents at intervals, political sociologists already have discovered
much about how voters decide their candidate choices during the
course of an election campaign. A panel design permits the same kind
of process analysis of turnout and nonvoting, subjects where most
research has lacked this time dimension. Chapters 1 and 10 in this
book report certain basic patterns by which voters' pre-election attitudes, social influences, and role prescriptions determine their turnout
rates on Election Day. In this paper I shall describe certain conditions
under which pre-election intention to vote subsequently is executed
into various turnout frequencies.

THE EXECUTION OF
TURNOUT INTENTIONS

VOTING is one kind of action that more people "intend" to perform
than do perform. Past research by Lazarsfeld (1948, p. xi), Berelson
(1954, p. 31), and Mosteller (1949, pp. 375-376, 384) has shown

Revised version of a paper previously published as "Intention and Voting
Turnout," *American Political Science Review,* 52 (December 1958), 1030-
1040.

that the number of people who vote is smaller than the number who expressed intentions, and the same over-all decline for the electorate appears in all the Regional Panels states. Our problem is to identify not only the conditions that correlate with intention in October and those that correlate with actual voting in November; but, even more important, any characteristics of voters that are associated with *fulfilling* an intention to vote, and any other characteristics that are associated with large-scale *desertion* of intentions.

People's characteristics may correlate with intention and the execution of intention in various ways.[1] In the Regional Panels data, voting intention and turnout follow these rules:

Intention. Voters with the strongest motivations, social influences, and role prescriptions express the highest rates of turnout intention before the election.

Trend. All categories of voters decline from their aggregate intention rates to some extent, but some do more than others. The strongest motivations, social stimuli, and role prescriptions—which are associated with the highest intention rates—also exercise greater "braking" influence on this tendency to decline. The largest declines characterize the voters with the weakest dispositions.

Executing a positive intention to vote. The stronger the motivations, social stimuli, and role prescriptions, the more likely the voter will carry out a previously expressed intention to participate. Types of voters with the weakest dispositions are most likely to desert such an intention.

Reversing an intention to abstain. According to Tables 9-1 and 9-2 on later pages, the social categories of voters possessing the strongest systems of dispositions are the persons most likely to desert prior abstention plans. Some exceptions occur in Table 9-3, when individual attitudes are singled out. In these special cases, sometimes reversals of abstention plans occur most frequently among the weakly disposed, usually as a consequence of a larger amount of general instability among the weakly motivated types of person.

Turnout. People with the strongest motivations, social influences, and role prescriptions have not only the highest pre-election inten-

---

1. They may correlate with the execution of intention positively, inversely, or not at all. The different possibilities are described and illustrated in my paper "Intention and Action" in Lazarsfeld (forthcoming). The characteristics that correlate with turnout intention also correlate positively with the carrying out of this intention.

tion rates, but also the highest turnouts. As a result of the aforementioned processes in the translation of intention into action (particularly differential execution of positive intentions to vote), the intergroup differences in turnout are larger than the earlier differences in intention.

DEMOGRAPHIC BACKGROUND VARIABLES

TABLES 9-1, 9-2, AND 9-3 present the data for all the respondents classified by the social statuses, social influence, and attitudes discovered by our questionnaires. An appendix at the end of this paper explains the construction of the tables.

Certain consistent patterns in the execution of intention appear in some of the social statuses in Table 9-1. Men, older persons, and higher-status voters have the highest intention rates, the smallest negative trends, and the highest turnout frequencies. In addition, these social categories are most likely to carry out an intention to vote, and they are most likely to reverse an intention to abstain. On the other hand, women, the young, and lower-class persons have the lowest intention rates, they show the largest declines in aggregate voting intention, they register the weakest executions of positive intentions, they maintain most firmly their intentions to abstain, and they have the lowest final turnout rates. Cross-sectional surveys, summarized in Lane (1959, pp. 46-52, 209-234), have previously demonstrated such social differences in turnout on Election Day, and our data show that such relationships are the final outcome of a systematic pattern that prevails throughout the campaign. The group differences in turnout are due to differences in the distribution of social stimuli and motivations that exert varying effects upon both the expression and fulfillment of turnout intentions. (That men, older persons, and the upper class have the strongest motivations and social stimuli is discussed further in Chapters 1 and 11 of this book.)

SOCIAL INFLUENCES

TABLE 9-2 describes the relationships and effects that various social influences exercise on the expression and execution of voting intentions. Nearly all cases follow the same pattern.

Table 9-1—Social Statuses, Intention, and Turnout

Demographic Group	Per Cent Who Expressed Intention to Vote in October	Trend in Percentage Points between October and November	PER CENT WHO VOTED IN NOVEMBER			NUMBER OF CASES		
			Total Per Cent Who Voted in November	Among Those Who Intended to Vote	Among Those Who Did Not Intend to Vote	Total	Intended to Vote	Did Not Intend to Vote
Sex								
Men	84%	— 8 pts.	76%	86%	29%	(641)	(536)	(105)
Women	78	—12	66	79	17	(707)	(554)	(153)
Age								
40 and over	86	— 8	78	87	27	(767)	(656)	(111)
30-39	81	—21	60	80	24	(333)	(270)	(63)
21-29	67	—18	49	67	13	(245)	(163)	(82)
Socioeconomic Status								
A and B	92	— 9	83	88	(3/9)	(115)	(106)	(9)
C	84	—11	73	82	26	(642)	(538)	(104)
D	71	—16	55	72	15	(214)	(152)	(62)
Money Income of Respondent's Family								
$3,000 and Over	78	— 5	73	87	23	(213)	(166)	(47)
Less than $3,000	77	— 8	69	86	9	(140)	(108)	(32)

Occupation of Respondent or His Breadwinner								
White Collar	86	— 8	78	86	30	(195)	(168)	(27)
Business and Farm	85	— 8	77	85	29	(447)	(378)	(69)
Skilled Labor	73	—11	62	80	12	(242)	(177)	(65)
Labor	76	—11	65	81	18	(365)	(277)	(88)
Social Class								
Upper	88	— 7	81	87	33	(336)	(297)	(39)
Middle	81	—10	71	83	23	(567)	(381)	(106)
Lower	75	—13	62	78	17	(445)	(332)	(113)
Education								
College	84	— 6	78	90	15	(293)	(246)	(47)
Completed High School	83	—12	71	80	28	(405)	(337)	(68)
Some High School	81	—17	64	76	12	(221)	(179)	(42)
Grade School, None	77	— 8	69	83	24	(245)	(326)	(99)
Marital Status								
Married	81	— 5	76	87	27	(505)	(411)	(94)
Not Married	79	—11	68	80	23	(103)	(81)	(22)
Religion								
Protestant	81	— 9	72	82	25	(718)	(584)	(134)
Catholic	85	—18	67	76	10	(203)	(173)	(30)

Table 9-2—Social Influences, Intention, and Turnout

	Per Cent Who Expressed Intention to Vote in October	Trend in Percentage Points between October and November	PER CENT WHO VOTED IN NOVEMBER			NUMBER OF CASES		
			Total Per Cent Who Voted in November	Among Those Who Intended to Vote	Among Those Who Did Not Intend to Vote	Total	Intended to Vote	Did Not Intend to Vote
Turnout of the Rest of the Respondent's Household								
All Others Voted	93%	— 6 pts.	87%	91%	(5/15)	(229)	(214)	(15)
Others Divided between Voting and Nonvoting	85	—23	62	68	(1/4)	(26)	(22)	(4)
No Others Voted	66	—34	32	44	9	(97)	(64)	(33)
Turnout of the Respondent's Spouse								
Spouse Voted	86	+ 1	87	93	47	(139)	(120)	(19)
Spouse Did Not Vote	79	—21	58	66	(3/10)	(48)	(38)	(10)

Turnout of the Respondent's Friends								
Most Friends Voted	83	—6	77	88	23	(299)	(247)	(52)
Some or Few Friends Voted	58	—6	52	76	19	(65)	(38)	(27)
Exposure to Mass Media								
High	93	—4	89	92	(5/10)	(138)	(128)	(10)
Medium High	88	—7	81	89	29	(252)	(221)	(31)
Medium Low	87	—16	71	79	22	(247)	(215)	(32)
Low	70	—16	54	69	18	(337)	(235)	(102)
Participation in Political Conversations								
Actively Participated	90	—9	81	88	20	(589)	(528)	(61)
Did Not Actively Participate	74	—11	63	78	22	(753)	(557)	(196)
Contact by Party Representatives								
Contacted	88	—10	78	84	28	(214)	(189)	(25)
Not Contacted	80	—12	68	80	21	(758)	(608)	(150)

The process may be understood clearly by examining the case of media exposure. The higher the exposure, the higher the intention rate in October, the higher the final turnout in November, and the smaller the negative trend between October and November. Among those who intended to vote, the differences in turnout between the persons standing at the low value and those at each successively higher value on the index of mass-media exposure represent the "preserving effects" that increments of exposure exercise upon a positive intention to vote. Among those who did not intend to vote, the differences in turnout rates between the low and higher index positions represent the "generating effects" by which increments of exposure induce change in a negative intention. The fourth and fifth columns of Table 9-2 show that the higher the mass-media exposure, the larger the preserving effects upon an intention to vote, and the larger the generating effects inducing reversals of intentions not to vote.

These patterns occur in nearly every part of Table 9-2. The stronger the social influences that might arouse an individual respondent's political awareness, the higher the intention rate in October, the higher the turnout rate in November, the smaller the decline during the campaign, the stronger the preserving effects upon an intention to vote, and the stronger the generating effects arousing change in an intention not to vote. (The only exception is a possible reversal in the generating effects associated with exposure to political conversations; this may result from the fact that nonparticipants are generally far more unstable in carrying out all kinds of intentions than are those persons who participate in conversations.)

ATTITUDES

NEARLY the same patterns govern attitudes as govern social influences, as Table 9-3 shows. Variations in attitudes are often associated with eccentric fluctuations in the amount of turnover, and systematic generating effects fail to appear. But for this irregularity, a consistent process can be found in Table 9-3. The stronger the attitudes denoting awareness of the campaign, the higher the intention rate in October, the higher the turnout rate in November, generally the lower the decline between October and November, and the stronger the preserving effects upon an intention to vote.

PREDICTING TURNOUT

PANEL ANALYSIS has enabled us to extend past knowledge about voting behavior in certain ways. We have long known that when pre-election turnout intentions or Election Day turnout are studied in separate cross-sectional surveys, men, persons over forty, and the upper class have higher rates for both intentions and turnout than do women, the young, and persons of lower status. Panel analysis now has shown that men, persons over forty, and the upper class have the highest rates in translating their intentions into action, thus demonstrating that a consistent and continuous social process operates over time to produce differential final turnout rates among the categories in the population.

We have long known that the unequal turnout rates by sex, age, class, and party identification are associated with the distribution of motivations, social stimuli, and role prescriptions among these groups. Panel analysis has shown that the strong stimuli and motivations possessed by the high-turnout group are associated with high pre-election intention rates; these stimuli and attitudes exercise strong preserving effects on a positive intention to vote; and they have effects generating change in intentions not to vote. We have also found that the weaker predispositions possessed by the low-turnout group are associated with lower intention rates, and they exercise weaker preserving and generating effects upon intentions. Consequently, the group differences in turnout behavior at separate points in time can be explained by the unequal distribution of certain predispositions and experiences, and by the different effects that these motivations and stimuli exert upon the *development* of this behavior over time.

These findings bear upon the familiar problem of turnout prediction, which long has interested pollsters and social scientists. Our analysis suggests certain new approaches. First of all, as Table 9-1 shows, when a respondent expresses any sort of voting intention in a pre-election interview, the predictive significance of that intention depends on the social identity of the person. As a rough beginning, a positive intention to vote is a more accurate predictor for men, for persons over forty, and for upper-class persons than it is for others. An intention not to vote will be followed more consistently by the women, the young, and the lower class than it will by others. An

Table 9-3—Attitudes, Intention, and Turnout

	Per Cent Who Expressed Intention to Vote in October	Trend in Percentage Points between October and November	Total Per Cent Who Voted in November	PER CENT WHO VOTED IN NOVEMBER		NUMBER OF CASES		
				Among Those Who Intended to Vote	Among Those Who Did Not Intend to Vote	Total	Intended to Vote	Did Not Intend to Vote
Amount of Interest in the Campaign								
Great Deal	94%	— 8 pts.	86%	91%	18%	(371)	(349)	(22)
Quite a Lot	89	—12	77	82	38	(463)	(411)	(52)
Not Much, None	70	—11	59	74	23	(464)	(324)	(140)
Amount of Issue Involvement								
High	91	— 2	89	93	50	(181)	(165)	(16)
Medium High	85	— 9	76	86	18	(299)	(255)	(44)
Medium	81	—12	69	80	19	(362)	(295)	(67)
Medium Low	77	—14	83	78	16	(323)	(249)	(74)
Low	69	— 9	60	76	25	(182)	(126)	(56)

Amount of Candidate Involvement								
High	90	— 7	83	88	36	(245)	(220)	(25)
Medium High	91	—18	73	79	(2/14)	(154)	(140)	(14)
Medium	85	—14	71	81	19	(274)	(232)	(42)
Medium Low	72	— 9	63	77	28	(115)	(83)	(32)
Low	67	—12	55	73	17	(184)	(124)	(60)
Knowledge about the Campaign								
Knew Name of One or Both Candidates	86	— 4	82	92	21	(211)	(182)	(29)
Knew Name of Neither Candidate	66	— 8	58	76	21	(158)	(105)	(53)

intention expressed by any person so identified will have a different likelihood of resulting in turnout, according to the level of motivations and interpersonal experiences that supports it. Some social influences (such as the turnout plans of the rest of the family and the respondent's exposure to mass media) may be especially useful in turnout prediction. A comparison of Tables 9-2 and 9-3 suggests that certain social influences exercise a more consistent patterning upon the expression and execution of intention than do the attitudes that survey analysts ordinarily examine. Pollsters' turnout scales until now usually have been weighted cross-tabulations of intention with interest and with a few other attitudes, which are so similar to interest that they are redundant. Perhaps more efficient prediction can be achieved by weighted cross-tabulations involving intention, demographic identity, interest, any other attitudes essentially different from interest, and exposure to certain crucial social influences. Some estimate of social supports and social barriers must be included, since they will determine how earlier intentions and motivations are acted upon.

INTENTION, TURNOUT, AND ELECTION OUTCOMES

UNDER CERTAIN CONDITIONS, the abandonment of intentions to vote by certain sections of the electorate may affect the outcome of elections. If one party depends more heavily than the other upon weakly motivated supporters, then its position may deteriorate during the election campaign, since it will lose supporters at a faster rate than the opposition. In a previous chapter of this book I described

Table 9-4—Party Identification, Intention, and Turnout

	Per Cent Who Expressed Intention to Vote in October	Trend in Percentage Points between October and November	Total Per Cent Who Voted in November
Republicans	87%	— 8 pts.	79%
Democrats	79	—13	66
Neither	78	— 8	70

how the President's party declines more than the opposition party in midterm elections if he were elected with the support of weakly motivated persons who fail to vote later. If such politically marginal people support one party or candidate more heavily than the other at the beginning of a campaign, the same kind of shift in party strength can occur *during* the campaign as well as *between* campaigns, since the electorate's general tendency to desert its turnout intentions would strike the parties unequally.

If candidate choices were based on party identifications alone, the general trend from intention-to-vote toward nonvoting would damage the Democrats more seriously than the Republicans. Table 9-1 showed that the lower class, Catholics, and the young decline more than the upper class, Protestants, and the old; and in recent American elections class, religion, and age correlate with party identification and with voting choices. Table 9-4 shows the expected result—compared to the Republicans, Democrats have lower rates of intention and of final turnout, they have a larger negative trend, they are more likely to abandon an intention to vote, and they are slightly less likely to reverse an intention to abstain. Consequently, in "normal" elections, Democratic candidates are more likely to lose their early supporters than are their opponents; and if the electorate were closely divided at the start of a campaign, a typical intention-to-vote to nonvoting trend among everybody would erase a pre-election Democratic lead and would produce a Democratic defeat.[2]

---

2. The possibility that the trend damages the Democrats more than the Republicans is corroborated by the one published study where I have found all the necessary data. In a representative national sample interviewed both before and after the 1948 election, the persons who intended to vote but then abstained favored Truman more often than Dewey (Mosteller, 1949, pp. 375, 379).

PER CENT WHO VOTED IN NOVEMBER		NUMBER OF CASES		
Among Those Who Intended to Vote	Among Those Who Did Not Intend to Vote	Total Number	Intended to Vote	Did Not Intend to Vote
87%	26%	(407)	(353)	(54)
78	21	(584)	(461)	(123)
84	21	(339)	(264)	(75)

Republican candidate should attract a large number of marginal people at the beginning of a campaign, his sup-....uld be subject to the same kind of deep erosion that normally most affects the Democrats. If the Republican leaders tried to arrest this trend by propaganda and canvassing, their efforts might partly boomerang. Stimulating an apathetic lower-class person who is casually interested in the Republican candidate early in the campaign might ensure that he will vote, but increasing his political awareness might activate his Democratic predispositions and lead to a switch in choice. A glamorous Republican candidate like Eisenhower is able to counter all these trends by attracting many people normally uninterested in politics, keeping them interested in voting throughout the campaign, keeping them loyal to him, and at the same time profiting from the fact that regular Republicans tend to carry out their intentions to vote. For such reasons, popular Republican candidates may win by landslides—but fortunately for the Democrats, such opponents are rare.

APPENDIX: THE ENTRIES
IN THE TABLES

THROUGHOUT THE TABLES, I combined all four samples when the data were available for all. Sometimes one or two samples could not be included, because the questions were not asked of them. In some topics, only one sample yielded the information. The following list indicates how many of the samples were included in the computations for each set of entries in the tables:

All four samples combined: sex, age, social class, occupation of the breadwinner, education, party identification, participation in conversations, interest, issue involvement

Colorado, Minnestota, and Iowa combined: socioeconomic status, religion, mass-media exposure, contact by party representatives, candidate involvement

Washington and Iowa combined: marital status

Washington alone: family income, turnout of the respondent's friends, knowledge about the campaign

Minnesota alone: turnout of the rest of the respondent's household

Iowa alone: turnout of the respondent's spouse

Most of the characteristics of respondents were elicited from the pre-election interviews. Where the determining variable was a social influence that took place during the campaign or on the eve of the election itself, this information was obtained in the postelection interview. Consequently, the relevant information about social statuses, attitudes, and party identification summarized in Tables 9-1, 9-3, and 9-4 were elicited in the pre-election interviews, and the social stimuli presented in Table 9-2 were taken from the postelection interviews. The definitions of SES levels and the construction of the indexes are described in Appendixes B and C, at the end of this book.

All the absolute numbers are presented explicitly in the last three columns of the tables, or they may be inferred from the entries. The numbers in the third column from the right are the base for both the percentage of persons who intended to vote and the percentage of persons who actually voted. The numbers in the two right-hand columns are the base numbers for the percentages in the fourth and fifth columns. For example, of the 641 men, 84 per cent (or 536) intended to vote, and 16 per cent (or 105) did not intend to vote. Of the same 641 men, 76 per cent finally voted. Of the 536 men who intended to vote, 86 per cent actually voted; and of the 105 who did not intend to vote, 29 per cent voted. Where the base number is less than 15, I have presented the turnout frequency as a fraction and not as a percentage.

10

THE PREDICTION OF TURNOUT

By Howard E. Freeman

The prediction of who votes is of interest to both the social scientist developing theories and hypotheses in the area of political behavior and to the pollster who is concerned with accurate election prediction. The two aims are not, of course, mutually exclusive. Indeed, it is often the same individuals, playing different roles, who are interested in accurate prediction per se, and accurate prediction as a test of a social-psychological hypothesis. The pollsters' pragmatic need of an instrument with which they might "pull out" the voters is the primary reason for the presentation of the findings contained in this paper.

Specifically, the purpose of this paper is to present some "hunches" that an analysis of the 1950 Regional Poll data indicated might serve as a filter in election prediction. Clearly, the adequacy of this study hinges upon the accuracy of our information on whether or not the individuals in the sample voted. All of the states utilized a second-wave interview, conducted shortly after the election, to obtain this information. Washington, in addition, checked the voting registration lists. An examination of the Washington data should provide a clue to the reliability of the respondents' replies.

The check in Washington of 438 of the 441 respondents indicated

Reproduced in part from *The Public Opinion Quarterly,* 17 (Summer, 1953), 288-293.

that 57.8 per cent of the sample voted. In the second wave of interviews 364 of these respondents were reinterviewed, and a cross-check reveals that the respondents' replies do not agree with the record in 17.9 per cent of the cases.

Table 10-1—Measures of Voting in the State of Washington

ELECTION CHECK	RESPONDENT STATEMENT	
	Voted	Did Not Vote
Voted	79%	8%*
Did Not Vote	21*	92
	100%	100%
	(n = 267)	(n = 107)

* Disagreement

Table 10-1 shows that most of the disagreement occurs in the expected category. While it is likely that some of the responses are false replies (individuals who did not vote but said they did), it may be that the record check is likewise partly in error. Errors in the record check could be due to the checkers' negligence, individuals voting under different names from those they used with the interviewer, and/or individuals voting in different districts from the ones they lived in when interviewed. There is evidence that the latter two possibilities occurred in some of the cases. We find the most disagreement among married women, who may still vote under their single names, and among residents of the Seattle and Spokane areas, where confusion in election districts is most likely.

The difference in proportion voting on the basis of the two measures is of both methodological and substantive concern. Of those polled in Washington, the respondents' figure indicates that 73.3 per cent of the second-wave sample voted but, on the basis of the record-check figure, only 57.8 per cent of the total sample. The second-wave samples in the other states indicate a similar high proportion of voters. It is quite apparent that individuals available and willing to be reinterviewed are more likely to constitute a sample of voters than the general population.

If we had utilized a third-wave interview, our proportion of voters would probably have increased even further. While not very practicable, a sample of people who can be interviewed on successive waves may be one device for securing a sample of voters. Although we have no data to support the idea, it is possible that such a sample might be accomplished through the development of items getting at the same variable(s). That is, it may be fruitful to develop "solid citizen" items, including such questions as, "How many evenings a week do you stay at home?" "Are you willing to make your opinions and election preferences known to public opinion polls?"[1]

Although the total samples are believed representative of the general population of the states considered, it may be that the second-wave samples are not particularly good ones from which to generalize. It was felt that the Washington record-check sample, despite the possibility of an inaccurate election check, was a better one to work with, utilizing the samples from the other states as a test of the findings.

FILTERING THE VOTERS

MANY SIGNIFICANT and interesting relationships were uncovered when several series of questions were related to voting in Washington. The most successful filter was the relationship between voting and interest in the election. Four items in this area approximate the conditions necessary for a Guttman-type scale.

This scale suffers from several defects—the main one being that it consists of only four questions. There is likewise the possibility that all of the errors are not of the random type necessary to conclude that only one unidimensional universe is being studied. The over-all reproducibility is, however, .92. Both the reproducibility of the individual scale types and that of the individual items are sufficiently high to justify the scale's use. The following questions were used:

A. How much difference would it make to you if your favorite candidate for senator lost this year?
    1. A lot
    2. Some
    3. Not too much
    4. No difference
    x. Don't know

---

1. We do have evidence in Washington that the respondents stating that they had discussed or heard talk about the election fell into the voter classification in greater proportion than respondents who stated that they had only heard about the election or had neither heard about nor discussed it. This *single item* did not, however, provide a strong enough predictive index to be of much value.

B. How much interest would you say you have in the November 7th election?
  1. A great deal
  2. Quite a lot
  3. Not very much
  4. None at all
  x. Don't know
C. How strongly do you feel about going to the polls in November? Will you
  1. Be sure to go
  2. Be fairly likely to go
  3. Go if you can find time
  4. Probably not go to the polls this year
  x. Don't know
D. Are you registered as a voter in the State of Washington?
  1. Yes
  2. No
  x. Don't know

Upon the necessary combination of categories, seven scale types resulted. As can be noted from Table 10-2, one may conclude that the more interest an individual has in the election, the more likely he is to go to the polls. A careful examination of Table 10-2 indicates that there is not much of a difference in the proportion voting in the first four scale types, although there is a rather sharp drop in the proportion voting in the scale types after that. To improve this scale as a predictive device, it would be necessary to develop scale items yielding scale types somewhere between types 5 and 6 and types 6 and 7.

Table 10-2—Relationship of Interest Scale Scores to Voting of 438 Respondents in the State of Washington, October, 1950

Scale Type	A	B	C	D	Voters in Per Cent	Nonvoters in Per Cent	Per Cent	Number
1	1	1	1	1	81%	19%	100%	(53)
2	2,3,4,x	1	1	1	81	19	100	(59)
3	2,3,4,x	2	1	1	77	23	100	(128)
4	2,3,4,x	3,4	1	1	74	26	100	(42)
5	2,3,4,x	3,4	2	1	53	47	100	(36)
6	2,3,4,x	3,4	3,4	1	30	70	100	(36)
7	2,3,4,x	3,4	3,4	2	4	96	100	(84)
All Respondents					58	42	100	(438)

It is important to note that the question that distinguishes type 6 from type 7—registration—shows the most significant drop. An unpublished study in Colorado also indicates the same results, that *pollsters should consider only the registered voters in their samples when making their predictions.*

A WEIGHTING SYSTEM BASED ON THE INTEREST SCALE

EVEN IN ITS preliminary stage, the interest scale can be utilized as a weighting device. For this purpose, the replies on the second-wave interview were employed as the basis of analysis. Since registration seemed a key, only registered voters replying to a postelection poll were considered. The discrimination obtained on items B and C provided what appears to be a good series of weights.

The use of only registered voters who were interviewed both before and after the election substantially reduced the samples in the four states. Categories were combined to yield three scale types. As shown in Table 10-3, the results are fairly uniform in all four states.

Table 10-3—*Proportion Voting by Scale Type in Revised Interest Scale*

Type	QUESTION C	B	Iowa	Washington	Colorado	Minnesota
1	1,2	1,2	87%	90%	92%	85%
2	2,2	3,4	77	83	85	75
3	3,4	1,2,3,4	46	50	50	36

The applicability of this revised scale to all four states is even more apparent when the difference in percentage between any two scale types is considered (see Table 10-4).

Table 10-4—*Difference in Proportion of Voters between Scale Types, in Percentage Points*

Between Types	Iowa	Washington	Colorado	Minnesota
1 and 2	11 pts.	7 pts.	8 pts.	10 pts.
2 and 3	30	33	35	39

The uniformity from state to state makes it possible for us to venture a series of weights on the basis of the revised scale. The best series appears to be:

$$\text{Revised Scale Type } 1 = 8$$
$$2 = 7$$
$$3 = 5$$

As a pragmatic device it seems profitable to weight respondents in terms of their scale scores, in other words, count the opinion of an individual in scale type 3 only five-eighths as much as an individual in scale type 1.

FURTHER RESEARCH

THE USUAL suggestion that additional studies be undertaken, of course, deserves mention. Two problems directly associated with the work reported here should receive consideration. First, we must know whether our samples' choices of politicial candidates in pre-election polls become significantly closer to that of the actual results when we weigh respondents on the basis of the above-described scheme.

We must also know whether other relationships can be used to develop a multiple weighing scheme. That is, can an individual's weight on the interest scale be combined with a weight derived, for example, on the basis of age to provide a better filter? Such a procedure was attempted with background factors in Washington. Age, marital status, veteran's status, and education all were found to be significantly related to voting. We were unable to increase our predictive power, however, when weights on these items were combined with the interest weight. This may, of course, have been a function of the size of the sample, and more rewarding findings might have resulted if the four samples had been combined.

CONCLUSIONS

A SERIES of items that appear to be highly correlated to voting form a rough Guttman scale. On the basis of these items, a rough weighing system applicable to the four states studied is possible. While this is but a tentative weighing system, it is believed that better election prediction could be expected if: (1) only registered voters were employed; and (2) opinions regarding choice of candidate were weighed on the basis of interest in the election.

EXTENSION

Based on the work of Arnold Simmel and Murray Gendell

After the preparation of Freeman's paper, Murray Gendell and Arnold Simmel of the Bureau of Applied Social Research used discriminant function analysis (Guttman, 1941, pp. 273-275) and latent structure analysis (Lazarsfeld, 1959) in attempts to assign weights to individual questionnaire items and to entire response patterns. Their goal was to estimate each person's probability of voting, on the basis of his response pattern on the set of predictor items. If a number of persons had a particular response pattern, a certain proportion of them might be expected to vote. It was hoped that the assignment of such item weights and such response-pattern probabilities would greatly improve prediction over the results of traditional turnout prediction scales. The usual prediction methods have used *all-or-nothing* cut-off points; that is, once the best predictive items are selected from a pre-election questionnaire and once the critical response pattern is identified, usually it is assumed that *everyone* giving these and "stronger" responses can be expected to vote, while *everyone* giving "weaker" responses can be disregarded as potential nonvoters. In place of the two oversimplified categories of certain voters and certain nonvoters, the present methods were intended to arrange respondents in a series of categories, each with an empirically realistic voting probability; instead of assuming that all or none of each category would vote, we hoped to estimate the proportion of each group who would vote. Figure 10-1 compares

By the editors.

the methods of prediction by dichotomies and by probability functions and shows the large number of mispredictions that the probability method aims to avoid.

10-1—Two Methods of Turnout Prediction

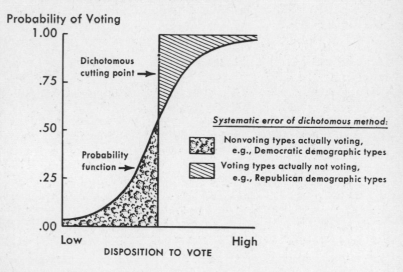

Discriminant function analysis is a test to see how much difference each questionnaire item makes in distinguishing voters from nonvoters with other items held constant. A comparison of pre-election interview responses and subsequent reported turnout by this method showed that five items in the Regional Panels interviews seemed to be the only independent predictors. Table 10-5 shows the items, the response categories, and the "Z scores" for each item; the scores show the relative weight of each item in predicting turnout. (The analysis is confined to respondents in Colorado and Washington; the registration question did not apply to Iowa, which had permanent personal registration, and the discussion item was not asked in the pre-election interview in Minnesota. The complete wording of each item appears in the pre-election questionnaire in Appendix B.)

As the Z scores show, registration is by far the most powerful item. Anyone who tells an interviewer he is not registered probably cannot and will not vote. (The small error resulting from the votes of reported nonregistrants is due partly to some respondents' failure to remember they are registered and partly to early interviewing of respondents before the close of registration.) If registration is used as a filter to distinguish the certain nonvoters from others, the remaining items can differentiate among those with greater or lesser likelihoods of voting. As the Z scores show, interest and participation in discussions carry much less weight than one might have expected from common sense.

Each person's probability of voting is determined by adding the separate Z scores for his entire five-item response pattern. Table 10-6 shows all the response patterns for the Colorado and Washington respondents who were interviewed both before and after the election. The table compares the voting probability of each response type with the proportion of such persons who actually voted (Columns 1 and 3). Discriminant function analysis still makes a number of erroneous predictions, although fewer than a dichotomous technique.

Arnold Simmel attempted to use latent structure analysis also in order to select predictive items and to compute a voting probability for each response pattern. Table 10-6 shows the probability with which each response pattern assigns a respondent to a latent class of probable voters. The latent structure method differs from discriminant function analysis in that it uses only pre-election information. Discriminant function analysis is a kind of retrospective pre-

Table 10-5

Question	Positive Response	Negative Response	Z Score
Registration	Registered	Not Registered, Don't Know	.62
Turnout in 1948	Voted	Did Not Vote, Doubtful	.15
Intention in 1950	Sure to Go	Fairly Likely, Go if Find Time, Probably Not Go, Don't Know	.13
Interest in Campaign	Great Deal, Quite a Lot	Not Very Much, None, Don't Know	.05
Participation in Discussions	Discussed	Paid No Attention to Discussions, Did Not Hear Discussions	.05
			1.00

diction, since it estimates the weights of items by correlating each with the respondent's actual turnout, as reported in the postelection interview. In contrast, latent structure uses only the intercorrelation of items from the single pre-election interview. This naturally achieves less accurate predictions than discriminant function analysis, as Table

Table 10-6—Estimated and Actual Voting Proportions, Discriminant Function Analysis and Latent Structure Analysis

	RESPONSE PATTERN					Probability of Belonging to	Actual	
Reg.	Past Vote	Int.	Inter.	Disc.	Total Z Score	Latent Class of Voters	Per Cent Who Voted	Number of Cases
+	+	+	+	+	1.00	1.00	96	208
+	+	+	+	−	.95	1.00	90	112
+	+	+	−	+	.95	.99	92	36
+	+	+	−	−	.90	.97	85	55
+	+	−	+	+	.87	.92	92	12
+	−	+	+	+	.85	.99	82	22
+	+	−	+	−	.82	.69	85	20
+	+	−	−	+	.82	.54	62	13
+	−	+	+	−	.80	.96	67	15
+	−	+	−	+	.80	.92	100	3
+	+	−	−	−	.77	.19	67	36
+	−	+	−	−	.75	.70	100	3
+	−	−	+	+	.72	.44	50	8
+	−	−	+	−	.67	.14	75	4
+	−	−	−	+	.67	.08	00	1
+	−	−	−	−	.62	.01	100	5
−	+	+	+	+	.38	.89	33	3
−	+	+	+	−	.33	.59	00	1
−	+	+	−	+	.33	.44	−	0
−	+	+	−	−	.28	.01	00	4
−	+	−	+	+	.25	.01	00	5
−	−	+	+	+	.23	.38	33	3
−	+	−	+	−	.20	.01	60	5
−	+	−	−	+	.20	.01	11	9
−	−	+	+	−	.18	.10	00	2
−	−	+	−	+	.18	.00	−	0
−	+	−	−	−	.15	.00	15	20
−	−	+	−	−	.13	.02	00	1
−	−	−	+	+	.10	.00	18	17
−	−	−	−	+	.05	.00	7	14
−	−	−	+	−	.05	.00	14	21
−	−	−	−	−	.00	.00	4	53
								711

10-6 shows. But since latent structure analysis need use only pre-election attitude data, it is useful before the particular outcome is known. It was used in this way to provide "live" input for the voting model tested during the Wisconsin presidential primary of 1960 and described by McPhee (1961).

In summary, the work by Gendell and Simmel has suggested an alternative to the pollster's method of all-or-nothing cut-off points. In practice, different types of voters have varying probabilities of voting, and to ignore this probably introduces systematic bias like that in Figure 10-1.

11

POLITICAL BEHAVIOR

IN MIDTERM ELECTIONS

By William A. Glaser and Charles Kadushin

*W*hen the Regional Panels surveys were conducted in 1950, many specific generalizations had already accumulated about voting behavior in presidential elections. One of the purposes of the project was to discover whether voting in midterm elections obeys the same principles. In this chapter, we shall list certain propositions that have been discovered in previous panel surveys of presidential elections, and we shall report whether they are confirmed in the four Regional Panels samples.

The complete list of propositions was published in Appendix A of *Voting* (Berelson, 1954). It was based on fourteen published and unpublished reports of panel survey results obtained from nation-wide and local samples interviewed during the American presidential elections of 1940, 1944, 1948, and 1952 and the British parliamentary elections of 1950 and 1951. Some of the findings occurred in more than one study, others in only one.

Not every proposition in the original inventory can be tested with our data. The Regional Panels questionnaires were intentionally limited in scope, and the inventory in *Voting* was not prepared until after our data were obtained. However, a majority of the findings can be replicated in at least one of our samples; and in most of these tests, simultaneous replication is possible on all four samples.

A typical book summarizing an election survey would devote most of its text to summaries and tables of these kinds of findings, but we have deliberately presented them in the form of a terse list of outcomes, since this book aims primarily at an intensive analysis of a few major research problems. Every table testing individual propositions in the following list is on file at the Bureau of Applied Social Research and may be consulted by any interested readers.

The inventory simply replicates the list of statements as they originally appeared in Appendix A of *Voting*. The list does not include any revisions of the original propositions, it does not add any statements from previous studies that might have been overlooked at the time it was first prepared, and it does not add any new findings from the Regional Panels analysis. The inventory is simply designed to show the results of a kind of work rarely attempted in social research, namely, the replication in a slightly different kind of context (that is, midterm elections) of a long and heterogeneous list of generalizations that were found true in another context (that is, presidential elections). As it appears in *Voting* and in this chapter, the inventory is not offered as a complete codification of knowledge about voting behavior, although in some form it does touch upon most of the important variables and relationships.

To develop a long list of crude empirical generalizations is an important achievement during the early stages of a science. But this is only preparatory work, and the ultimate goal is to construct theories that combine and "explain" such discrete findings and from which valid new hypotheses can be deduced. Other parts of this book have attempted to build upon our inventory of findings in these ways. For example, the computer model in Chapter 5 was constructed from most of these separate propositions. The turnout theory of Chapter 1 was developed by combining many of the propositions about turnout and about the distribution of motivations and stimuli among the electorate. Chapter 4 is an elaboration of the conditions governing one of the propositions (Number 183). These essays represent a stage of theory and analysis of data beyond the empirical generalizations listed in this chapter. All such further syntheses assume the dependability of the original raw findings, and it is this kind of accuracy that is tested on the following pages.

When replicating the propositions, wherever possible we have used the same kinds of survey questions, measurements, and tables as those in the studies that first yielded the findings. Therefore, the reader can discover the operational meaning of the following generalizations by consulting the tables published in these original sources.

The table on pages 259-272 reproduces the same wording and proposition numbers as Appendix A of *Voting*. Where a number is missing, the proposition could not be tested by any Regional Panels data. When a state has no entry, the data for testing that proposition were not obtained from that particular sample. An entry of "yes" means that the generalization was verified in the sample—that is, the direction of the correlation was the same as in the original study. "No" means that the predicted relationship did not occur, and sometimes the opposite relationship appeared. "Mostly yes" signifies that the data tended to support the generalization, but statistical irregularities existed. "Mostly no" means that the data tended to go in the opposite direction from the predicted rule, but irregularities occurred. "Mixed" means that in some ways the data supported the rule, but contradictory tendencies also appeared. When a generalization consists of two parts, the entry in the table has two parts—such as "yes; yes" or "yes; no." Since we are dealing with a cumulative body of knowledge in a series of independent studies, we did not use statistical tests of significance on individual tables but instead we were interested in whether the results show a consistent direction.

Replication has various aims. An investigator may wish to check the accuracy of his original variables and their interrelations by performing a retest in a situation closely resembling the original conditions. Or, by testing the original relationship in a new and slightly different situation, he may determine whether the relationship is so general that it is always true, or whether it is true only under particular conditions. The first type of replication is a test of methodological reliability and empirical validity. The second attempts to elaborate the relationship by introducing new specifying variables.

Retesting the original voting propositions in the Regional Panels data represents a change in institutional context from presidential to midterm elections and therefore a change in many of the conditions that might have been expected to affect the relationships. The following table shows, however, that most of the findings hold true in these midterm election samples as well as in the presidential election data where they were first discovered. These confirmations reflect the many important similarities between voting behavior in the two kinds of elections.

Some findings were not consistently supported in the four Regional Panels samples. Four types of failure occur. In many cases the findings might be true in presidential elections but not in the different situation created by a midterm election. Other findings might be true in certain local contexts where previous research was done, but not in the areas providing the Regional Panels samples. Some propositions were once true in American politics, but historical changes have produced new situations in which the relationships among the variables have altered or in which the content of the original variables themselves has changed. Finally, some failures in replication suggest that the original propositions may have been mistaken.

SOME DIFFERENCES BETWEEN MIDTERM AND PRESIDENTIAL ELECTIONS

IN COMPARISON with presidential elections, less publicity is given to midterm elections and less seems at stake. Consequently, certain propositions assuming high levels of interest and activity may be true only of presidential elections. For example, Propositions 57 and 58 fail in most of the Regional Panels samples because of the lower numbers of people who are "greatly" interested in midterm campaigns and who are active participants. Conversations about the midterm campaign may be so perfunctory that even the uninterested and undecided persons get more political information from the mass media than from conversations. The latter are more important for such people in the more intensely discussed presidential elections. (This would explain why Proposition 108 fails to replicate consistently in the Regional Panels samples.)

The shorter duration and weaker stimuli of midterm election campaigns result in their exerting weaker and less orderly effects than a presidential campaign. The midterm campaign may have little power to crystallize and accelerate a national trend. If there has been a trend between campaigns for one party and against the other, it may already be close to its maximum at the start of the midterm campaign, and the period of the campaign itself may add little to this trend (Proposition 182). While the stimuli of presidential elections may lead people to understand and avoid inconsistencies among their opinions, the pressures to do so are weaker in midterm campaigns. Consequently, some persons continue to hold inconsistent opinions, others perform random opinion changes that result in new inconsistencies, and the electorate consequently fails to polarize into mutually exclusive factions (Propositions 183 and 183A). Compared to presidential campaigns, during which changes from one candidate to another are relatively uncommon and follow some orderly direction in accordance either with voters' predispositions or with historical trends, greater random change apparently occurs during midterm campaigns (Propositions 179B and D). Finally, political stimuli (such as candidate involvement and issue involvement) are not strong enough and the midterm campaign is not long enough to enable such stimuli to supersede social predispositions (age, education, social class, and so on) as the principal determinants of interest in the election (Proposition 67).

In summary, midterm and presidential campaigns constitute different kinds of social situation, because the former present fewer strong stimuli, the electorate is less interested and less active, and there exist fewer pressures inducing voters to make orderly, consistent, and stable decisions.

SOME DIFFERENCES AMONG COMMUNITY CONTEXTS

ONE OF THE PURPOSES of the Regional Panels Project was to discover how certain generalizations about voting behavior depend on the local context. Some of the reversals in our list of findings are due to differences between the Regional Panels contexts and the settings where earlier voting research was performed. Therefore, some of the generalizations should be amended to be conditional upon the specific social environment.

For example, Proposition 3B should be revised, taking account of the fact that whether a social group has more or less solidarity than other groups will depend on whether it is in the political majority or minority. White-collar and business groups have greater solidarity than workers in areas where the Republicans have a clear majority, such as Elmira and Iowa; but they may have less or equal solidarity where the Democrats have a majority or where the parties are evenly divided, such as Colorado, Washington, or the Minnesota Twin-Cities area.

Similarly, the effect of an intensifying variable may depend on whether the political environment is favorable or unfavorable to one's predispositions. For example, in 1948 in Republican Elmira, involvement in politics tended to direct Catholics away from Democratic voting (Proposition 7). But in the Democratic areas of Minnesota and Colorado in 1950, political participation intensified Catholics' Democratic preferences.

Religious and other ethnic statuses have different meanings and different effects in various communities depending on how these positions have been assimilated into the environment. Consequently, religion has different meanings and correlates with political participation in various ways, depending on the characteristics of both the religious groups and the social context (Proposition 45).

CORRECTION OF HISTORICALLY BOUNDED GENERALIZATIONS

AN INVENTORY of empirical generalizations should avoid presenting as timeless rules any statements that are peculiar to the particular situation existing at one historical period. Our replications in the 1950 election suggest that certain propositions found in previous studies were true for those specific times, but changes in American society have made them obsolete.

At all historical periods, high or low social status correlates with voting, but the concrete indicators of status may change. In early research about voting behavior, income correlated strongly with party preference, but occupation did not when material style of life was controlled (Propositions 2 and 3A). However, during the 1940's and 1950's, full employment and powerful industrial unions raised the incomes and living standards of many blue-collar workers. In social status and in voting behavior, occupation has become a more important predictor than income. In contrast to the income variable, occupation brings people together into the kinds of organized social groupings that influence individual political behavior.

Certain long-term historical trends may change the relationships between age and party. During periods of national stability and equal party divisions, age may not correlate with party independently of socioeconomic status (Proposition 12A). But by the time of the Regional Panels surveys, nearly twenty years of the New and Fair Deals had made young adults Democratic in many parts of the country, even with socioeconomic status controlled. A long period of Republican ascendancy in the future might produce a new generation of predominantly Republican voters.

Other voting propositions may depend on short-term historical trends. For example, during some periods few citizens may agree with all the policies of their parties (Proposition 124). But if crises or intense partisan conflicts suddenly arise, then one or both parties may gain their followers' strong support in ideology as well as in votes. The Regional Panels data show that the Truman Administration was so vigorously criticized in 1950 that most Republican voters agreed with all the Republican positions on issues.

CORRECTION OF
INACCURATE GENERALIZATIONS

REPLICATION ON four independent samples in the Regional Panels surveys permits correction of previous generalizations that were based on single samples and that are probably inaccurate. For example, interest in politics may intensify one's class predispositions instead of counteracting them (Proposition 73). Such a revision is more consistent with Suchman's (1955) summary of the existing knowledge about intensifying variables than is the original statement of Proposition 73.

Sometimes a failure to replicate a finding leads to re-examination of the previous research and discovery that the original proposition was based on methodological errors or on an atypical sample. Proposition 40A reported Kitt's (1950, pp. 406-407) finding that men have proportionately more turnout intentions than women but carry out these expectations less diligently. At the time, this proposition was offered as the only known exception to a general rule stating that the greater the motivation, the higher the frequency in both the expression and the fulfillment of voting intentions. Chapter 9 shows that the general rule is true for sex as well as for other statuses, and therefore Proposition 40A is probably inaccurate. Re-examination of Kitt's sample shows that her finding was due to unusually great instability by young men; it would not have been true if she had analyzed the available Elmira data only for middle-aged and older persons, and probably it would not have been true in 1948 if she had drawn other samples of young voters.

Other failures in replication may be due to the ambiguous and unreliable statement of the original proposition, and therefore any retest would be impossible. For example, Proposition 192 predicted that most voting changes should involve "moderate" positions, but the meaning of "moderate" was not specified, and replication with plausibly designed voting categories produced consistent reversals. Reliable propositions should not raise doubts about the research operations necessary for replication.

All in all, however, the dependability we find in this replication is "mostly yes."

Finding or Generalization	Number	Colorado	Washington	Minnesota	Iowa
SOCIOECONOMIC STATUS					
Class Status (SES level): The Higher the Status, the More Republican	1	Yes		Yes	Yes
Income: The Higher the Income, the More Republican	2	Yes	No	Mostly Yes	Yes
Occupation: The "Higher" the Occupation, the More Republican	3		Yes		Yes
but: (a) With SES Controlled, Occupation Does Not Correlate with Vote		No	No	No	Mostly No
and: (b) White-Collar and Business Groups Have Greater Political Solidarity Than Workers, as Indicated by Party Preference		No	No	No	Yes
RELIGION					
Catholics Vote More Democratic Than Protestants	5	Yes		Yes	Yes
and: (a) Catholics Vote More Democratic Than Protestants Regardless of Their "Liberalism" or "Conservatism" in Attitudes on Political Issues		No		Mostly Yes	Yes
Catholics Personally Involved in Political Affairs Follow the Religious Lead in Voting Less Than Catholics Not So Involved	7	No		No	
Young People Are More Likely to Resolve the Cross-Pressures of Religion and SES in Favor of Class (in the Contemporary Era)	9				Yes
RESIDENCE					
Size of Community: Urban Residents Vote More Democratic Than Rural Residents	10	Mostly Yes	Yes	Yes	Yes
but: (a) Residents of Metropolitan Areas and Open Country Vote More Democratic Than Residents of Middle-size Towns and Cities		Yes; Yes	Yes; No	Yes	Yes; Yes

Finding or Generalization	Number	Colorado	Washington	Minnesota	Iowa
AGE					
Younger People Vote More Democratic Than Older People	12	Yes	Yes	No	Yes
but: (a) With SES Controlled, There Is No Age Difference		No	No	Yes	Mostly No
(b) The Age-Vote Relation Is Different in Different Religious Groups: Younger People Follow the Political Tendency of Their Religion Less—i.e., Younger Catholics Vote More Republican Than Older Catholics, and Younger Protestants Vote More Democratic Than Older Protestants		No; Yes		Yes; No	Yes; Yes
EDUCATION					
The Higher the Educational Level, the More Republican	13	Yes	Yes	Mostly Yes	Mostly Yes
but: (a) With SES Controlled, There Is No Relation between Education and Vote		Mostly Yes	Mostly No	No	Mostly Yes
SEX					
Women Vote More Republican Than Men	14	Yes	Yes	Yes	No
Women—Less Politicized Than Men—Follow the Class Lead in Voting Less Than Men	15	Mostly Yes	No	Mixed	Mixed
ORGANIZATIONAL MEMBERSHIP					
Organizational Membership Brings Out Latent Political Predispositions (e.g., Class Effects on Vote), Especially For the Less Interested	21	Yes; No		Yes; Yes	Yes; No
Membership in Labor Unions, by Self or Breadwinner, Is Correlated with Democratic Vote (in Some Studies with Other Factors Controlled)	22	Yes		Yes	No
FAMILY					
In the Overwhelming Majority of Cases (from 80	24				

Finding or Generalization	Number	Colorado	Washington	Minnesota	Iowa
Per Cent Up) the Respondent and His Immediate Family Agree in the Vote	25				Yes
The Vote of the Present Generation Is Correlated with the Vote of the Parents, Although Less So When in Conflict with Class or Religion			Yes		Yes
(c) The New Generation Is at First Only Superficially Involved in Politics		Yes	Mostly Yes	Mostly Yes	Yes
PERSONAL ASSOCIATIONS (FRIENDS AND CO-WORKERS) People Generally Agree in Vote with Their Friends and Coworkers	26				
and: (b) Political Homogeneity among Friends Increases with Age			Yes		
Voters Predisposed to the Republican Position by Class or Religion Have More Republican Friends	27		Mixed		
The more Homogeneous the Personal Associates, the Stronger the Conviction in Support of a Candidate	28		Yes		
TIME OF VOTE DECISION Low Degree of Interest in the Election Delays the Final Vote Decision	30		Yes	Yes	Yes
The More Cross-Pressures the Voter is Subject to, the Later His Final Vote Decision (Cross-Pressures, e.g., between Religion and SES, the Voter and His Family, Attitudes on Diffferent Issues, etc.)	31		Yes	Yes	Yes
and: (a) Low Interest and Cross-Pressures Are About Equally Strong in Delaying Decision and Their Joint Effect Is Quite Powerful			No	Yes	Mixed
Voters in Families Whose Other Members Have No Vote Intentions Decide Later Than Voters in Families Whose Other Members Do Have Vote Intentions	32		Yes; No	Yes; No	Yes; Yes
					Yes

Finding or Generalization	Number	Colorado	Washington	Minnesota	Iowa
Democratic Voters Decide Later Than Republican Voters	33		Yes	Yes	Yes
Voters Constant between Two Elections (1948 and 1952) Decide Earlier Than New or Shifting Voters	34		Yes	No	Yes
The Weaker the Voter's Partisanship, the Later His Final Decision	35		Mixed	Mixed	Mixed
There Is No Difference in Time of Decision by Educational Level of the Voters	36		No	Yes	No
Late Deciders Are More Likely to Split Their Vote between Parties Than Early Deciders	38		Yes	Yes	Yes
TURNOUT (i.e., Casting a Vote)					
The Higher the Political Interest, the Greater the Turnout	39	Yes	Yes	Yes	Yes
Men Vote More Than Women	40	Yes	Yes	Yes	Yes
but: (a) If Women Say They Intend to Vote, They Are More Apt Than Men Actually to Do So		No	No	No	No
The Higher the Educational Level, the More the Turnout	41	Mostly Yes	Mixed	Yes	Mostly Yes
but: (a) With Economic Status Controlled, Education Does Not Correlate with Turnout		Mostly Yes	Yes	Mostly Yes	Mostly Yes
(b) With Interest Controlled, Education Does Not Correlate with Turnout		Mostly Yes	Mostly Yes	Mostly Yes	Mostly Yes
The Older, the More Turnout	42	Yes	Yes	Yes	Yes
but: (a) There Is a Reversal Toward Less Turnout among People Over Fifty-five		No	Yes	Yes	No
The Higher the Economic Status, the Greater the Turnout	43	Yes	Yes	Yes	Yes
The Higher the Occupation, the Greater the Turnout	44	Mostly Yes	Mixed	Mostly Yes	Yes
Jews Vote More Than Catholics, and Protestants Slightly Less Than Catholics	45	No Data; No		No; No	No Data; Yes
Residents of Metropolitan Areas Vote More Than Residents of Towns and Cities, and They, in Turn, More Than Rural Residents	46	No; Yes	Yes; No		No Data; Yes
Members of Labor Unions Turn Out More Than Nonmembers in the Same Occupations	47	Mostly Yes	Mostly No	Mostly No	Mixed

Finding or Generalization	Number	Colorado	Washington	Minnesota	Iowa
People Whose Primary Groups (Family, Friends, Coworkers) Do Not Vote Tend Not to Vote Themselves	48		Yes	Yes	Yes
The Higher the Level of Political Information, the More Turnout	49		Mostly Yes	Yes	
The Less Firm the Position on Issues (i.e., the Less Differentiation or the More Indecision), the Less Turnout	50	Yes	Yes	Yes	Mostly Yes
The Stronger the Partisanship and Identification with the Party, the More Turnout	51	Yes	Yes	Yes	Yes
Constants in Vote Intention Vote More Than Party Changers or Crystallizers	52	Mostly Yes	Mixed	Mostly Yes	Mostly Yes
In This Period, People with a Republican Vote Intention Turn Out More Than People with a Democratic Vote Intention	53	Yes	Yes	Yes	Yes
Contact by Party Representatives Increases Turnout Especially among the Less Interested	54	Yes		Mixed	Yes
The More Communication Exposure, the More Turnout	55	Yes	Yes	Yes	Yes
More People Actually Vote on Election Day Than Are Interested in the Election or Than Express Their Interest in Political Activity of Any Other Kind	56	Yes	Yes	Yes	Yes
POLITICAL INTEREST AND ACTIVITY *Amount*					
About a Third of the Electorate Is Greatly Interested in the Election	57	No	No	Yes	No
About One-Fourth of the Electorate Do Anything to Get Their Candidate Elected (Including Attempts at Persuasion of Others)	58	Yes	Mostly Yes	Mostly Yes	Mostly Yes
Interest Increases Slightly During the Campaign but: (a) Although There Is Little Net Change in Interest During the Campaign, There Is a Considerable Amount of Gross Turnover	59	Yes	Yes	Yes	Yes

Finding or Generalization	Number	Colorado	Washington	Minnesota	Iowa
Sources of Political Interest					
The Higher the Educational Level, the Greater the Interest	60	Mostly Yes	Mostly Yes	Mostly Yes	Mostly Yes
The Higher the Socioeconomic Status, the Greater the Interest	61	Yes	Yes	Yes	Yes
and: (a) In This Period Republicans Are More Interested Than Democrats, and They Care More Who Wins		Yes	Yes	Yes	Yes
Men Have More Interest Than Women	62	Yes	Yes	No	Yes
Older People Have Greater Interest Than Younger	63	Mostly Yes	Yes	Yes	Yes
The More Cross-Pressures, the Lower the Interest	64	Yes	Yes	Yes	Mixed
The Greater the Partisanship, the Greater the Interest	66	Yes	Yes	Yes	Yes
As the Campaign Goes On, Political Factors Come to Influence Interest More and Social Factors Less	67	No	No	No	Mixed
Consequences of Political Interest					
Interested or Active Voters Have More Opinions on Political Issues Than Uninterested or Inactive Voters	68	Yes	Yes	Yes	Yes
Interested Voters Participate More in the Campaign Than Uninterested	69			Yes	Yes
Interested Voters Read and Listen More to Campaign Communications than Uninterested	70	Yes		Yes	Yes
The More Interested Voters Support Their Own Candidate More Fully on the Subsidiary Issues of Campaign	71	Yes	No	Mostly Yes	Yes
The More Interested Voters Are More Likely to Think That Their Own Candidate Will Win	72	Yes	Yes	Yes	Yes
Interested Voters Follow Their Own Class Dispositions Less Strongly Than the Uninterested	73	No	Yes	No	No
Although the Voters' Estimate of Their Political Interest Does Not Change on the Average during the Campaign, Certain Types of Behavior That Manifest Political Interest Increase (e.g., Political Discussion)	74	No			Yes

Finding or Generalization	Number	Colorado	Washington	Minnesota	Iowa
Opinion Leadership					
Opinion Leaders Exist in All Strata and Groups	75	Yes	Yes	Yes	Yes
Opinion Leaders Are Characterized by Their Greater Interest and Competence in Politics and by Their Greater Activity in Social Affairs	76		Yes		
Opinion Leaders Support Their Own Party Position More Strongly on the Subsidiary Issues Than Do Others	77		Yes		
Sources of Political Activity					
The More Extreme the Partisan Position on Issues, the More Political Activity	78	No	Mostly Yes	Mostly Yes	No
The More Concern with Issues, the More Political Activity	79	Yes	Yes	Yes	Yes
The Stronger the Feelings about the Candidate as a Personality, the More Political Activity	80	Yes	Mostly Yes	Yes	Yes
COMMUNICATION AND CONTACT					
Distribution by Volume					
Campaign Exposure Generates More of the Same, e.g., Exposure at an Earlier Time Increases Exposure at a Later	86	Mostly Yes			No
The Higher the Educational Level, the More Exposure to Campaign Communications	87	Mostly Yes		Mostly Yes	Mostly Yes
The Higher the SES Level, the More Exposure to Campaign Communications	88	Yes		Yes	Yes
Older People Expose to Campaign Communications More Than Younger	89	Mostly Yes		Mostly Yes	Mostly Yes
Men Expose to Campaign Communications More Than Women	90	Yes		Mostly Yes	Yes
Urban Residents Expose to Campaign Communications More Than Rural	91	Mostly Yes			No
People Already Decided on Their Vote Intention Expose to Campaign Communication More Than the Undecided, the Changers, or the Nonvoters	94	Yes		Yes	Yes

Finding or Generalization	Number	Colorado	Washington	Minnesota	Iowa
The People Who Expose More to Campaign Communications at One Period of the Campaign Also Tend to Do So at Another Period	96				Mostly Yes
People Who Tend to Expose More to Campaign Communications in One Medium Tend to Do So in Other Media	97	Yes		Mostly Yes	Yes
By Partisanship					
The Stronger the Partisanship, the More Exposure to Campaign Communications	98	Yes		No	Mixed
(c) People Are More Likely to Know Party Workers from Their Own Side	99	Yes		Yes	Yes
By Channels					
There Is a Differential Use of Newspapers and Radio by Republicans and Democrats: (a) Republicans Expose More to Newspapers, and Democrats to Radio	102	Yes; No		Yes; No	Yes; Yes
(b) Republicans Generally Prefer Newspapers, and Democrats Radio as Sources of Information about the Campaign	103	Yes; No	Yes; Yes	Yes; No	Yes; Yes
Much Political Talk is Centered in the Family; and Married Women Report Discussing Politics in the Family More Than Married Men, Especially in Quiet Times	105				Yes
Political Discussions Are Made Up Much More of Mutual Agreement Than of Disagreement	106		Yes		
Voters Who Talk Politics the Least Are Most Likely to Agree in Vote with Their Friends			Mixed		
Private Conversation Is Used More Than the Media as a Source of Political Arguments by Those Undecided in Vote Intention	108	No	No	Yes	No

Finding or Generalization	Number	Colorado	Washington	Minnesota	Iowa
Those Interested in Politics Are More Likely to Know Party Workers	109	Yes		Yes	Yes
Those Better Integrated into the Community Are More Likely to Know Party Workers	110				No
By Consequences					
The More Communication Exposure, the Less Indecision on Political Issues	111	Yes		Yes	Yes
Communication Exposure to Campaign Material Increases Interest in the Election	112	Yes		Yes	Yes
The More Exposure to the Campaign in the Mass Media, the More Strongly Voters Come to Feel about Their Candidate	113	Yes		Yes	Yes
The More Exposure to the Campaign in the Mass Media, the More Correct Information the Voters Have About the Campaign and the More Correct Their Perception of Where the Candidates Stand on the Issues	114	Yes			Yes
The More Exposure to the Campaign in the Mass Media, the Less Voters Change Their Position and the More They Turn Out on Election Day	116	Yes; Yes		Yes; Yes	No; Yes
Party Contact Increases Turnout Most Among Those Least Likely to Vote	121	Yes		No	Yes
and: (a) Party Contact Increases Turnout Most Among People of Long Residence in the Community					Mostly Yes
Party Contact Is Not Particularly Effective in Converting Voters from One Party to the Other	122	Yes		Yes	Yes
Party Contact Increases the Level of Interest in the Campaign	123	Yes		No	Yes
ISSUES					
Agreement on Issues					
Only a Small Minority of the Voters in a Party	124				

Finding or Generalization	Number	Colorado	Washington	Minnesota	Iowa
Agree with Their Candidate on "All" the Important Issues		No	No	No	No
and: (a) There Is Little Difference between Republicans and Democrats in Voting a Straight or Split Ticket		Yes	Yes	No	Yes
Republicans and Democrats Hold Different Opinions on a Variety of Particular Issues (e.g., Rich-Man/Poor-Man Issues, Foreign Affairs)	126	Yes	Yes	Yes	Yes
People in Different Class Positions Hold Different Opinions on Political Issues	128	Yes	Yes	Yes	Yes
Regular Republicans Hold Substantially the Same Opinions on Political Issues Regardless of Their Occupational, Educational, Union, or Religious Characteristics; the Same for Regular Democrats	133	Yes	Yes	Mostly Yes	Yes
The Stronger the Partisan Position on the Parties, the Issues, or the Candidates, the Stronger the Support Given the Candidates	136	No	Yes	Mostly Yes	No
and: (a) The Stronger the Partisan Position on the Parties, the Issues, or the Candidates, the More Straight-Ticket Voting		Yes	Mostly Yes	Yes	Yes
(b) The Stronger the Partisan Position on the Parties, the Issues, or the Candidates, the Less Consideration Given the Opposing Candidate			Mostly No		Mostly Yes
The Greater the Interest in the Election, the Sharper the Differences between Partisans on the Issues	137	Yes	Yes	Yes	Yes
Expectation of Winner There Is a Correlation between Expectation of Winner and Vote Intention	141	Yes	Yes	Yes	Mostly No
but: (a) There Are Different Explanations of That Fact: 1. Bandwagon Effect 2. Projection			Projection		

Finding or Generalization	Number	Colorado	Washington	Minnesota	Iowa
The Greater the Interest in the Election, the Closer the Relationship between Expectation of Winner and Vote Intention	142		Mostly Yes	Mostly Yes	Yes
The Greater the Interest in the Election, the Less Change in Expectation of Winner	143		Yes		
Expectation of Winner is More Variable Than Vote Intention	144		Yes		
Postelection Opinions					
There Was Less Anxiety about Result of Election after It Was Over Than There Was Anxiety about Its Possible Result Before	145		Yes		
Voters Believe More Strongly After the Election That Their Own Party Is Generally Superior on the Issues Than Before (i.e., Opinions Within a Party "Harden" During the Campaign)	147		Yes		
POLITICAL PERCEPTION					
Perception of Parties					
About Three-Fourths of the Voters Usually Think of Themselves as Republicans or Democrats (Party Identification)	159	Yes	Yes	Yes	No (Two-Thirds)
CHANGE IN POLITICAL POSITION					
Amount of Change					
From One Election to the Next, Over Three-Fourths of the Voters in Both Do Not Change Party Position	175	Mostly Yes	Yes	Mostly Yes	Mostly Yes
Changes in Party Position During the Campaign Are Fewer Than Changes between Campaigns	177	Yes	Yes	Yes	Yes
(a) In Over Half the Cases the Over-all Effect of the Campaign Is to Reinforce an Existing Party Position	179	Yes	Yes	Yes	Mostly Yes

Finding or Generalization	Number	Colorado	Washington	Minnesota	Iowa
(b) In About One-Sixth of the Cases the Campaign Has No Effect		No	Yes	No	No
(c) For Another One-Sixth It Has an Activating Effect		No	No	No	Mostly No
(d) For the Final One-Sixth It Has a Converting Effect		No	No	No	No
Only a Small Proportion (Under 10 Per Cent) of the Changers During a Campaign Move from One Party to the Other	180	12%	5%	12%	13%
Partisanship in Political Support Increases During the Campaign	181	Yes	Mixed	Yes	Mostly Yes
Direction of Change					
The Over-all Effect of the Campaign Was to Speed Up the between-Campaign Trend of Vote Movement	182	No	No	Yes	No
During a Campaign, When Voters Hold Opinions on Particular Issues Contrary to the Position of the Party They Support, There Is a Tendency for Them to Change Such "Inconsistent" Opinions to Fit Their Vote Intention	183				
and: (a) Hence the Campaign Results in Increased Consistency within Individuals and Groups and Increased Polarization between Groups within the Society		Yes	Mostly No	Mostly No	Mixed
The Majority of Voters Who Change Their Vote Intention Change It in the Direction of the Prevailing Vote of Their Group	184	Mostly No	Mostly No	Mixed	Mostly No
The People Who Do Not Expect to Vote During the Campaign but Then Actually Do Vote on Election Day Tend to Follow the Predominant Party Pressure	189	Yes	Probably No, but the Regional Panels Data Are Few and Inconclusive	Yes	No

Finding or Generalization	Number	Colorado	Washington	Minnesota	Iowa
in Their Locale					
Most of the Voters Who Leave Their Party Position for Indecision Later Return to Their Original Party Position; Most of Those Who Leave for the Other Party Do Not Return	190	Yes; Yes	Yes; Mixed	Yes; Yes	Yes; Mixed
Most Conversion in Vote During the Campaign Is Composed of Movement between Moderate Positions on the Two Sides	192	No	No	No	No
Conditions of Change					
Voting Changes between Generations Are Affected by the Political Preferences of Social Strata: among Catholics, Republican Fathers "Lose" More Children to the Opposition; among Protestants, Democratic Fathers "Lose" More (and Similarly for Occupational Groups)	193		Yes		Yes
and: (a) Between Generations—and Especially in Homogeneous Social Strata—It Is the Group Tradition in Voting That Survives Better than Individual Father-to-Son Preferences			Mostly Yes		Mostly Yes
Turnover in Vote During the Campaign Is Not So Great As Turnover in Opinion on Issues	195	Yes		Yes	Yes
The Less Homogeneous the Family in Its Political Position, the More Change among Its Members	196				No
The Less Homogeneous One's Friends and Coworkers in Political Position, the More Change	197		Yes		
and: (a) Shifts in a Vote are Related to the Political Inclination of One's Friends (i.e., Those with Republican Friends Shift More toward the Republicans, and Those with Democratic Friends Shift More toward the Democrats)			Yes		
The Less Interested the Voter Is in the Election, the More Likely He Is to Change His Vote Preference During the Campaign, in Any Direction	198	Yes	Yes	Yes	Yes

Finding or Generalization	Number	Colorado	Washington	Minnesota	Iowa
The More Cross-Pressures and Inconsistencies the Voter Is Subject to, the More Change in His Vote Preference	199	Yes	No	Yes	Yes
People Who Do Not Discuss Politics Much Are Relatively Unstable in Their Voting	200	Yes	Yes	Yes	Yes
and: (a) People Who Do Not Discuss Politics Much Are More Likely to Follow the Secular Trend of the Times		Yes	No	Yes	Yes
Voters Who Have Previously Changed Their Party Position Are More Likely to Change Again Than Those Who Had Not Previously Changed	201	Yes	Yes	Yes	Yes
The Changers Who Moved from One Party to the Other During the Campaign Were	202				
(a) Least Interested in the Election		Yes	Yes	Mostly Yes	Mostly Yes
(b) Least Concerned about the Outcome			Yes	Yes	Yes
(c) Least Attentive to Campaign Communications		Yes	Yes	Yes	Yes
(d) Last to Decide on Their Vote Decision					
(e) Most Likely to Be Influenced by Personal Persuasion Than by Political Issues		No		No	
Voters Who Change from One Party to the Other Support Their Initial Candidate on the Issues Less Strongly Than the Nonchangers	203	Yes	Yes	Yes	Yes
Voters Who Change from One Election to Another (1948-1952) Hold Opinions on a Variety of Political Issues in between the Opinions of Regular Republicans and Regular Democrats	205	Yes	Yes	Yes	Yes
Voters Who Change Parties Occupy an Intermediate Position in Social Class between the Nonchangers	207	No	Yes	Yes	No
Within Social Strata with Unambiguous Political Preferences the Political Majority Is More Stable Than the Political Minority	208	Mostly Yes	Yes	Yes	Yes

12

HINDSIGHT AND SIGNIFICANCE

By William A. Glaser

Critics often claim that surveys collect miscellaneous facts in a haphazard way that misses the "true meaning" of an election. And so it seemed, as they conducted the Regional Panels surveys of 1950, that the pollsters were designing questionnaires without important central themes and were reporting heterogeneous and meaningless facts about voters whose behavior as individuals lacked critical significance.[1] But if one looks back at 1950, no one else seemed to have divined any central meanings in the election results. Indeed, the outcome of American midterm elections usually have such a heterogeneous appearance, as Key (1953, Chap. 17) and others have noted, that off year balloting usually is thought to have no central meaning.

By accident, we are publishing our study over a decade after the surveys were conducted, and as a result, we can write as historians as well as pollsters. A report of a survey usually focuses on the situation during that particular year, but now we can look back at 1950 in the perspective of previous and subsequent elections and can discern its meaning in historical perspective. Probably the significance of any event is best discovered by hindsight. In retrospect, we can now see that we selected topical events and contemporary

---

1. The questionnaire is chiefly to be blamed on McPhee, then of the *Denver Post* Poll.

rhetoric when designing and first analyzing the Regional Panels surveys, and we missed certain crucial historical themes. But although our present hindsight is superior to our assumptions at that time, it is also superior to the guesses of other onlookers then—including some who might have thought the polls were missing something.

AN OVERVIEW

During the campaign, the Truman administration had tried to secure a national endorsement of its policies, while its Republican critics had predicted that a national tide would destroy the Fair Deal. But the election returns at first inspection seemed to lack any clear-cut outcome. Just as in most midterm election campaigns, different issues had been emphasized by local candidates in different parts of the country, and the kinds of candidates who won in some districts lost in others. The Republicans gained seats in the Senate and House and captured a majority of the governorships, but neither party won a decisive majority on a national scale.

In retrospect, however, certain major themes appear. 1950 was a critical election in a period of political change. It was a final stage in the erosion of the New Deal majority, and it foreshadowed the Republican return to power in 1952. A sifting of leaders and of issues took place, and the result was a weakening of the national Democratic Party and a strengthening of its opposition. By emphasizing the kinds of issues that would appeal to their local electorates and by making effective personal contacts with local constituents, certain new leaders arose and other old leaders were re-elected. Some new issues were tested and found to be effective vote-getters, while some old issues were found to be obsolete and passed out of partisan rhetoric thereafter.[2]

2. Detailed descriptions of the 1950 campaign and election results have been published elsewhere. The outcomes of the races for national offices appear in Clerk of the House (1951) and *The New International Year Book* (1950, pp. 169-170). Summaries of the propaganda and tactics by principal pressure groups in 1950 have been written by LaPalombara (1952), Calkins (1952), and Kelley (1956, Chap. 3). Some articles have been published about the campaigns in three of the four states where the Regional Panels surveys were conducted. About Iowa, see Millsap (1951) and *The New York Times* for June 4 and November 1, 1950. About Colorado, see Martin (1951), Irwin (1955), and *The New York Times* for October 20, 1950. Washington was described by Bone (1951) and by *The New York Times* for May 14, May 15, and October 23, 1950.

LEADERS

Emergence of New Leaders

In every midterm election, balloting in certain localities will project some previously lesser-known men into power. Some new faces and some unexpected sources of power were revealed by the 1950 election results, and the short-run consequences were detrimental to the Democrats.

Above all, the election was a springboard for Senator Joseph McCarthy of Wisconsin. He had first become nationally noticed in early 1950 by his charges that a pro-Communist fifth column dominated the State Department and the White House. A Senate subcommittee headed by Senator Millard Tydings of Maryland had rejected his charges. In the 1950 election Tydings and Senator Scott Lucas of Illinois were both defeated for re-election by Republican candidates who repeated McCarthy's charges and who were aided by him in their campaigns. Victories by some other McCarthy supporters in Senate and House races convinced many political leaders that McCarthy had widespread support among American voters. The Senator himself was not a candidate in 1950, but the victories of his allies made the election the beginning of his four-year period of national influence.

Some other leaders gained new offices in 1950 and were destined to rise higher in later years during the Eisenhower Administration. Representative Richard M. Nixon was elected Senator from California, and former Representative Everett M. Dirksen won the Senate seat from Illinois.

Few important new leaders were produced by the 1950 election results in the states where the Regional Panels surveys were conducted. One of them, however, was to contribute important influence in swinging the western states behind Dwight Eisenhower in 1952. When the 1950 campaign began, Dan Thornton was a wealthy cattle rancher with little political experience beyond service in the Colorado State Senate. When the popular Republican gubernatorial candidate died in Colorado six weeks before election day, a Republican vacancy committee hastily substituted Thornton. Campaigning effectively and benefiting from a Republican trend, Thornton unseated the less colorful Democratic governor. In subsequent years Thornton acted as a counterweight to the Old Guard who had previously dominated the Republican Party in Colorado, and at the 1952 national convention he was one of Eisenhower's principal supporters.

In the Regional Panels states, the election results spurred the careers of two Democrats but they were not to achieve high-level leadership until after the rise and decline of the Eisenhower Administration. In 1950 Representative Eugene McCarthy was re-elected to his second term by a large majority in the fourth District in Minnesota. In Colorado, Representative John Carroll was defeated for the United States Senate by only a narrow margin, despite the Republican trend in the country. When the liberal wing of the Democratic Party staged its comeback in the 1958 elections, both McCarthy and Carroll were elected to the United States Senate.

Re-election of Old Leaders

In the sorting-out of American political leaders in the election of 1950, some gained increased power by re-election. In Congress, maintenance of power depends on seniority and demonstrations of electoral strength, and in 1950 some of the impressive re-election victories benefited Republican opponents of the Truman Administration. The most notable victory that year was the overwhelming re-election of Senator Robert Taft in Ohio. The size of his majority convinced him and his supporters that he possessed heretofore unsuspected popularity at the grass roots and led to his bid for the 1952 presidential nomination. But while the Ohio results encouraged the power and hopes of the Old Guard Republicans, elsewhere other re-election victories strengthened those who wanted another kind of presidential nominee. While Taft was winning his biggest majority in Ohio, the rival who repeatedly frustrated his presidential ambitions, Governor Thomas Dewey, was receiving an equally strong mandate from the voters of New York. Thus, 1950 not only strengthened the Republican Party, but it increased the power of the two rival factions within the party and led to the bitter convention disputes of 1952.

In the Regional Panels states, some re-election victories enhanced the positions of Old Guard Republicans in Congress. One was Senator Eugene Millikin, chairman of the Senate Republican Policy Committee and an ally of Senator Taft; another was Senator Bourke Hickenlooper of Iowa; a third was Representative Ben Jensen of the Seventh District of Iowa. A Congressman since 1938 and a member of the strategic Committee on Appropriations, Jensen then (and now) has been gradually following the kind of career that produces great power in the House of Representatives, namely, a combination of regular re-election from a one-party agricultural district and conscientious but unpublicized legislative work. In the Fifth Congressional District of Minnesota, a convincing re-election victory went to Walter Judd, a more liberal Republican who was one of the principal critics of the Truman administration's policy on China.

But not all the re-election victories contributed to the Republican tide of the early 1950's. Since midterm elections are conducted in a decentralized manner, they result in victories for some leaders whose positions are contrary to the national trend and who will become the nucleus for a comeback by the defeated party. For example, in the Regional Panels state of Washington, Senator Warren Magnuson was re-elected by a large majority. A New Deal Democrat, he won because of his effective electioneering, because he had secured many economic benefits for the state, and because the Democratic Party and its labor union allies campaigned efficiently for him.

Defeat of Old Leaders

A midterm election can become an important stage in a national trend if it results in the defeat of some important leaders. No major election upsets occurred in the Regional Panels states, but elsewhere four of the principal Democratic Senators were defeated. They were Scott Lucas of Illinois, Majority Leader of the Senate; Francis J. Myers of Pennsylvania, Majority Whip of the Senate; Millard Tydings of Maryland, Chairman of the Armed Services Committee; and Elbert Thomas, Chairman of the Labor Committee. The simultaneous defeat of four such important leaders weakened the power and prestige of the Democrats. No comparable defeats of incumbents were experienced by the Republican Party in 1950.

ISSUES

Emergence of New Issues

A midterm election not only is a sifting of leaders in accordance with certain national trends, but also it is a testing and selection among issues. In 1950, certain new issues were tested for their vote-getting effectiveness, and other older issues were again introduced. Just as in the sifting of leaders, the selection of issues in 1950 was detrimental to the Democrats and pointed forward to the national Republican victory two years later.

The three main issues that keynoted the 1952 Republican campaign—Korea, Communism, and corruption—were first used widely by Republican campaigners in 1950. The Truman administration was blamed for failing to prevent the Korean conflict. Korea was to become a more embarrassing issue for the Administration a month after election day, when the Chinese defeated the American army and when the protracted military stalemate began. The Communism-in-government issue had been intensified during 1950 because of the convictions of Alger Hiss and Judith Coplon and because of Senator McCarthy's accusations, and the issue would increase under McCarthy's leadership during the next few years. The corruption charges were first leveled against the Truman administration and the Democratic Party as the result of the Kefauver Committee's work in 1950, and new scandals would later be revealed by other congressional investigations. Because nearly all the victorious Republicans in 1950 had campaigned against Korea, Communism, and corruption, and because later circumstances would underscore these issues further, these topics soon came to dominate American politics.

Continuation of Old Issues

Some of the traditional partisan rhetoric was again used by Republican and Democratic campaigners in 1950 and seemed successful enough to remain in each party's arsenal for the next election. Most Republicans—including nearly all candidates in the Regional Panels states—denounced the Democrats for excessive government spending, waste, bureaucracy, and regimentation. On the other hand, most Democrats pointed to their party's past accomplishments in social welfare, and some candidates proposed extensions in housing and in pensions.

Even these traditional issues foreshadowed the imminent defeat of the Democrats. After being in power nationally for nearly twenty years and after having enacted much of their program, the Democrats had very few attractive vote-getting issues left. In a full-employment economy, the welfare issue seemed boring, less urgent than it once had been, and less important than some conflicting goals. For example, in the Regional Panels state of Washington, the voters in 1950 adopted a referendum *reducing* the state's pension system in order to make it financially solvent.

Defeat of Old Issues

When advocates of certain positions are defeated in midterm elections, their viewpoints will be avoided by the survivors who run the government and who conduct the next election. In 1950, a number of the Truman administration's principal policies succumbed in this way.

One of the Regional Panels states, Iowa, became the electoral testing site for the Administration's farm program. The so-called Brannan Plan was designed to keep consumer prices low by permitting farm goods to sell at competitive market prices, but farmers' incomes would be supported by subsidies. Iowa seemed a reasonable choice for a vote of confidence in the Administration's farm program, since Truman himself had carried the state in 1948 and since the Republican Senator Hickenlooper seemed vulnerable. Therefore, against Hickenlooper the Democrats nominated Albert J. Loveland, the Undersecretary of Agriculture and an author of the Brannan Plan. Hickenlooper won by an unexpected landslide, Republicans won most other Senate and House seats in the Western farm states, and the Brannan Plan was dead.

Another of the Truman administration's policies was national health insurance. Like the Brannan Plan, it had been pigeon-holed by hostile Congressional committees during 1950 and became a major issue during the election. The American Medical Association conducted a nation-wide campaign against the proposal, and most Republicans publicly condemned the plan. The election in the Regional Panels state of Colorado was considered one of the principal tests since the Senate race pitted an Old Guard Republican against a New Dealer and since many of the state's doctors participated in the Republican campaign. The victories of Senator Millikin in Colorado and of other Republican opponents of national health insurance were generally interpreted as the voters' mandate against the proposal.

Certain other Fair Deal issues were raised by leaders of the Truman administration, but their minor role in the campaign and in the election results seemed to eliminate them as important forces thereafter. For example, during his successful campaign for re-election in 1948, President Truman had advocated Taft-Hartley Act revisions and price controls. Congress had failed to adopt his recommendations after his re-election, and by 1950 these promises seemed to be half-forgotten issues of the past. Price controls and excess profits taxes were advocated by some officials as an emergency measure during the Korean crisis, but such policies were no longer an important element in the Fair Deal's domestic economic program. The facts that the Taft-Hartley Act and price controls were rarely debated in the 1950 campaign and that many of the Fair Deal's critics in Congress were re-elected were further evidence of how the Democrats were losing many of the important issues they needed in order to win a national presidential election.

Erosion of Democratic Strength

The weakening of the Fair Deal issues and the increased allure of Republican arguments produced a fundamental vulnerability in Democratic voting support while solidifying Republican unity. During 1948, as in most presidential elections, voters who identified themselves with each party tended to agree with the issue positions of that party (Berelson, 1954, pp. 194-199). Such a compatibility of party identification and opinions always serves to rally and stabilize the voting strength of each party.

But during 1950, the decline of Democratic issues and the rise of Republican issues began to unstabilize the voting strength of the Democratic Party. Many Democrats were becoming critical of the Truman administration on few or many issues, a condition that foreshadowed the massive Democratic defections to the Republican presidential candidate in 1952 and 1956. Meanwhile during 1950, Republican voters were becoming increasingly wedded to their party's issue positions.

Evidence of these trends appears in the Regional Panels survey data. Table 12-1 shows the relationship between party identification and scores on the Index of Issue Opinion described in Appendix C; the index measures whether Democratic or Republican opinions were held on five leading issues.[2] Less than half the Democrats

2. Many of the issues of 1950 were charges against the Truman administration, and the Regional Panels questionnaires were based on the topical controversies of the time. Therefore, some of the items are "loaded" against the Democrats in the sense that only an extreme partisan would adopt an in-

agreed with their party on most or all issues; over one-quarter tended to hold Republican views. On the other hand, nearly all the Republicans agreed with their party. Another indication of future trouble for Democratic candidates was that most respondents giving no party identification held Republican opinions. (Table 12-1 gives the pre-election opinions of all the Regional Panels respondents. The distribution of opinions remained almost the same during the campaign.)

Table 12-1—Party Identification and Opinions about Five Issues

	Democrats	Republicans	No Party
All Republican	12%	64%	37%
Majority Republican	16	23	20
Split	31	9	24
Majority Democratic	26	2	10
All Democratic	15	2	9
	100%	100%	100%
	(n = 765)	(n = 559)	(n = 481)

CONCLUSION

THE 1950 ELECTION, like other midterm campaigns, thus combined certain local characteristics with other features that fit into a long-term national trend. The fate of many Democratic candidates and issues showed that 1950 would be the New Deal's last stand. Important Democrats were defeated, and some of the Administration's most adamant opponents were strengthened. Some of the Truman administration's new proposals were discredited in electoral tests, and some of its old issues were becoming obsolete. While the Administration was running out of issues, the 1950 campaign showed the vote-getting effectiveness of new issues that would keynote the Republicans' victorious campaign of 1952—namely Korea, Communism, and corruption. 1950 did not produce the united Republican leadership that would take over the party and country in 1952, but it did strengthen the party as a whole and it did provide an impetus

---

flexibly pro-Democratic position—for example, asking whether the respondent agrees with the statement, "Democratic administrations have made many bad mistakes in foreign affairs." However, not all our items are "loaded" in this way. Whether the individual items seem pro-Democratic, pro-Republican, or neutral, issue loyalty is greater among Republicans than among Democrats.

to the various factions who would compete for the presidential nomination at the 1952 convention.

Probably many midterm elections play such a historical role as
a rehearsal for the fundamental political changes effected in subsequent presidential elections. Other midterm elections may perform
other functions for the political system, such as consolidating
previous changes, aggravating or moderating national political dead-
locks, or reinforcing political apathy. Key (1955) has suggested
ways of differentiating types of elections, particularly the presidential
elections that produce basic historical changes. In similar vein, types
of midterm election probably can be identified in American political
history. And in making such judgments, contemporary survey data
can be combined advantageously with historical hindsight.

SAMPLES

THE POPULATIONS sampled were as follows: the entire states of Colorado and Washington; the Third, Fourth, and Fifth Congressional Districts of Minnesota, comprising the cities and suburbs of Minneapolis and St. Paul; and the Seventh Congressional District in southwestern Iowa. Representative samples of each of these populations were drawn by area sampling in Colorado, Washington, and Iowa, and by quota sampling in Minnesota. The pre-election interviews were conducted during the first and second weeks of October, and the sample sizes were: Colorado 473; Washington 441; Minnesota 492; and Iowa 476.

The postelection reinterviews with the same respondents were held in mid-November. Not all of the respondents could be contacted because of the project's limited money, time, and personnel. Such "panel mortality" reduced the number of cases successfully reinterviewed to: Colorado 336; Washington 378; Minnesota 397; and Iowa 251. (Statistics derived from the complete pre-election samples, may be accurate estimates of magnitudes in the population; but the readers of this book should realize that, since panel mortality reduces the uninterested and unstable members of samples more heavily than the others, statistics based on the postelection interviews should be interpreted only as evidence for relations among variables and not as literal estimates of population magnitudes.)

QUESTIONNAIRES

TWO BASIC QUESTIONNAIRES were prepared, one for the pre-election interview and one for the postelection interview. Each of the basic questionnaires was used in all four states. Each polling organization added extra questions, either about politics or about other topics. Occasionally one of the basic questions was omitted or modified in one of the states, usually because it did not apply to the election campaign there.

Following are the basic questionnaires plus many of the extra questions asked in individual states. Throughout this book, we have indicated when the basic questions were asked in all four states and when a question was omitted from one of the interviews. There were slight variations among the samples in the order of questions. All the questionnaires and codebooks are on file at the Roper Opinion Research Center, Williams College, Williamstown, Mass.

I. Pre-election Questionnaire

(A) Basic questions:
  (Introduction read by interviewer): This study is being made by members of the American Association for Public Opinion Research. Time and money is being donated by staff members of Central Surveys, Inc., The Colorado Poll, Columbia University, The Minnesota Poll, The University of Chicago, Washington State College, and others. Your opinions are strictly confidential. Statistical results of all interviews averaged together will be published in scientific journals, newspapers, and college publications.
  1. How much interest would you say you have in this year's elections—a great deal, quite a lot, not very much, or none at all?

  A great deal_____   Not very much_____   Don't know_____
  Quite a lot_____   None at all_____

2. During the past week (7 days), can you recall reading anything in the newspapers about the elections or election candidates?
Yes, read something past week_____
Saw, did not read (volunteered)_____
No, not read or don't know_____

2a. (IF READ OR SAW) What was it? (Story, editorial, ad? Who said it? What was it about?)

3. During the past week (7 days), can you recall hearing anything on the radio about the elections or election candidates?
Yes, heard something past week_____
Heard, paid no attention (volunteered)_____
No, not heard or don't know_____

3a. (IF HEARD EITHER WAY) What was it? (News, commentator, speech, commercial? What was it about? Who said it?)

4. During the past week (7 days), can you recall discussing the elections and election candidates, or hearing talk about them?
Yes, heard actively, discussed_____
Heard, paid no attention (volunteered)_____
No, not heard or don't know_____

4a. (IF HEARD EITHER WAY) What was this occasion? (With family, friends, work people? What was it about?)

5. Regardless of how you hope the _____(state)_____ elections will come out, what do you *really expect*—a Democratic win, OR a very close Democratic edge, OR a very close Republican edge, OR a Republican win?

Democratic win_____	Republican edge, close_____
Democratic edge, close_____	Republican win_____
Tossup, very close_____	Don't know_____

6. A lot of people didn't get to vote last time in 1948—did you happen *not* to get to the polls then?
Respondent voted in 1948_____
Respondent did not, doubtful_____

6a. (ASK ALL) Which man did you prefer—Truman or Dewey?
Voted (or would have) for Truman_____
Voted (or would have) for Dewey_____
No choice, don't recall_____

7. (Interviewer then ascertained respondent's registration status by informal questioning)
Registered_____
Intend to register_____
Not registered, or vague (skip to 9)_____

8. (IF REGISTERED OR INTEND TO) how strongly do you feel about going to the polls to vote *this year*—will you be sure to go, OR fairly likely to go, OR go if you can find time, OR probably not go *this year?*

Sure to go_____   Probably not go_____

Fairly likely_____   Don't know_____

Go if find time_____

(INCLUDE NON-VOTERS IN ALL SUBSEQUENT QUESTIONING, WITH APPROPRIATE WORDING)

9. When (if) you vote(d) for ____(major office)____, between _____ and _____, which is more important to you: The man himself, OR the stand he takes on public issues, OR his political party?

Mainly the man, his ability, judgment_____

Mainly his stand on issues, his ideas_____

Mainly his political party, vote party_____

Combination (what?)_____

Don't know_____

10. Do you think a man in Washington, like _____ or _____, should decide questions according to his own judgment or according to the desires of people back home?

Mainly according own judgment_____

According both, but final decision own judgment_____

According both, but final decision on what people want_____

Mainly according people desires_____

Other qualities (what?)_____

Don't know_____

11. I'm going to read you some arguments that come up in the election. For each will you tell me if you agree or disagree?

11a. (FOR EACH) How strongly do you feel about that?

	Agree	Disagree	Mixed— Don't Know	Strongly	Not Quite So Strongly
The *Republicans* would cut down *waste and bureaucracy* in government?	_____	_____	_____	_____	_____
We need strict price controls and *excess profits taxes immediately?*	_____	_____	_____	_____	_____
Defense and war problems can best be handled by the *Democrats?*	_____	_____	_____	_____	_____
Democratic administrations have made many *bad* mistakes in *foreign affairs?*	_____	_____	_____	_____	_____
Democrats have been too easy on *Communists in America?*	_____	_____	_____	_____	_____
The Taft-Hartley *labor* law is *unfair* to working people?	_____	_____	_____	_____	_____

	Agree	Disagree	Mixed— Don't Know	Strongly	Not Quite So Strongly
We should go *even farther* with *government welfare benefits* such as housing, medical care, and farm price supports?	_____	_____	_____	_____	_____
President Truman is a *poor* leader	_____	_____	_____	_____	_____

12. Which of the men on this list do you feel you know a little something about? (Who he is or what he does.)

Check Those Known:	Democrats	Republicans
Senatorial candidates	_____	_____
Congressional candidates	_____	_____
Gubernatorial candidates	_____	_____
_____ (other state) candidates	_____	_____
_____ (other state) candidates	_____	_____

(All questions about lists of candidates and lists of issues were answered with the aid of cards handed to respondents. For the names of all candidates in the Regional Panels states, see Appendix D, *infra*.)

13. As things look *now* (If you were going to vote), how would you choose in each of these contests? (Well, which man would you lean toward?)

13a. (FOR EACH) How strongly do you feel about that one?

	Democrat	Republican	No Leaning	Strongly	Not So Strongly
Senate	_____	_____	_____	_____	_____
Congress	_____	_____	_____	_____	_____
Governor	_____	_____	_____	_____	_____
_____ (other state)	_____	_____	_____	_____	_____
_____ (other state)	_____	_____	_____	_____	_____

14. (IF STRONGLY IN MAJOR CONTEST) Do you have any special reasons for feeling strongly on the _____ vs. _____ contest?

15. Is this the first time you have thought much about the ___(major race)___ vs. _____ contest, or had you decided before? When did you decide?

Just now, hadn't thought much_____
This month, since Oct. 1st_____
Earlier fall, Aug. to Sept._____
May to August, last summer_____
Before May, always for him_____
Don't know, very vague_____

16. Which political party did your parents generally favor?

Democratic mainly_____	Vote men both parties_____
Republican mainly_____	Don't recall_____

17. *All in all,* do you consider yourself mainly a Democrat, mainly a Republican, or neither one?
Mainly Democrat____   Mainly Republican____
Neither, other party, don't know____

18. (Sex of respondent estimated by interviewer):
Male____   Female____

19. (Age of respondent asked by interviewer):
21-29____   40-54____
30-39____   55 and over____

20. (Occupation of family breadwinner asked by interviewer):
Job_____   Industry_____

21. (Union of family breadwinner asked by interviewer):
C.I.O.____   Other union____
A.F.L.____   No union____

22. What was the last school you attended?
Grade____   Completed high____
Some high____   College____

23. (Religion of respondent asked by interviewer):
Protestant____   Jewish____
Catholic____   None____

24. (City size estimated by interviewer):
Metropolitan district____   Rural non-farm (under 25,000)____
10,000 to 50,000____   Rural farm____
2,500 to 9,999____

25. (Socioeconomic Status, or SES: In Colorado, Minnesota, and Iowa, interviewers rated each respondent according to his visible socioeconomic level. The categories are those widely used in polling: A ("wealthy"), B ("upper middle class"), C ("middle class"), and D ("poor"). In Colorado and Iowa, the middle class was divided into C+ and C−. In selecting specific indicators of socioeconomic status and in assigning respondents to particular categories, interviewers followed the instructions in *Interviewing for N.O.R.C.* (Denver: National Opinion Research Center, 1945), pp. 62-67. In the Washington sample, respondents were asked their annual family income, and we have used this information instead of S.E.S.)

(B) Special Colorado questions:
1. From what you've heard or read about _____, what do you like most about him? (Asked separately about the Democratic and Republican candidates for Governor and Senator.)
2. What do you like least about _____? (Asked separately about the Democratic and Republican candidates for Governor and Senator.)

(C) Special Minnesota question:
   In the 1948 race for Govenor, did you vote for _____ or
   _____?
   Democratic candidate_____   Don't remember_____
   Republican candidate_____   Didn't vote for governor_____
   Other candidate_____

(D) Special Washington questions:
   1. Of all these problems listed, which four do you feel are of most concern to you and people like yourself? Please rank them in order of
   importance. Feel free to suggest any problems which you feel should
   be added to the list.
      General foreign policy_____
      Communism in the United States_____
      Recession and unemployment
      Strikes and labor disputes_____
      Inflation and high cost of living_____
      Columbia Valley Authority_____
      How much aid should we give to aged
         (referenda 176 and 178 in state election)_____
      The state going into debt (income vs. sales tax)_____
      Public vs. private electric power_____
   2. Since this is an election year, we would like to know which political
   party you feel has the best program to meet the problems you have
   mentioned:
      Democratic_____   Both_____
      Republican_____   Don't know_____
   3. (IF RESPONDENT REPORTED DISCUSSING POLITICS, IN
   ANSWER TO BASIC QUESTION 4, *supra*): When you and your
   friends discuss political questions, do you usually:
      Just listen_____
      Take an equal share in the conversation_____
      Especially try to convince the others of your ideas_____
   4. In the coming election, are most of the people you associate with:
      Definitely planning to go to the polls_____
      Undecided about going to the polls_____
      Or, will they probably not go to the polls_____
      Some are, some are not_____
      Don't know_____
   5. Which political party do most of the people you associate with generally support:
      Democratic_____
      Republican_____
      Socialist Labor_____

Support no party, independent voters_____
Back both Democrats and Republicans_____
Don't know_____

6. (IF RESPONDENT HAS ALREADY DECIDED TO VOTE FOR A CANDIDATE FOR SENATE): How much difference would it make to you if your favorite candidate for Senator lost this year?

A lot_____   Not too much_____
Some_____   No difference at all_____

7. Would any of these things keep you from voting: unpleasant weather? big lines at polling places? unexpected guests?

One or more of them would_____
One or more of them might_____

8. Would you mind telling me who won the Democratic nomination for Senator in the recent primary election

9. Would you mind telling me who won the Republican nomination for Senator in the recent primary election?

10. Both candidates for Senator, Mr. Williams and Mr. Magnuson, have made various statements regarding the problems you mentioned. Which of the two candidates has the best approach to the solution of the problems you chose?

Williams, Republican_____   Both_____
Magnuson, Democrat_____   Don't know_____

11. For whom did you vote for Senator in the recent primary election?

Magnuson, Democrat_____   Don't remember_____
Williams, Republican_____   Didn't vote_____
Others_____

12. How about the last time you remember discussing the elections, or hearing talk about them, was it mainly about:

Democratic candidates_____   Neutral, both_____
Or about Republican candidates_____   Can't say, no answer_____

13. How long have you lived in the State of Washington?

Less than one year_____   Eleven to fifteen years_____
One to five years_____   Sixteen to twenty years_____
Six to ten years_____

(E) Special Iowa questions:

1. How about your (husband, wife) . . . is there any chance (he, she) won't go to the polls and vote this year?

Spouse will vote_____
Will not vote_____
No spouse_____
Spouse, but don't know, doubtful, some chance not_____

1a. (ASK ALL) What party does (he, she) generally favor?

Democrats, mainly_____   Vote for men in both parties_____
Republicans_____   Don't know which_____

2. Think of your best friend outside the family—(pause). Would you guess there's a chance he or she won't go to the polls and vote this year?
> Friend will vote_____
> Will not vote_____
> Don't know, doubtful, some chance not_____

2a. (ASK ALL) What party does he or she generally favor?
> Democrats mainly_____   Votes for men in both parties_____
> Republicans_____   Don't know which_____

3. (AFTER BASIC QUESTION 11): If your candidate for Senator, Mr. Hickenlooper or Mr. Loveland, disagreed with you on a lot of these things we have been talking about, would you vote against him, OR respect his judgment enough to stick with him?
> Vote against him_____   Stick with him_____
> Consider it, depends_____   Don't know_____

4. Have you ever met any of these men or seen them personally? (CHECK THOSE MET OR SEEN PERSONALLY.)

	Democrats	*Republicans*
Senate	_____	_____
Congress	_____	_____
Governor	_____	_____
(other state)	_____	_____
(other state)	_____	_____

5. How long have you lived in _____(county or city)_____ ?
> Less than year_____   Eleven to twenty years_____
> One to five years_____   More than twenty_____
> Six to ten years_____

II. Post-election Questionnaire

(A) Basic questions:

1. How much interest would you say you had in this year's elections:
> Great deal_____   Not very much_____   Don't know_____
> Quite a lot_____ None at all_____

2. According to your impressions of the election campaign, which of these issues or questions were talked about most often right here in _____? (CHECK ALL MENTIONED)
> Govt. spending and economy_____
> Controls on prices and profits_____
> Defense and war preparedness_____
> Foreign affairs (Russia, China, Korea, Europe)_____
> Communists in America_____
> Labor unions and strikes_____
> The job President Truman has been doing_____
> Government welfare programs of the New Deal and Fair Deal_____
> None, don't know_____

3. Were any of these things especially important in helping you decide for ___(major contest)___ or _____? (Even if you didn't vote?)

      Govt. spending and economy_____
      Controls on prices and profits_____
      Defense and war preparedness_____
      Foreign affairs (Russia, China, Korea, Europe)_____
      Communists in America_____
      Labor unions and strikes_____
      The job President Truman has been doing_____
      Government welfare programs of the New Deal and Fair Deal_____
      None, don't know_____

4. Here are some arguments that came up in the elections. For each would you tell me if you agree or disagree?

4a. (FOR EACH) How strongly do you feel about that one:

	Agree	Disagree	Mixed—Don't Know	Strongly	Not Quite So Strongly
The *Republicans* would cut down *waste and bureaucracy* in government?	___	___	___	___	___
We need strict price controls and *excress profits taxes* immediately?	___	___	___	___	___
Defense and war problems can best be handled by the *Democrats?*	___	___	___	___	___
Democratic administrations have made many *bad* mistakes in *foreign affairs?*	___	___	___	___	___
The *Taft-Hartley* labor law is *unfair* to working people?	___	___	___	___	___
We should go *even farther* with *government welfare programs,* such as housing, medical care, and farm price supports?	___	___	___	___	___
President Truman is a *poor* leader?	___	___	___	___	___
In *Europe and Asia,* we are trying to take *too much responsibility* for other people's problems	___	___	___	___	___
Democrats have been too easy on *Communists in America*	___	___	___	___	___

5. Did you happen to discuss the ___(major contest)___ with your family during the campaign?
   Yes, discussed_____   No_____
   Heard, paid no attention_____

6. How about your friends and people where you work—did you happen to discuss ___(major contest)___ with them during the campaign?
   Yes, discussed_____   No_____
   Heard, paid no attention_____

7. Did you stop and read anything about ___(major contest)___ *in the papers* during the campaign, or did you just glance over things about them?
   Yes, read_____   Didn't read_____
   Glanced, didn't read_____

   7a. (IF READ OR GLANCED) Which did you notice: news stories and articles; editorials; advertisements, or what? (CHECK AS MANY AS MENTIONED)
   Stories, articles_____   Ads_____
   Editorials_____   Don'tknow_____

8. Did you stop and listen to anything *on the radio* about ___(major contest)___, or didn't you pay any attention to things about them?
   Yes, listened, heard_____   Didn't listen_____
   Heard, paid no attention_____

   8a. (IF LISTENED OR HEARD AT ALL) Which do you recall listening to: Speeches, commercial announcement, news broadcasts or what? (CHECK ALL MENTIONED)
   News_____   Commercials_____
   Speeches_____   Don't know_____

9. What about billboards, placards, signs, and posters—did you take a really good look at any of them about ___(major contest)___, or didn't you pay any attention to them?
   Yes, look well, read_____
   Saw, paid no attention_____
   No_____

   9a. (IF SAW AT ALL) What kinds of signs did you see? Any others? (CHECK ALL MENTIONED)
   Billboards, large signs_____   Placards, posters, small signs_____
   Bus, streetcar cards_____   Don't know_____

10. How about letters, handbills, pamphlets, sample ballots, and such things concerning ___(major contest)___ —did you read any of them?
    Yes, read_____   No_____
    Glanced, didn't read_____

    10a. (IF ANY MENTIONED) What was it you read? Any other things? (CHECK ALL MENTIONED)
    Letters_____   Sample ballots_____

Pamphlets, booklets_____   Cards_____
Handbills, flyers_____   Don't know_____

11. Did you go to any meeting or gatherings where any of the election candidates appeared personally or somebody spoke in behalf of any of the candidates?
_____ and _____ appeared for
_____

12. During the campaign, did anybody telephone or see you about registering, or voting for somebody, or getting to the polls? What was that? (EXPLAIN BRIEFLY)
Democrats_____   No, no one_____
Republicans_____

13. Here's a list of the things we've been talking about—would you pick out the ones that have been most important to you in learning about ___(major contest)___? (PROBE FOR DETAIL, CHECK ALL MENTIONED)
Newspaper stories_____
Newspaper editorials_____
Newspaper ads_____
Radio news_____
Radio speeches_____
Radio commercials_____
Large signs, billboards_____
Small signs, posters_____
Doctors, dentists_____
Letters_____
Booklets, pamphlets_____
Handbills, leaflets_____
Meetings where ___(major contest)___ appeared_____
Other meetings_____
Talk with family_____
Friends, work associates_____
Calls, party workers_____
Don't know, none of them_____

14. A lot of people didn't get to vote in the elections this year. Did you happen NOT to vote?
Respondent voted, definitely_____   Didn't vote, not sure_____

14a. (IF DIDN'T VOTE) was there any special reason why you didn't get registered or didn't happen to vote this year? (EXPLAIN TO NON-VOTERS THAT EVEN IF THEY DIDN'T GET TO VOTE WE'D LIKE TO KNOW WHAT THEY WOULD HAVE DONE IF THEY HAD.)

15. (ASK ALL, INCLUDING NON-VOTERS) Regardless of which men you really prefer now, how did you vote on each of these contests

on election day? (Or, how would you have voted?)

15a. (FOR EACH) How strongly did you feel about that one?

	Democrat	Republican	No Choice	Strongly	Not So Strongly
Senate	___	___	___	___	___
Congress	___	___	___	___	___
Governor	___	___	___	___	___
(other state)	___	___	___	___	___
(other state)	___	___	___	___	___

16. Which of these things were important to you in choosing (major contest) for ___(major contest)___? (CHECK ALL MENTIONED)

He's a Democrat or Republican___
He's better qualified personally ___
His ideas and stand on issues were better___
People said he was better, he was well endorsed___
He was better known to me___
I didn't want other man at all___
None, don't know___

17. About how long before election day did you decide or find out that _____ was the man you wanted for___(major contest)___?

(B) Special Colorado questions:

1. Did you get any doctor's or dentist's opinion on the Carroll-Millikin contests—for example through personal discussion, or a speech, or a letter? (CHECK ALL MENTIONED)

Yes, personal discussion with one___
Yes, heard doctor speak publicly___
Yes, got letter, pamphlet from doctor___
Yes, not personally but hearsay___
No, got no doctor's opinion specifically___

2. All in all, what were your most important reasons for preferring _____ for Senator? (PROBE AND FOLLOW UP ANSWERS)

3. Here's the last question—I'm going to read you some "mud-slinging" charges made in the elections, some true and some not true, of course. For example, "Senator Ed . . ."

(a) Did you hear that during the campaign?
(b) (IF HEARD) Did you think it was true or false?

	Heard It and "True"	"False"	Didn't Hear
Senator Ed Johnson was against John Carroll	___	___	___
Senator Millikin is an isolationist	___	___	___
Carroll is for socialized medicine	___	___	___
Millikin is too friendly with big business and against profits taxes	___	___	___

	Heard It and		Didn't
	"True"	"False"	Hear
Carroll is a left-winger who protected Communists	____	____	____
John Metzger made a fool of himself over the Russian Flag	____	____	/
Governor Johnson was controlled by backroom politicians	____	____	____
Dan Thornton is a rich Texan who just recently came to Colorado	____	____	____
Governor Johnson made a mess of the Warden Best prison investigation	____	____	____

(C) Special Minnesota questions:
1. About how long before election day did you decide or find out that _____ was the man you wanted for Congress?
2. All in all, what were your most important reasons for preferring _____ for Congress?
3. (ASKED AFTER BASIC QUESTION 4): Was there any other question that came up in the Congressional race in this district that impressed you this fall? What was that?
4. Were there any (other) people in this household who voted?
5. Were there any (other) voting-age people in this household who did not vote?

(D) Special Washington questions:
1. Of all these problems listed, which four do you now feel are of most concern to you and people like yourself?
    General foreign policy____
    Communism in the United States____
    Recession and unemployment____
    Strikes and labor disputes____
    Inflation and high cost of living____
    Columbia Valley Authority____
    How much aid should we give to aged
        (referenda 176 and 178 in state election)____
    The state going into debt (income vs. sales tax)____
    Public vs. private electric power____
2. Both Mr. Magnuson and Mr. Williams made various statements regarding the problems you have mentioned. Which of these two candidates did you feel had the best approach to the solution of the problems?
    Williams, Republican____   Other____
    Magnuson, Democrat____   Don't know____

3. Which political party do you feel has the best program to meet the problems mentioned above?

Republicans_____   Other_____
Democrats_____   Don't know_____

4. Concerning the outcome of the recent elections, would you say that on the whole you are:

Very satisfied_____   Not at all satisfied_____
Fairly satisfied_____

5. In the recent elections did you think that most of your friends, or some of your friends, or only a few of your friends were able to get to the polls and vote?

Most_____   Only a few_____
Some_____   Don't know_____

6. Which political party do you think most of the people you associate with supported last Tuesday?

Democratic_____
Republican_____
Socialist Labor_____
Support no party, independent voters_____
Back both Democrats and Republicans_____
Don't know_____

7. Regardless of how the state election came out, what did you really expect?

A clearcut Democratic win_____   Close Republican win_____
A close Democratic win_____   Tossup, mixed, even_____
Clearcut Republican win_____   Don't know_____

8. How much difference did it make to you that Mr. Williams (the Republican candidate for Senator) lost this year?

A lot_____   Or not too much_____
Some_____   No difference at all_____

9. Did you ever seriously consider voting for the opposition candidate?

No_____   Yes_____

10. All in all, which political party do you generally favor?

Democrats_____
Republicans_____
Socialist Labor_____
Favor none, independent voter_____
Both Democrats and Republicans_____

(E) Special Iowa questions:

1. Were any of these things especially important in helping you decide for Jensen or Hart (Congressional candidates)?

Government spending and economy_____
Government controls on prices and profits_____

Defense and war preparedness_____
Foreign affairs (Russia, China, etc.)_____
Communists in America_____
Labor unions and strikes_____
The job President Truman has been doing_____
Government welfare programs of the New Deal and Fair Deal_____
Rural electrification_____
The threat of socialism in this country_____
The Brannan Plan_____

2. I'm going to read you some statements about the election, some of which are true and some not.
   (a) For each, would you tell me whether you think it's true, or false, or if you hadn't heard of it?
   (b) (FOR EACH TRUE) Was this an important point against the man named, in your opinion?

	Heard It and "True"	"False"	Hadn't Heard	Believe It True and Important	Not Important
Hickenlooper (Republican Senate candidate) only went to a few of the meetings he was supposed to attend in Washington.	_____	_____	_____	_____	_____
Loveland (Democratic Senate candidate) was sent out from Washington as a Truman Administration stooge to beat Hickenlooper.	_____	_____	_____	_____	_____
Hickenlooper is a tool of the private utility interests.	_____	_____	_____	_____	_____
Loveland is in favor of the Brannan Plan, but dodged the issue during the campaign.	_____	_____	_____	_____	_____
Jensen (Republican Congressional candidate) is against soil conservation	_____	_____	_____	_____	_____
Hart (Democratic Congressional candidate) moved to Iowa from Nebraska just to run for Congress.	_____	_____	_____	_____	_____

3. Were you ever in doubt or not sure about who you wanted in the Hickenlooper-Loveland Senate contest?
4. Did your husband (wife) vote in this election or not?
   Yes_____   No_____

INDEXES

THE FOLLOWING indexes were constructed from questionnaire items and were used in the text of this book.

INDEX OF SOCIAL CLASS

Items: Based on SES, breadwinner's occupation, and respondent's education. In Washington, annual family income was used instead of SES.

Scoring: Upper, middle, and lower classes are constructed by combining the items as follows:

		Professional, Semi-Professional, Managerial, Executive, Farmers, Clerical-Sales		Skilled Labor, Semi Skilled, Unskilled, Farm Labor, and Service Workers	
	SES or Annual Family Income	High School Graduates and Above	Some High School and Below	High School Graduates and Above	Some High School and Below
A and B	Over $5,000	Upper	Upper	Middle	Middle
C+	$3,000-$5,000	Upper	Middle	Middle	Middle
C—	$2,000-$3,000	Middle	Middle	Middle	Lower
D	Under $2,000	Middle	Middle	Lower	Lower

Distribution of the samples:

Index Type	Colorado	Washington	Minnesota	Iowa
Upper	122	106	105	149
Middle	188	200	199	183
Lower	163	135	188	144
	473	441	492	476

INDEX OF CANDIDATE INVOLVEMENT

Items: Based on strength of feelings about candidates (regardless of the direction of choice) in five contests. In Colorado, Minnesota, and Iowa, every respondent was asked his pre-election and post-election choices for United States Congressman, governor, and state attorney general. In addition, in Colorado and Iowa, he was asked about United States Senator, in Minnesota and Iowa about state lieutenant governor, and in Colorado and Minnesota about state secretary of state. Separate indexes were computed from the pre-election and postelection interviews, since the same items were repeated.

Scoring: A *strong* choice in any contest is scored + 2.
A choice *without* strong feeling is scored + 1.
No choice is scored 0.

Distribution of the samples for the two separate indexes computed from the pre-election and postelection interviews:

Index Type	Total Score	COLORADO Pre	COLORADO Post	MINNESOTA Pre	MINNESOTA Post	IOWA Pre	IOWA Post
High	10, 9	147	171	111	117	92	107
Medium High	8, 7	62	67	109	78	47	4
Medium	6, 5	123	70	148	153	104	97
Medium Low	4, 3	40	10	64	26	71	12
Low	2, 1, 0	101	18	60	23	162	31
		473	336	492	397	476	251

A complete index cannot be computed for Washington, since only the contests for Senator and Congressman were covered in the questionnaire. However, some inferences may be made about candidate involvement in this sample by examining the intensity of choice for these two offices and also by means of a separate question included in the Washington questionnaire: "How much difference would it make to you if your favorite candidate for Senator lost this year?" Answers: "A lot," "Some," "Not too much," "No difference at all," and "Not yet decided on a candidate."

INDEX OF STRAIGHTNESS
OF TICKET

Items: Based on party choice in five contests (regardless of the strength of feelings). The contests were the same as those used in the Index of Candidate Involvement, described earlier. The index could be computed for the Colorado, Minnesota, and Iowa samples. Separate pre-election and postelection indexes could be computed for each respondent, since the same questions were asked in both interviews.

Scoring:

Index Type	Combination of Choices
Straight Republican	All Choices (1-5) Republican
Majority Republican	2 of 3, 3 of 4, or 4 of 5 Choices Republican
Split Ticket	1 of 2, 2 of 4, 2 of 5, or 3 of 5 Choices Republican or Democratic
Majority Democrat	2 of 3, 3 of 4, or 4 of 5 Choices Democratic
Straight Democrat	All Choices (1-5) Democratic
No Choice	All 5 Questions Answered "Undecided" or "No Choice"

Distribution of the samples for the two separate indexes computed from the pre-election and postelection interviews:

Index Type	COLORADO Pre	Post	MINNESOTA Pre	Post	IOWA Pre	Post
Straight Republican	95	103	188	143	228	130
Majority Republican	36	34	76	55	28	10
Split Ticket	80	52	88	78	23	25
Majority Democrat	67	38	59	42	20	9
Straigth Democrat	135	101	59	65	56	50
No Choice	60	8	22	14	121	27
	473	336	492	397	476	251

A complete index cannot be computed for Washington, where only the contests for Senator and Congressman were covered in the questionnaire.

INDEX OF ISSUE INVOLVEMENT

Items: Based on strength of feelings about five issues (regardless of agreement or disagreement with each issue position stated in the question). The same questions were asked in all four states. Separate indexes were computed from the pre-election and post-election interviews, since the same items were repeated. Each respondent was asked to express his degree of agreement or disagreement with each of the following statements:

a. "The Republicans would cut down waste and bureaucracy in government."
b. "Defense and war problems can best be handled by the Democrats."
c. "Democratic administrations have made many bad mistakes in foreign affairs."
d. "Democrats have been too easy on Communists in America."
e. "The Taft-Hartley Labor Law is unfair to working people."

Scoring: A *strong* choice on any issue is scored + 2.
A choice *without* strong feeling is scored + 1.
No choice is scored 0.

Distribution of the samples for the two separate indexes computed from the pre-election and postelection interviews:

Index Type	Total Score	COLORADO		WASHINGTON		MINNESOTA		IOWA	
		Pre	Post	Pre	Post	Pre	Post	Pre	Post
High	10, 9	87	70	18	9	93	97	37	35
Medium High	8, 7	138	111	63	44	135	130	78	48
Medium	6, 5	115	79	130	119	137	85	119	76
Medium Low	4, 3	80	44	166	145	78	58	119	57
Low	2, 1, 0	53	32	64	61	49	27	123	35
		473	336	441	378	492	397	476	251

INDEX OF ISSUE OPINION

Items: Based on direction of opinion on five issues (regardless of the strength of feelings). The issues were the same as those used in the Index of Issue Involvement, described earlier. The same questions were asked in all four states. Separate indexes were computed from the pre-election and postelection interviews, since the same items were repeated.

Scoring:

Index Type	Combination of Opinions
Consistent Republican	All Opinions (1-5) Republican
Majority Republican	2 of 3, 3 of 4, or 4 of 5 Opinions Republican
Split	1 of 2, 2 of 4, 2 of 5, or 3 of 5 Opinions Republican or Democratic
Majority Democrat	2 of 3, 3 of 4, or 4 of 5 Opinions Democratic
Consistent Democrat	All Opinions (1-5) Democratic
No Opinion	All 5 Questions Answered "Undecided"

Distribution of the samples for the two separate indexes computed from the pre-election and postelection interviews:

	COLORADO		WASHINGTON		MINNESOTA		IOWA	
	Pre	Post	Pre	Post	Pre	Post	Pre	Post
Index Type								
Consistent Republican	125	98	138	123	124	110	246	122
Majority Republican	102	70	78	76	92	75	81	59
Split	118	83	91	82	127	87	64	28
Majority Democrat	73	48	79	55	84	75	26	17
Consistent Democrat	36	28	44	30	52	43	34	15
No Opinion	19	9	11	12	13	7	25	10
	473	336	441	378	492	397	476	251

INDEX OF MEDIA EXPOSURE

Items and Scoring: Based on amount of exposure to news about the campaign in four mass media. The index was computed from questions asked in Colorado, Minnesota, and Iowa in the postelection interview. The questions and scoring were as follows (The blanks were filled with reference to the principal contests in each state):

a. "Did you stop and read anything about ———— and ———— in the papers during the campaign, or did you just glance over things about them?" ("Yes, read something" scored + 1. "Glanced, didn't read" scored 0. "No" and "Don't recall" scored 0).
b. "Did you stop and listen to anything on the radio about ———— and ————, or didn't you pay any attention to things about

them?" ("Yes, listened to something" scored + 1. "Heard, paid no attention" scored 0. "Didn't listen" or "Don't recall" scored 0).

c. "How about billboards, placards, signs, and posters? Did you take a really good look at any of them about ——— and ———, or didn't you pay any attention to any of them?" ("Yes, took good look, read" scored + 1. "Saw, paid no attention" scored 0. "No" and "Don't recall" scored 0).

d. "How about letters, handbills, pamphlets, sample ballots, and such things concerning ——— and ———? Did you read any of them?" ("Yes, read something" scored + 1. "Glanced, didn't read" scored 0. "No" and "Don't recall" scored 0).

Distribution of the samples for the index computed from the postelection interview:

Index Type	Total Score	Colorado	Minnesota	Iowa
High	4, 3	65	59	15
Medium High	2	96	97	60
Medium Low	1	72	115	61
Low	0	103	126	115
		336	397	251

INDEX OF PARTY HABIT

Items: Based on party identification and presidential preference in the 1948 election.

Scoring: Six categories are constructed by combining the items. Index types are formed by combining the categories.

Preference in 1948	PARTY IDENTIFICATION		
	Democratic	Other	Republican
Truman	6	4	2
Dewey	5	3	1

Distribution of the samples according to party regularity:

Index Type	Colorado	Washington	Minnesota	Iowa
Regulars (6, 1)	317	262	267	287
Changers (5, 2)	38	45	98	48
Irregulars (4, 3)	118	134	127	141
	473	441	492	476

Distribution of the samples according to partisan tendencies:

Index Type	Colorado	Washington	Minnesota	Iowa
Strong Democrats (6)	207	168	141	115
Weak Democrats (5, 4)	81	102	128	98
Weak Republicans (3, 2)	75	77	97	91
Strong Republicans (1)	110	94	126	172
	473	441	492	476

INDEX OF
PARTICIPATION INVOLVEMENT

Items: Based on answers to three questions in the pre-election interview in all four states. The questions were: turnout in 1948; interest in the 1950 election campaign; intention to vote in 1950.

Scoring: Four index types are constructed by combining the items as follows:

Intention to Vote in 1950	VOTED IN 1948			DID NOT VOTE IN 1948
	Great Deal of Interest	Quite a Lot of Interest	Not Much, No Interest	All Levels of Interest
Sure to Go	High	Medium High	Medium Low	Low
Fairly Likely	Medium High	Medium Low	Medium Low	Low
Go if Find Time, Probably Not Go	Medium Low	Medium Low	Low	Low

Distribution of the samples:

Index Type	Colorado	Washington	Minnesota	Iowa
High	100	107	112	73
Medium High	93	113	123	110
Medium Low	156	84	123	161
Low	124	137	134	132
	473	441	492	476

APPENDIX *D*

CANDIDATES

THE FOLLOWING are the principal candidates for offices in the districts where the Regional Panels surveys were conducted. The winners are starred (*).

	Republican	Democrat
COLORADO		
Governor	Dan Thornton*	Walter W. Johnson
Lieutenant Governor	Gordon Allott*	Lacy Wilkinson
Secretary of State	Clarence Stafford	George Baker*
Attorney General	Duke Dunbar*	John Metzger
United States Senator	Eugene Millikin*	John Carroll
United States House of Representatives		
First District	Richard Luxford	Byron Rogers*
Second District	William Hill*	George Bickel
Third District	J.Edgar Chenoweth*	John Marsalis
Fourth District	Jack Evans	Wayne Aspinall*
WASHINGTON		
United States Senator	Walter Williams	Warren Magnuson*
United States House of Representatives		
First District	Mildred T. Powell	Hugh Mitchell*
Second District	Herb Wilson	Henry Jackson*
Third District	Russell Mack*	Gordon Quarnstrom
Fourth District	Hal Holmes*	Ted Little
Fifth District	Walt Horan*	Robert Dellwo
Sixth District	Thor Tollefson*	John Coffee
MINNESOTA		
Governor	Luther Youngdahl*	Harry Peterson
Lieutenant Governor	C. Elmer Anderson*	Frank Murphy
Secretary of State	Mike Holm*	Marie McGuire
Attorney General	Joseph A. A. Burnquist*	Orville Freeman
United States House of Representatives		
Third District	Alfred Lindley	Roy Wier*
Fourth District	Ward Fleming	Eugene McCarthy*
Fifth District	Walter Judd*	Marcella Killen

IOWA

Governor	William Beardsley*	Lester Gillette
Lieutenant Governor	W. H. Nicholas*	Iver Christofferson
Secretary of State	Melvin Synhorst*	Mary Kelleher
Attorney General	Robert Larson*	Harold Fleck
United States Senator	Bourke Hickenlooper*	Albert Loveland
United States House of Representatives		
Seventh District	Ben Jensen*	James Hart

REFERENCES

"AAPOR Forms Committee on Research Development," *The Public Opinion Quarterly,* 14 (Spring, 1950), 200.

Adams, John. *A Defense of the Constitutions of Government of the United States of America,* in *The Works of John Adams.* Boston: Little, Brown and Company, 1850-1856.

Agger, Robert E. "Independents and Party Identifiers," in *American Voting Behavior,* eds. Eugene Burdick and Arthur J. Brodbeck, pp. 308-329. New York: The Free Press, 1959.

Bean, Louis. *How to Predict Elections.* New York: Alfred A. Knopf, 1948.

Bendix, Reinhard. "Social Stratification and Political Power," *The American Political Science Review,* 46 (June, 1952), 357-375.

Benney, Mark, *et al. How People Vote.* London: Routledge & Kegan Paul, 1956.

Benson, Lee. "Research Problems in American Political Historiography," in *Common Frontiers of the Social Sciences,* ed. Mirra Komarovsky, pp. 113-183. New York: The Free Press, 1957.

——. *The Concept of Jacksonian Democracy: New York as a Test Case.* Princeton: Princeton University Press, 1961.

Berelson, B., Paul Lazarsfeld, and William McPhee. *Voting.* Chicago: The University of Chicago Press, 1954.

Blau, Peter M. "Formal Organization: Dimensions of Analysis," *The American Journal of Sociology,* 63 (July, 1957), 58-69.

Bone, Hugh. "The 1950 Elections in Washington," *The Western Political Quarterly,* 4 (March, 1951), 93-94.

Boulding, Kenneth. *Economic Analysis.* New York: Harper & Brothers, 2nd ed., 1948.

Bryce, James. *Modern Democracies*. New York: The Macmillan Company, 1929.

Burnham, W. Dean. *Presidential Ballots 1836-1892*. Baltimore: The Johns Hopkins Press, 1955.

Calkins, Fay. *The C.I.O. and the Democratic Party*. Chicago: University of Chicago Press, 1952.

Campbell, Angus. "Surge and Decline: A Study of Electoral Change," *The Public Opinion Quarterly,* XXIV (Fall, 1960), pp. 397-418.

————, Philip E. Converse, Warren E. Miller, and Donald E. Stokes. *The American Voter*. New York: John Wiley & Sons, 1960.

————, and Homer C. Cooper. *Group Differences in Attitudes and Votes*. Ann Arbor, Mich.: Institute for Social Research, 1956.

————, Gerald Gurin, and Warren Miller. *The Voter Decides*. Evanston: Row, Peterson and Company, 1954.

Clerk of the House of Representatives. *Statistics of the Congressional Election of November 7, 1950*. Washington: United States Government Printing Office, 1951.

Coleman, James S. *The Adolescent Society*. New York: The Free Press, 1961.

Cutright, Phillips, and Peter H. Rossi. "Party Organization in Primary Elections," *The American Journal of Sociology,* 64 (November, 1958), 262-269.

Davis, James A. *Great Books and Small Groups*. New York: The Free Press, 1961.

Dittmann, Wilhelm. *Das Politische Deutschland vor Hitler*. Zurich: Europa Verlag, 1945.

Duverger, Maurice. *The Political Role of Women*. Paris: UNESCO, 1955.

Eldersveld, Samuel J. "The Independent Vote," *The American Political Science Review,* 46 (September, 1952), 732-753.

Eulau, Heinz, and Peter Schneider. "Dimensions of Political Involvement," *The Public Opinion Quarterly,* 20 (Spring, 1956), 128-142.

Ewing, Cortez A. M. *Congressional Elections 1896-1944*. Norman: University of Oklahoma Press, 1947.

Feller, William. *An Introduction to Probability Theory and Its Applications*. New York: John Wiley & Sons, 2nd ed. 1957.

Festinger, Leon. *Theory of Cognitive Dissonance*. Evanston: Row, Peterson and Company, 1957.

Friedman, B. "A Simple Urn Model," *Communications on Pure and Applied Mathematics,* 2 (1949), 59-70.

Gallup, George. *The Political Almanac—1952.* New York: B. C. Forbes, 1952.

Glock, C. Y. "Participation Bias and Re-Interview Effect in Panel Studies." Unpublished Ph.D. thesis, Columbia University, 1952.

Gosnell, Harold F. *Getting Out the Vote.* Chicago: Chicago Press, 1927.

Guttman, Louis. "Mathematical and Tabulation Techniques," in *The Prediction of Personal Adjustment,* ed. Paul Horst, pp. 251-364. New York: Social Science Research Council, 1941.

Hamilton, Alexander, John Jay, and James Madison. *The Federalist.* New York: The Modern Library, n.d.

Harris, Louis. *Is There a Republican Majority?* New York: Harper & Brothers, 1954.

Hastings, Philip K. "The Non-Voter in 1952: A Study of Pittsfield, Massachusetts," *The Journal of Psychology,* 38 (1954), 301-312.

Havemann, Ernest, and Patricia West. *They Went to College.* New York: Harcourt, Brace and World, 1952.

Heberle, Rudolf. *From Democracy to Nazism.* Baton Rouge: Louisiana State University Press, 1945.

Hofstadter, Richard. *The Age of Reform.* New York: Alfred A. Knopf, 1955.

Hoggatt, Austin C., and F. E. Balderston. "Continuity of Relationships among Organizations Imbedded in a Communication Network," unpublished papers available from the authors, Management Science Institute, University of California, Berkeley.

Hovland, Carl I., *et al. Experiments in Mass Communications.* Princeton: Princeton University Press, 1949.

Hyman, Herbert. *Survey Design and Analysis.* New York: The Free Press, 1955.

————. *Political Socialization.* New York: The Free Press, 1959.

Irwin, William. "Politics of Colorado." Unpublished doctoral dissertation in the University of Colorado Library. Boulder, Colorado, 1955.

Jones, W. H. Morris, "In Defense of Apathy: Some Doubts on the Duty to Vote," *Political Studies,* 2 (February, 1954), 25-37.

Kelley, Stanley. *Professional Public Relations and Political Power.* Baltimore: The Johns Hopkins Press, 1956.

Kendall, Patricia. *Conflict and Mood.* New York: The Free Press, 1954.

Key, V. O. *Politics, Parties and Pressure Groups.* New York: Thomas Y. Crowell Company, 3rd. ed., 1952.

―――. *Southern Politics.* New York: Alfred A. Knopf, 1949.

―――. "A Theory of Critical Elections," *The Journal of Politics,* 17 (February, 1955), 3-18.

―――. *American State Politics: An Introduction.* New York: Alfred A. Knopf, 1956.

―――, and Frank Munger. "Social Determinism and Electoral Decision: The Case of Indiana," in *American Voting Behavior,* eds. Eugene Burdick and Arthur J. Brodbeck, pp. 281-299. New York: The Free Press, 1959.

Kitt, Alice S., and David B. Gleicher. "Determinants of Voting Behavior," *Public Opinion Quarterly,* 14 (Fall, 1950), 393-412.

Kornhauser, Arthur, *et al. When Labor Votes.* New York: University Books, 1956.

Kornhauser, William. *The Politics of Mass Society.* New York: The Free Press, 1959.

Krueger, William C. "Rate of Progress as Related to Difficulty of Assignment," *Journal of Educational Psychology,* 37 (April, 1946), 247-249.

Lane, Robert E. *Political Life.* New York: The Free Press, 1959.

LaPalombara, Joseph G. "Pressure, Propaganda and Political Action in the Elections of 1950," *The Journal of Politics,* XIV (May, 1952), pp. 300-325.

Lawrence, David. Column in *The New York Herald Tribune,* September 26, 1952.

Lazarsfeld, Paul F. "The Logical and Mathematical Foundation of Latent Structure Analysis," in *Measurement and Prediction,* ed. Samuel A. Stouffer, pp. 362-472. Princeton: Princeton University Press, 1950.

―――. "A Conceptual Introduction to Latent Structure Analysis," in *Mathematical Thinking in the Social Sciences,* pp. 349-387. New York: The Free Press, 1954(a).

―――. "Latent Structure Analysis," in *Psychology: A Study of a Science,* ed. Sigmund Koch, pp. 476-543. New York: McGraw-Hill Book Company, 1959.

―――, *et al. The Panel Method.* Forthcoming, 1962.

————, Bernard Berelson, and Hazel Gaudet, *The People's Choice.* New York: Columbia University Press, 2nd ed., 1948.

————, and Raymond H. Franzen. "Prediction of Political Behavior in America," *American Sociological Review,* 10 (April, 1945), 261-273.

————, and Robert K. Merton. "Friendship as Social Process: A Substantive and Methodological Analysis," in *Freedom and Control in Modern Society,* eds. Morroe Berger *et al.,* pp. 18-66. New York: D. Van Nostrand Co., 1954(b).

————, and Morris Rosenberg. "The Contribution of the Regional Poll to Political Understanding," *The Public Opinion Quarterly,* 13 (Winter 1949-1950), 569-586.

————, and Wagner Thielens. *The Academic Mind.* New York: The Free Press, 1958.

Lipset, Seymour M. "The Political Animal: Genus Americana," *The Public Opinion Quarterly,* 23 (Winter 1959-1960), 554-562.

————, Paul F. Lazarsfeld, Allen H. Barton, and Juan Linz. "The Psychology of Voting: An Analysis of Political Behavior," in *Handbook of Social Psychology,* ed. Gardner Lindzey, pp. 1124-1175. Reading, Mass.: Addison-Wesley Publishing Company, 1954.

————, Martin Trow, and James Coleman. *Union Democracy.* New York: The Free Press, 1956.

Lord, Frederic M. "The Relation of Test Score to the Trait Underlying the Test," *Educational and Psychological Measurement,* 13 (Winter, 1953), 517-549.

Lubell, Samuel. *The Future of American Politics.* New York: Harper and Brothers, 1952.

Lynd, Robert S., and Helen M. Lynd. *Middletown in Transition.* New York: Harcourt Brace, 1937.

McPhee, William N. "Note on a Campaign Simulator," *The Public Opinion Quarterly,* 25 (July, 1961), 184-193. See also, McPhee, W. N., *Formal Theories of Mass Behavior.* New York: The Free Press, 1962 (in press).

MacRae, Duncan. "Occupations and the Congressional Vote, 1940-1950," *American Sociological Review,* 20 (June, 1955), 332-340.

————, and James A. Meldrum. "Critical Elections in Illinois: 1888-1958," *The American Political Science Review,* 54 (September, 1960), 669-683.

Martin, Curtis. "The 1950 Elections in Colorado," *The Western Political Quarterly,* 4 (March, 1951).

Merton, Robert K. *Social Theory and Social Structure.* New York: The Free Press, 2nd ed., 1957.

Meyers, Marvin. *The Jacksonian Persuasion.* Stanford, Calif.: Stanford University Press, 1957.

Mill, John Stuart. *Utilitarianism, Liberty and Representative Government.* London: J. M. Dent & Sons, 1910.

Miller, Mungo. "The Waukegan Study of Voter Turnout Prediction," *The Public Opinion Quarterly,* 16 (Fall, 1952), 381-398.

Miller, Warren E. "One Party Politics and the Voter," *The American Political Science Review,* 50 (September, 1956), 707-725.

Mills, C. Wright. "The Middle Classes in Middle Sized Cities," in *Reader in Urban Sociology,* eds. Paul K. Hatt and Albert J. Reiss, Jr., pp. 359-371. New York: The Free Press, 1951.

Millsap, Kenneth. "Iowa Politics," *The Palimpsest,* 22 (September, 1951), 351-360.

Moos, Malcolm. *Politics, Presidents and Coattails.* Baltimore: The Johns Hopkins Press, 1952.

Mosteller, Frederick, *et al. The Pre-Election Polls of 1948.* New York: Social Science Research Council, 1949.

The New International Year Book for 1950. New York: Funk & Wagnalls Company, 1950.

Newell, Allen, J. C. Shaw, and Herbert A. Simon. "Empirical Explorations of the Logic Theory Machine," *Proceedings of the Western Joint Computer Conference* (February 26-28, 1957), 218-230. A bibliography is available from the authors at Carnegie Institute of Technology, Pittsburgh, Pa.

Ogburn, William F., and A. J. Jaffe. "Independent Voting and Presidential Elections," *The American Journal of Sociology,* 42 (September, 1936), 186-201.

Press, O. Charles. "The Prediction of Midterm Elections," *The Western Political Quarterly,* 9 (September, 1956), 691-698.

"Proceedings of the American Association for Public Opinion Research," *The Public Opinion Quarterly,* 13 (Winter 1949-1950), 737-808.

"Proceedings of the American Association for Public Opinion Research," *The Public Opinion Quarterly,* 14 (Winter 1950-1951), 820-868.

"Proceedings of the American Association for Public Opinion Research," *The Public Opinion Quarterly,* 15 (Winter 1951-1952), 768-819.

Robinson, Edgar Eugene. *The Presidential Vote 1896-1932.* Stanford, Calif.: Stanford University Press, 1934.

Roper, Elmo. Column in *The New York Herald Tribune* (June 30, 1952).

Rossi, Peter H. "Four Landmarks in Voting Research," in *American Voting Behavior,* eds. Eugene Burdick and Arthur J. Brodbeck, pp. 5-54. New York: The Free Press, 1959.

Saenger, Gerhart H. "Social Status and Political Behavior," in *Class, Status and Power,* eds. Reinhard Bendix and Seymour M. Lipset, pp. 348-358. New York: The Free Press, 1953.

Selvin, Hanan C. *The Effects of Leadership.* New York: The Free Press, 1960.

Simon, Walter. "The Political Parties of Austria." Unpublished doctoral dissertation in the Columbia University Library, New York, 1958.

Slocum, Walter L., and Herman M. Case. "Are Neighborhoods Meaningful Social Groups throughout Rural America?," *Rural Sociology,* 18 (March, 1953), 52-59.

Suchman, Edward, and Herbert Menzel. "The Interplay of Demographic and Psychological Variables in the Analysis of Voting Surveys," in *The Language of Social Research,* eds. Paul F. Lazarsfeld and Morris Rosenberg, pp. 148-155. New York: The Free Press, 1955.

Torgeson, W. S. *Theory and Methods of Scaling.* New York: John Wiley & Sons, 1960.

Toynbee, Arnold. In *The New York Times,* Sec. 11 (April 30, 1961).

Warner, Lloyd, and P. S. Lunt. *The Social Life of a Modern Community.* New Haven: Yale University Press, 1941.

Wiggins, Lee M. "Mathematical Models for the Interpretation of Attitude and Behavior Change: The Analysis of Multi-Wave Panels." Unpublished doctoral dissertation, in the Columbia University Library, New York, 1955. Also, a condensation to appear in Lazarsfeld, *et al.,* volume on panel analysis to appear in 1962.

Wilson, Francis G. "The Inactive Electorate and Social Revolution," *The Southwestern Social Science Quarterly,* 16 (March, 1936), 73-84.

Zetterberg, Hans L. *On Theory and Verification in Sociology.* Stockholm: Almqvist & Wiksell, 1954.

NAME INDEX

Abelson, H. I., 79n
Acheson, Dean, 198, 205
Adams, John, 69
Agger, Robert E., 66
American Medical Association, 279
Anderson, Bo, 5, 78

Bachelder, Joseph, 51, 104n
Balderston, C. C., 127
Bean, Louis, 48
Beiler, Ross, 51
Bendix, Reinhard, 48n
Benney, Mark, 27, 46
Benson, Lee, 140, 181, 181n
Berelson, B., 1, 26, 33, 49, 71, 78n, 88,
    106, 127n, 142, 180, 181, 183, 225,
    251, 280
Blau, Peter M., 181, 181n
Bone, Hugh, 274n
Boulding, Kenneth, 34
Bryce, James, 65
Bureau of Applied Social Research, 123n,
    180n, 246, 252

Calkins, Fay, 274n
Campbell, Angus, 14, 15, 19n, 26, 27,
    28n, 41, 43, 45, 46, 47n, 66, 68,
    173, 181, 187
Carnegie Institute of Technology, 123n,
    126
Carroll, John, 276
Case, Herman M., 192
Chiang Kai-shek, 198
Clerk of the House of Representatives,
    274n
Coleman, James, 142, 181
Columbia University, 123n, 155n
Cooper, Homer C., 187
Coplon, Judith, 278
Cutright, James A., 181, 181n

Davis, James A., 181, 181n
Dewey, Thomas, 237n, 276
Dirksen, Everett M., 275
Dittmann, Wilhelm, 310
Durkheim, Émile, 181n
Duverger, Maurice, 41

Eisenhower, Dwight D., 47, 47n, 64, 143,
    238, 275, 276
Eldersveld, Samuel J., 66
Emery, Jane, 78
Emery, John, 51
Ennis, Philip, 9, 10, 11, 83n
Eulau, Heinz, 28

Feller, William, 142-142n
Ferguson, Jack, 8, 15, 155
Ferguson, LeRoy, 8, 15, 27n, 41
Festinger, Leon, 79n, 79
Ford Foundation, 78, 123n, 155n
Freeman, Howard E., 9, 10, 11, 13, 212,
    240
Friedman, B., 142

Gallup, George, 160
Garabedian, Gladys, 154n
Gaudet, H, 78
Gendell, Murray, 13, 246, 250
Glaser, William A., 3, 4, 14, 15, 19, 44,
    127n, 173, 225, 251, 273
Glock, C. Y. 80
Goldish, Sidney, 51
Gosnell, Harold F., 33
Guttman, Louis, 133, 246

Hamilton, Alexander, 69
Harris, Louis, 47n
Hastings, Philip K., 45, 46
Havemann, Ernest, 75
Heberle, Rudolf, 181n, 186, 188
Heider, Fritz, 79n
Hickenlooper, Bourke, 276, 279
Hiss, Alger, 278
Hofstadter, Richard, 185
Hoggatt, Austin C., 127
Hovland, Carl I., 20
Hyman, Herbert, 66, 127

International Business Machines, Inc.,
    123n, 154n
Irwin, William, 274n

Jensen, Ben, 276
Judd, Walter, 198, 199, 205, 207, 277

317

SUBJECT INDEX